2001: A Baseball Odyssey

2001: A BASEBALL ODYSSEY

▼

Writers Club Press
San Jose New York Lincoln Shanghai

2001: A Baseball Odyssey

Writers Club Press
an imprint of iUniverse, Inc.

For information address:
iUniverse, Inc.
5220 S. 16th St., Suite 200
Lincoln, NE 68512
www.iuniverse.com

ISBN: 0-595-21169-0

Printed in the United States of America

*This book is dedicated to
Gabby and Lani,
the best parents a kid could ask for*

CONTENTS

INTRODUCTION

I guess you could say that my love of baseball and my love of writing first crossed paths in the spring of 2000. I was invited to Spring Training with the Montreal Expos in hopes of making their Class AA team, and while I was in Florida, I began keeping a journal for friends and family. I would write every two or three days to discuss the goings-on in the Sunshine State, and the responses I received were quite favorable. A good friend of mine, Mark Kingston, at the time an assistant baseball coach at the University of Miami (FL), told me about Baseball America's website and how there is a Player Journal section. He then told me basically that I could outwrite the contributing ballplayers with one thesaurus tied behind my back, so I checked into it. Before long, I was writing a semi-monthly column for the website.

My entries continued throughout the summer and winter, and when I found out that I was to play in Taiwan in March of 2001, I knew that my writing would take a huge leap forward; after all, it's not every day that a small town, white boy goes to the Orient to play baseball. Once again, I began chronicling the events of my life, and it seemed as though the circle of "Bo-followers" had grown ten fold. Apparently, random people, not just friends and family, enjoyed my musings. To me, the greatest compliments I would receive from my readers are those that came from the non-baseball fans: they simply enjoyed the stories. Whether it was a journal entry from Taiwan or an article on clubhouse nudity—perhaps the *pièce de résistance* of my brief writing career—I kept my readers anxiously awaiting my next musing. Now for the ironic part: Writing, which I've been doing for basically a year and a half, is easy compared to baseball, which I've been doing for ten years.

In one of my Baseball America journal entries from January of 2001, I wrote a lengthy piece on athletic talent. The theme of the article was that talent, far more often than not, wins out in the advancement of an athlete's career. I mentioned the quote that sums up the American way: "You can do/have/be anything you want in life if you work hard enough at it." I then proceeded to shatter dreams all over this country by saying that the statement is true in any line of work *except* sports. You see, hundreds of thousands of athletes all over the world work tirelessly at their sports in order to get their hands on the money that professional athletes earn nowadays. What separates those who reach the highest level of their sports from those who never make past the junior college level? Talent. Certainly not all the time, but pretty damn close. What's my point? The talent that I so blatantly lacked as a ballplayer is apparently rather abundant in my writing ability.

As a position player in baseball, your natural ability is rated by the following five "tools" rate: hitting for average, hitting for power, running speed, fielding, and throwing. I have always been both unfailingly objective and keenly aware of my abilities—traits unbelievably rare in most ballplayers; it's an athlete's nature to think he is better than what he really is—and I would have to rank my "tools" like this: above average, below average, poor, average, average, respectively. Yes, some baseball people may think otherwise in certain categories, but I think these assessments are pretty accurate. It's no secret that my "God-given" ability to play baseball is relatively paltry compared to most professional players, and I've had to work my ass off just to get to the level of WBL All-Star. Such a label wasn't exactly what I sought out when I began my life in baseball in the fall of 1991 as a freshman at the University of North Carolina.

I have played with and against so many guys that were so unbelievably gifted that I secretly envied them. Whether it was a picture-perfect swing, a Howitzer for an arm, blinding speed, or a body chiseled out of marble, I always felt short-changed on the baseball field. How I am still playing professionally, in spite of my shortcomings, is equally bewildering and satisfying. I've hit .330 or better for three straight years now with a swing that you won't exactly make you drool, and I was the best third baseman, percentage-wise at least, twice in the WBL with an arm that on a good day might elicit a yawn. I've had to *think* to make it this far. I've had to *work* to make it this far. Discussing hitting with one of my former teammates, a guy who is in the Top Five of pure hitters that I've seen, is pretty much a microcosm of the talent factor. I would ask him what he looks for at the plate, questions like, "Were you sitting on that changeup?" or "Did you look for that inside fastball on that 2-0 pitch?" He would just say, "Bo, I don't worry about stuff like that. I just look for the ball to appear in the strike zone and then hammer it." I wanted to choke him. If I went up to the plate with that mindset, I'd have been out of baseball a long time ago.

When I write, though, the words just flow. I don't sit around reading books looking for quotations (even though I used to, not to augment my writing but because I have always found them to be quite interesting). I am not constantly thumbing through a dictionary looking for words. True, I have an outstanding memory, and I remember rules of grammar, syntax, and spelling from my high school days rather easily. But when people would read my stuff and say, "Jeez, Bo, you write so well," I just shake my head. I don't get it. I have asked people, honestly, "Can't anybody do this?" They tell me no. I still don't get it. I simply sit down at my computer and start typing. Whatever comes into my mind goes onto the pages, but I guess I do it pretty well. As much blood, sweat and tears as I put into baseball over the years, I put the opposite amount into my writing. I am a firm believer that everyone has some form of talent, obviously some more than others, and I guess my talent is writing. It certainly isn't in baseball.

Now, I want you to sit back and enjoy my journey to the Far East and back home. I want you to enjoy the experiences, the people, and the trials and tribulations that I faced during the summer of 2001. I tried to be as visual as I could be with my imagery, so you can "be there" with me. I comment on religion, racism, government, women, coaching, and those God-awful bus trips. I try to mix in all the emotions that envelop a ballplayer: humor, sadness, frustration, elation, pangs of guilt, and loneliness. And I set everything against a baseball backdrop. Baseball has been my life. Now, let it be yours.

PROLOGUE: THE FIRE INSIDE

On July 20, 1985, I had an epiphany. I had just thrown a no-hitter—actually, one walk from a perfect game—in a Little League District 7 All-Star game against our archrivals in front of probably 2000 fans. That evening, my mom threw a surprise 40th birthday party for my dad on our farm. As my parents' friends entertained themselves, my "girlfriend" at the time (you know how relationships are when you're 12) called several times wanting to speak to me, much to the ire of my mom. Although I can't remember why, I simply didn't want to talk to her. My friends couldn't believe it. After all, this was Georgia Cypher, the prettiest, most fully developed twelve-year-old around. And I was blowing her off. Later, as we sat in the barn on the tractors and shot around the basketball, my friends were needling me mercilessly, insinuating that I cared more about baseball than I did about Georgia. You know what? They were right. Later that night, after the party had died down and the house was quiet, I retreated to the darkness of our basement to sleep on the waterbed. I had just pitched the game of my life, and I was on top of the world. At that moment I realized that I had a chance to make something of myself in sports. And before I closed my eyes to fall asleep, I actually kissed my right arm. The great Ted Williams wrote in his autobiography that every man has ten days in his life that he'll never forget. To me, July 20, 1985 seems like yesterday.

Today, when people find out that I am a professional baseball player, some of them ask, "Is that something you always wanted to do?" The answer is a resounding, "Hell yes!" Honestly, what red-blooded American male doesn't dream of playing major league baseball someday? I feel that most kids start out with big league aspirations, but eventually, they discover that they simply don't have the ability to play baseball and therefore move their focus to another sport or leave the world of athletics altogether. Fortunately, I did have just enough ability, and combined with desire and hard work, I accomplished my goal.

Growing up in the small, rural town of Kittanning, PA, I was a pretty good four-sport athlete in high school, and I knew that I was going to pursue a life in athletics. Eventually, though, I focused on baseball because I had the best chance of going to the "big time" in that sport, and when I signed to become a University of North Carolina Tar Heel in May of 1991, I realized my dream. I consider August of 1991 as the beginning of my baseball career, as it was when I set foot in Chapel Hill and promptly devoted my life to becoming the best baseball player I could be.

When I arrived in Chapel Hill, I knew no one, and I didn't really care. All I cared about was that I was on scholarship to play baseball at UNC. What was my major going to be? Didn't matter. Was I going to make any friends? Didn't matter. Was I going to meet my future wife? Didn't matter. I *burned* with desire. I was all-everything in Western Pennsylvania sports, but I knew that I was going to have to put in overtime to keep up with the other, more physically gifted players. The funny thing, though, is that I couldn't *wait* to get started. I would work out for an hour and a half before practice started and two hours after it ended. Everyday. I couldn't get enough. Eventually, coach Mike Roberts had to give me my own key to the stadium because he became sick and tired of waiting around for me to finish my workouts. It wasn't too long before I started hearing little comments made by the other players about my incessant practicing. I knew they were snickering behind my back, but you know what? I didn't care. I was going to *make* it. The only guy I keep in touch with from that year is Mark Kingston, who was a senior then and is currently an assistant coach at Tulane University. We hit it off from day one because we had a similar drive. When the others would chirp about our basically living in the hitting cages, he would say, "People mock what they do not understand." I couldn't agree more.

At the end of that year, I was more or less asked to transfer. Every speech Coach Roberts gave that year began and ended with work ethic, and no one worked harder than I did. The problem was that I simply wasn't very good. I hit .226 and fielded around .870. I was slow, and I hit with little power. He wanted to bring in some new junior college transfers, and he apparently had already promised them my scholarship money, something that infuriated my mother—and still does to this day. During our exit interviews in May of 1992, he told me that he didn't think I'd make the team in the future but if I wanted to stay as a regular student, I could still have my scholarship. As it turned out, unbeknownst to my parents and me, it was against UNC policy to rescind an athlete's scholarship for poor performance. Roberts knew how much I loved baseball and that I would never stay at UNC if I could not be on the team. He was right. Before I got into the car on the way back to Kittanning, I knew I would no longer be a Tar Heel.

That summer, I played in the Northeast Collegiate Baseball League (NCBL), and, once again, my intense craving for improvement alienated me from a lot of my teammates. I would beg the coaches to hit me groundballs after each practice. I would plead with them to throw me extra batting practice. I jumped rope at 9:00 PM to increase my foot quickness. I played Wiffle Ball on off days. Nobody understood, but you know what? I didn't care.

During that summer I decided to transfer to Virginia Tech, and for the second straight August, I enrolled at a 24,000-student campus not knowing a soul. I moved into an apartment with four other baseball players—one a junior, one a senior, and the other two had just completed their senior years in the spring. Typical of most upperclassmen who come to the conclusion that their baseball careers would end at the collegiate level, they had little passion for the game. They certainly enjoyed being on the team, but they didn't thirst for baseball like I did. I don't know if they were ready for me and all of my badgering. I was constantly trying to talk baseball with them, but rarely were they interested. To this day, whenever I talk to them, they still laugh (and so do I) about how intense I was. To exacerbate further my situation, I had no vehicle while living off-campus. Therefore, I had to rely on the Blacksburg Transit System to get me to and from campus on a daily basis. I would catch the bus at 7:00 AM from the apartment, go to class, go to practice, go to study hall, and then catch the bus at about 7:00 PM back to home. And, yes, I did most of these activities alone. Part of the reason is my disdain for waiting for other people. The other part, though, is that I had a goal to accomplish.

After fall workouts, we had no official practices until spring, so we could do whatever we wanted. Some guys lifted. Some guys did nothing. I went by myself to Rector Fieldhouse five days a week. As I was pushing myself through grueling speed and agility workouts and hitting off the batting tee, my inner voice would speak to me, and I found myself quoting the *Rocky* movies. One prominent voice was that of *Rocky III*'s Clubber Lang, who told reporters, "I live alone. I train alone. I win the championship alone." I then envisioned the scene of Lang's moaning and groaning as he worked out in his small, dirty, dimly lit apartment while Rocky was loafing. (Do I **really** need to make a symbolic connection here between Rocky and the upperclassmen?) The other line was from Rocky's trainer (and Apollo Creed's former trainer) in *Rocky IV* when Rocky went to the Soviet Union to train for his fight with Drago: "….Now, you're going to have to go through hell, worse than any nightmare, but in the end, I know you'll be the one standing. You know what you have to do. Do it. DO IT!" Usually, there was no one in the fieldhouse but me. Need I make another connection?

All that hard work paid off because during the following spring, for the first time in two years, I had some success on the field. I hit .423, leading the Metro conference. Needless to say, the gratification and sense of accomplishment were overwhelming. The two successive springs were equally rewarding, as I established myself as a *bona fide* collegiate third baseman. Unfortunately, the scouts didn't think too highly of me during the Amateur Draft of 1995; instead of receiving the phone call that I felt I deserved, I had to pick up the phone. If I didn't, I wouldn't have been able to play professionally.

I eventually decided to pack up my car and drive to Romeoville, IL, to play for the Will County Claws of the North Central League, a league that would fold in three weeks. In fact, I never even received a paycheck. To give you an idea of how poorly the league was operated, there was one team in Illinois and three in Minnesota. A four-team league. Are you kidding me? It gets better.

We opened on the road in Hibbing, MN, about 100 miles from the Canadian border, and before our first game, someone from our team had to go to K-Mart to buy bats for us. For those of you unfamiliar with bat quality, comparing K-Mart wooden bats to real professional wooden bats is like comparing Sandra Bernhard to Nicole Kidman. Because there was no clubhouse at the stadium, we drove the eight hours home without showering.

For our two opening home games, they didn't even charge admission in hopes of bringing out the fans. As it turned out, probably only 150 people showed up anyway. During one point in the game, the umpires ran out of official baseballs, so once again, someone had to go to the local sporting good store to buy more. Our resident genius returned with nylon balls with plastic cores (as opposed to leather ones).

In spite of everything, I did quite well on the field, hitting seven home-runs in twenty-one games. I didn't care about all the extraneous stuff; I just wanted to play ball. Sure, it bothered me that I was in some bullshit independent league when I felt as though I had earned a shot to play in the real minors, but what were my options? I could have done what a lot of snubbed ballplayers do and sit around the house that summer waiting for the phone to ring. Sorry, but I had dreams.

Anyway, after the league folded, I received an opportunity to join the Adirondack Lumberjacks of the newly formed Northeast League. The league was light-years better than the NCL, and upon my arrival, manager Dave LaPoint inserted me into the starting lineup, where I remained. I helped the Lumberjacks win the league championship, and I was named playoff MVP. It was a nice ending to a frustrating summer, but things soon went downhill fast. I spent that fall finishing up my degree at Virginia Tech and preparing a résumé to send out to all the major league teams. Here I was, a career .360 hitter at a major university, a .290 hitter in a decent independent league, and a playoff MVP, and no one gave me a chance. I suddenly began to understand why excessive pride is a deadly sin. I could have waited for that damn phone to ring, but, once again, I had dreams. Fulfilling these dreams meant swallowing what was left of my pride and going to Florida for tryout camps.

Every spring major league organizations hold tryout camps for recently released players or for players who fell through the cracks in the system. I went to the Spring Training sites of Philadelphia, Florida, St. Louis in order to catch on with one of those organizations—and talk about humiliation. You should *see* some of the guys that show up for an open tryout. Half of them probably didn't make their high school teams, and most of the rest of them that did play college ball were playing at a low level of competition and *still* didn't do well. I wasn't the first one to practice and the last one to leave, honing my skills, living and dying with every at-bat for four years of college to be lumped together with a guy who wore those white, plastic-soled cleats and a Jack Daniels tank-top. I suppose the business world equivalent would be graduating from a top-notch business school with a 3.5 GPA, going to a job fair with IBM, and seeing the members of Podunk High School's metal shop there as your competition.

Unfortunately, no one offered me a contract—signing at one of these tryouts is rare for anyone, let alone someone with my lack of "tools"—so I retreated to Blacksburg with my tail between my legs and tears gushing from my eyes. As luck would have it, however, I connected with the expansion Arizona Diamondbacks organization, and after a one-on-one workout with a scout, I signed my first real minor league contract. I then proceeded to play for two years, 1996 and 1997, in their minor league system before being released in December of 1997. Playing in the "real" minors was quite the humbling experience. Although I performed reasonably well, all I had to do was look around me to see the talent level that existed. Lots of guys, like me, can play in Class A. The big question is, "Can you play at the big league level?" Apparently, Arizona, Houston (spring training, 1998) and Montreal (spring training, 2000) all thought not.

I then moved on to Chico, CA, to play for the Chico Heat, and after three successful years, I decided to try my luck overseas. Certainly, I was hoping for another chance at spring training with an organization, but my chances were next to zero. When I found out that I had been selected to go, I reacted not with the youthful enthusiasm I exhibited upon signing my first contract but rather with the ho-hum of making a simple business decision. Baseball can suck the joy right out of you.

My point to this prologue is for you to understand who I am and what baseball has done to me and for me. I want you to understand that for every drop of gasoline that feeds the fire, there is a drop of water that extinguishes it. When I was younger—say, from 18 to 23—I used all these aforementioned trials and tribulations as reasons to continue the pursuit. Now, at the ripe and cynical old age of 28, they have become reasons to end it. I grew tired of having to deal with the "system." I grew tired of watching younger, better players from all over the world leapfrog past me at breakneck speed. I grew tired of being "average." I grew tired of seeing friends and family members with "stuff." I want "stuff," too, and baseball won't provide me with what I want. Six years ago, I didn't give a damn that

I could fit everything I owned into my 1988 Dodge Daytona. Today, the fact that I can nearly do that with my 1998 Chevy Camaro is quite disturbing. As you'll see in the journal, I like to sprinkle quotations throughout my stories. Allow me to end this prologue with the last line from "The Fire Inside" by *Bob Seger and the Silver Bullet Band*: "…like wind on the plains, sand through the glass, waves rolling in with the tide/Dreams die hard and we watch them erode but we cannot be denied…. The fire inside…. Burning you up…. Burning you up…. The fire inside."

CHAPTER 1

▼

SEEKING THE RICHES OF THE EAST

Tuesday, February 27, 2001 (12:45 AM PST)
Somewhere over the Pacific Ocean

Well, as I crank this out, I am sitting in a humongous 747 jet. For those of you who have been clamoring for my next entry, the reason that I have been *incommunicado* for the past few weeks is the same reason that I am on this aircraft: I am on my way to Taiwan. I had been vigorously closing up shop in Chico: paying bills, distributing my furniture, and generally tying up loose ends for about 10 days in preparation for my journey into the abyss known as the Orient. By the way, I *will* have access to my e-mail address as well as my Website address, so please feel free to inundate me with as much correspondence as possible to help me maintain my sanity as the proverbial "Stranger in a Strange Land."

As I listen to the flight attendants belt out their instructions in Chinese, which I'm certain are as inane and pointless as they are in English, I must admit that various thoughts are racing through my head, ranging from excitement to anxiety to nervousness, and all points in between. Other than the brief comments that a Chico teammate of mine who played in Taiwan last spring has told me, I know next to nothing about what to expect. The one thing I do know is my salary, and that is why I'm going in the first place. I did a live interview with a local TV station in Chico last week, where I came out and said, "You know, you hear all the time about athletes' saying that 'it's not about the money.' Well, this is *definitely* about the money."

Now, to avoid sounding like a money-hungry, unappreciative big leaguer, let me qualify that quote by saying that it's not as if I'm turning down $8 million a year in search of $12 million. Basically, I have a chance to make in a month and a half what I would make for an entire summer in Chico. Because of the Western Baseball League's salary cap restrictions, a player's earnings are somewhat limited, and that is why several players in recent years have decided to give the Taiwan Major League a try.

Nevertheless, I have to admit that I feel somewhat guilty about leaving the Heat because had it not been for former manager Bill Plummer's constantly working with me, I wouldn't even be in the position to go overseas. I'll be the first one to admit that Plummer deserves almost all the credit for making me the hitter I am today. Furthermore, I was involved in the Chico Heat Reading Program. In this program, Rory Miller, our tireless play-by-play announcer, Heater the mascot, and I went around to local elementary schools to speak about the importance of reading, and it pains me greatly to leave in the middle of our 12-week endeavor. Unfortunately, though, at 28-years-old, with about no chance of catching on with an organization, and finding myself increasingly unhappy with my financial situation, Taiwan is the only logical choice for me at this point in my life.

One common question I have gotten from many people is, "Aren't you going to miss Chico?" Hell, yes! This will be the first time in four seasons that I won't be playing for the Heat, but once you sign that first pro contract, you basically sell your soul to baseball. If it means living a nomadic, everything-you-own-you-can-fit-in-your-car existence for six or ten or fourteen years, so be it. If it means seeing your friends paying a mortgage rather than rent or hearing them discuss 401K's while you talk about your ERA, so be it. And if it means leaving your comfort zone for the Pacific Rim to augment your bank account, well, you gotta do it.

I suppose that sounds as though I'm complaining a little bit too much, and my mother constantly reassures me that if most people had the opportunity to do what I have done and what I am doing now, they'd jump at it. Now, even though in my heart of hearts I know that what she says is true, the bottom line is that "love don't pay the rent." Don't get me wrong; I absolutely love being a "celebrity" (believe me, my tongue is firmly imbedded in my cheek) in Chico and being a positive influence in the community and hearing the crowd yell, "Let's Go Bo!" when I come up to the plate. However, when it comes time to sit across from that loan officer, all the interviews and autographs and cheers don't mean Jack Squat.

Finally, let me say once again that I don't really know for sure how long I will be here in Taiwan. Spring training, which begins on March 1, lasts about a month, and then the manager will decide if I am the type of player he wants on his team. If so, I would like to play the entire season—which, incidentally, parallels an American major league season—and then return stateside in October. If, for some reason, he decides that I am not what he is looking for, I'll be back in time for the start of Chico's spring training. As I said, I just don't know what to expect, other than my salary and the fact that the team consists of all Taiwanese players except for a Japanese pitcher and me. Can you say communication breakdown?

Fortunately, though, baseball is baseball, and once I get on the field, I should be okay, with the possible exception of trying to figure out what in Sam Hill the umpires are saying. Other than that, it's go time. "Have bat, will travel, reads the card of a man/A summer without English in a savage land." Out.

Wednesday, February 28, 2001 (4:00 PM)
Taichung

After a 14-hour, uneventful flight, I landed in the mysterious and exotic Taipei, where my contact, Jeremy Chou, greeted me and then promptly put me on a bus to Tai-chung (also spelled Tai-chong or Taijung). The trip was about two hours long, and for all you who are into that type of stuff, the landscape was nothing special. Other than seeing English words on buildings and signs, the only "Western" thing I saw was a billboard of Britney Spears. By the way, unlike American buses, the bus I was on featured one row on each side of the aisle with *one seat* per row. Even better, the seat was like a big Lazy Boy, sans leg rest, and able to recline about 30 degrees.

At the bus terminal, I was met by our team's equipment manager, Abai, and our interpreter, "Kevin." Actually, Kevin, whose real name is difficult to pronounce and spell in English, will be *my* interpreter—wow, don't I feel special!—since I'm the only American on the team. After some pleasantries, I asked him what his position was, and he told me was the interpreter, to which I responded, "OK, so you and I are best friends, right?" He chuckled, telling me that humor is humor, no matter where you are.

We then proceeded to the apartment complex of the entire team, and Kevin showed me to my room. I must admit that I was pleased to hear that I get a room all to myself, as does every player, and that the team pays the rent on it. Unfortunately, though, since the team basically "owns" the room, no one has set foot in it since the last player left, and the room was in disarray, to say the least. So, doing my best Martha Stewart imitation, I cleaned the quarters to the best of my ability. The upside to having left the room unkempt since last fall, however, is that much of the former (American) player's stuff was still here. Such remnants include a few books on learning Chinese, cleaning supplies, linens, and cookware.

The room itself is more than adequate for anyone, and it comes complete with a color TV and satellite, refrigerator, phone, Internet access, and a washer and dryer. Not too shabby, huh? It's a far cry from my Colombian excursion two winters ago where my roommate and I shared a smaller room with far fewer amenities. Incidentally, the washer and dryer will be used on a daily basis because we players have to launder our own uniforms after each practice and game. This is a decidedly un-American policy, but it's not as though we have to go to a laundromat and wait two hours for it, so I refuse to complain about it.

Near our apartment complex, in which I reside on the 18th of 19 floors in my particular building, is a KFC and a McDonalds, where I snarfed down a Sausage McMuffin with Egg Combo Meal for breakfast. Something tells me that I am going to develop an even greater affinity for the cuisine of The Colonel and Ronald, which could eventually invite comparisons of Babe Ruth, but only in his prodigious girth. According to Kevin, Chinese food here is quite inexpensive, and if it tastes at all like "American" Chinese food, I'll be happy.

Let me close with a few points of interest. Taichung is the third largest city in Taiwan, with Taipei, the capital, as the most populous, and it is located on the NW coast of the island. The weather here today was about 70 degrees and overcast. In the Taiwan Major League (TML), there are four teams, and in the Chinese Professional League (CPBL), there are four teams; I am in the TML. Apparently, a few years ago, the CPBL was tainted by a game-fixing scandal, and it is now known as the "dirtier" of the two leagues, but Kevin says that preliminary talks are underway to have "interleague" play, if not an amalgamation of the two leagues. My team's name is Agan, which means, roughly, "Hercules." As I learn more, I will include the other teams' names. Kevin says Taichung averaged roughly 4,000 fans per game last summer, and he thinks that the figure will rise slightly this year as the Taiwanese people slowly rinse the rotten taste out of their mouths from the past. Practice starts tomorrow, so I am anxious to see how everything goes. Out.

Friday, March 2, 2001 (11:00 AM)
Taichung

As I write this entry, I am on the team bus as we travel to our second practice. I'm not sure why, but we have a 90 minute bus ride to our practice facility for the first three practices, and since I have read cover-to-cover all the *Sports Illustrateds* and *ESPN The Magazines* that I brought—even the X games articles (ugh!)—I figured this is an opportune time to write my journal entries.

Yesterday, we had our first practice, and needless to say, it was quite different from an American spring training workout. We had a brief meeting at the beginning, during which all the players had to remove their hats while the manager, Mr. Wu, spoke. Then, he asked me if I wanted to say anything, and, through Kevin, of course, I said that I was happy to be here and willing to do whatever it took to win a championship. Normally, that's just lip service for most athletes, but when I found out that in 1999, after Agan won the league and the team was taken to Hawaii on an all-expense paid victory vacation, I truly meant it. Not too shabby, huh?

One positive thing I found out from Mr. Wu was that he is willing to let me spend the first ten days or so preparing at my own pace. I explained to him about my knee surgery last year and that spring training, with all of its extra conditioning, can cause me quite a bit of discomfort. He then told me that I could do whatever conditioning I wanted to do. While I appreciate such leeway, I don't want to come across as the "lazy American," especially in a culture where hard work and discipline are such highly regarded virtues. I am trying to walk the narrow line of caring for my knee and earning the respect of my teammates. If I were to err, though, I would rather do so on the cautionary side because, as the old saying goes, "You can't make the club in the tub."

I estimate that we spent roughly an hour warming up, stretching, and conditioning before I even touched a baseball, and having played independent league baseball for the past few years, it was certainly a change of pace. Most of the stretching exercises were familiar, but some of the conditioning drills were not. I watched the guys go through all of them until we ended with some sprints, and then I joined in. I must say that I was quite nervous about how my knee was going to hold up during the sprints, but I ran about 10 of them with no problems. We then got the balls out and began throwing, and since I hadn't thrown anything but a long outlet pass on the basketball court since last spring, I had to force myself to take it easy. Next, we split up into our positions to take fungoes (groundballs), and I was happy with the fact that I didn't miss a single one, even more so when I saw the other third baseman miss several.

On a side note, one thing I have been maybe the most proud of in my baseball career is my defensive skill at third base, especially when you consider that I had no idea how to properly field a groundball until the fall of 1992. My high school baseball coaches were both former pitchers, and looking back at what Mike Roberts, my coach at UNC, was trying to teach us defensively, I just shake my head. Whatever strides I have made defensively are a result of the teachings of Jay Phillips, my infield coach at Virginia Tech; it was through his instruction and my own diligent practice habits that I am now a pretty good defensive third baseman in spite of not having tremendously quick feet or a rocket for an arm. Furthermore, unlike most baseball players, I haven't fallen subject to the Peter Principle, the theory that an employee will climb the corporate ladder until he reaches his level of incompetence. Since I don't have the foot speed to play the outfield, the agility to play the middle infield, or the arm strength to be a catcher (notice how I didn't say 'play catcher'?), I have been at the hot corner for what is now my tenth season. Therefore, I have learned the nuances of fielding all those tricky hops, slow rollers, and hot smashes, and, in doing so, I have developed into a fine defensive third baseman. So many of the more-gifted players spend their whole careers bouncing around from one position to the next, becoming a "Jack of all trades, master of none," but fortunately my average athletic ability has actually made me better. Go figure.

After fielding practice, we broke off into our hitting groups, and the way we did it was definitely different. In an American batting practice session of, say, four groups, one group is hitting live BP on the field, one is hitting in a batting cage, one is fielding fungoes from the coaches or pitchers, and one is shagging in the outfield. Yesterday, though, we had three groups, and two groups would shag in the outfield while the other group was hitting, and that group was hitting three people *at a time*. The coaches wheeled out a bunch of screens, which were carefully set up so the three BP pitchers were properly protected. It looks odd to the newcomer, but it is very efficient and safe, the only danger being that a batted ball could ricochet off one the screens and strike a batter. The only problem, however, is that after 20 swings or so, I tired, so I found myself having to take mini-breaks to keep myself fresh. I'm a firm believer that "tired" swings lead to bad swings, and I would rather spend my allotted three minutes taking 40 quality swings with a few breaks mixed in than 25 good ones and then 40 half-assed ones.

All in all, for the first day, it went rather well considering I hadn't swung a bat since last fall. My shoulders and arms and hands are sore from all the swings, but that it is to be expected. We'll see how it goes today. On the way home, we were all given "Rice Boxes," a healthy concoction of white rice, seaweed, pork, green beans, and cabbage, all to be eaten with chopsticks. Normally, when I'm hungry after a workout, I eat with all the daintiness of an emaciated pit bull, but my unfamiliarity with these chop sticks has forced me to slow down. Apparently, it's "healthier" to eat slowly— like I care—so maybe the chop sticks will have some long-term health benefits to counteract my short-term aggravation.

One thing I neglected to mention is that on Wednesday night, I was given my uniform and peripheries, and I made out like a bandit. I received the following: two pairs of sliding shorts, four pairs of socks, two pairs of pants, four different-colored game shirts, one jacket, one pullover, four white sleeveless undershirts, four blue undershirts, four pairs of wristbands, a hat, a belt, a bag, and two bats, with a pair of white cleats (ugh!)

and a glove to arrive soon. That's more free stuff than I have gotten in my 6 previous years of pro ball. Because of my gigantic cranium, Abai, the equipment manager had to dig through several boxes to find a hat for me (Kevin said that no one has ever worn that size before), and while he was looking, I picked up a three-gallon bucket and proceeded to put it on my head, much to their delight.

Also, I've found that one of the truisms of spring training is that no team has ever had a batting helmet in stock that fits me, and Agan was no different. Normally, I have to cut out some of the padding of an existing helmet to make it fit, but Abai said he would get me one as soon as possible. Here, all the helmets have one protective earflap, so as a switch hitter, I had to decide if I wanted to have two one-flap helmets or one two-flap helmet. For convenience reasons only, I chose one helmet, and the search is on to find the appropriate headgear.

I am without Kevin today, as he went to Taipei for an exam—he is taking classes at a college there—but last night, he wrote down on a piece of paper what to order at two different eateries, so I was able to purchase food without a problem. I have found a very tasty and healthy local dish, which is basically a pork and cabbage dumpling, and one dumpling costs $4 NT (currently, $1 US = approx. $30 NT) if you eat it there. However, if you take home and prepare frozen dumplings, they only cost $3 NT. So, I bought 50 frozen dumplings, and a bowl of soup for $210 NT, but when you consider that I ate only 17 dumplings and the soup, the meal itself cost me only about $3.75 American. I can live with that.

Well, we are almost to the field now, so I have to go. Until next time.... Out.

Saturday, March 3, 2001 (4:00 PM)
Taichung

Today's entry will encompass both Friday's and today's workouts. On Friday, we practiced in the afternoon, and it was sure a hot one. I wore one of those plastic pullovers, and I was sweating like Wilt Chamberlain at a paternity test. My hands and forearms were pretty sore, but I still did okay. The Taiwanese love their music during practice, and the loudspeakers were blaring everything from Enrique Iglesias to Destiny's Child to Eminem—boy, I gotta learn how to say, "I'm the real Slim Shady" in Taiwanese.

We practiced at Luka's field again, and I introduced myself to a couple of Australians. One of them, Gavin Fingleson, played in the independent Northern League, and this is his first year in Taiwan. The other guy, Matt Buckley, was a member of the Intercontinental Cup team in 1999, when I represented the USA. I remembered the name, but I don't remember what type of player he is. I do know that they won the Cup that year and that he was also a member of their Olympic team last fall. Typical of the Australians whom I have met, they were both very friendly. This is Buckley's third year in the league, and he told me to just play hard and don't rock the boat. I told him that I agreed.

At the end of practice, Mr. Wu said he felt that I wasn't ready to play in a game yet, so I would have to be a spectator for Saturday's scrimmage. Although I disagreed with him, I said that I understood. The Taiwanese expect you to be in peak physical condition, which to them means that you should be able to run a damn marathon. I just wanted to play to work on my batting eye and not worry about how I do, but I bit my tongue.

It's funny, but in the first few days, I noticed the contrasts this culture can have at times. For example, Kevin and I went to McDonald's that first day, and we sat on small, plastic stools whose surface was about the size of a Kennedy Half-Dollar, yet the seating on the bus is *far* more spacious than anything I have seen in America. Also, one would think that with all the conditioning we do, smoking and drinking would be frowned upon, but I estimate that 90% of the team smokes, even during the game, and at our post-scrimmage party, the booze flowed like Niagara Falls. I don't quite understand it, but it certainly is interesting.

Last night, while Kevin was still in Taipei, I was on my own for dinner, so I just boiled up those dumplings. Now, I know what you're thinking: Jeez, Bo, how many nights in a row can you eat the same meal? Well, anyone that knows me knows that I am not afraid to eat the same meals over and over again. One of my brother's all-time favorite "Boisms" is when my roommate in High Desert in 1997 asked me how I could eat my bacon, egg, and cheese sandwiches every freakin' morning, and I asked him, "Well, how can you wake up next to the same woman every morning?" He loves that one. In fact, I found a little diner-type place (hell, they're *all* pretty much diner-type places) which specializes in breakfast cuisine, and I ordered, yep, three bacon, egg, and cheese sandwiches and a sweetened iced tea for $95 NT, roughly $3.25 US. Not bad. The first day I ordered them, the cook put pickles and tomatoes on them, and so I told Kevin to nix that. Now, when I walk in, he knows exactly what to prepare, and I don't have to hold Kevin's hand every freakin' minute of the day.

Today, we had an early morning, and we left the hotel at 8:00 AM. We got to the field at about 9:20 AM and started our pregame routine at about 9:30 AM. It was another hot one, and I was soaked by the end of our practice session. As I said before, the Taiwanese don't skimp on their preparation and conditioning. We finished our "boot camp" and proceeded into batting practice and fielding practice, and everything went smoothly for me. Because I wasn't scheduled to play in the scrimmage, Mr. Wu wanted me to take some swings in the batting cage and then to do some running. So, in about the third inning, I took a few hacks and then ran ten poles, which means I ran along the warning track from foul pole to foul pole ten times. I can say with virtual certainty that it was the most I had run at one time in my entire pro baseball career, but I did it to look as if I was trying to get in better shape. In my opinion distance running for position players is pointless, but I wanted to oblige Mr. Wu.

After the game, we did some abdominal work, some light sprint work, and hit the showers. We then went to a barbeque-style party, where the cooks prepared the food right in front of us. The cuisine included bread and butter—have you ever tried to spread butter with chopsticks?—fresh seafood, pork, soup, noodles, rice, and beer. I ate well.

Finally, we returned to the apartment, where one of the pitchers asked me to go "clubbing" with some of the guys, and I said okay. But, when we got into the apartment, he told me that a last-minute birthday party popped up, and he suggested that I meet them at the club. Normally, I consider it to be a travesty to sit at home on a Saturday night, no matter where one finds himself, but since Kevin wasn't going to be with me (he had made plans himself), I didn't feel comfortable taking a cab by myself to a new dance club in a foreign country. Maybe next time, I told him, I could meet them there, but for the first time, I wanted Kevin with me. Thus, I spent the night setting up my Internet service, which is going to be quite reasonable financially. That is a *huge* load off my mind; without cheap Internet access, I would undoubtedly go stir crazy. Being without my beloved laptop/Internet in Taiwan is no different from being without a telephone in America, *i.e.*, unbearable. All in all, after four days, everything has gone well, but you never know what tomorrow will bring. Out.

Monday, March 5, 2001 (3:30 PM)
Taichung

Not a whole lot happened between Saturday night and now, so this entry will be short. I spent Sunday surfing the Internet and fending for myself food-wise, as Kevin was once again in Taipei. You're probably thinking that if he is my interpreter and I don't speak a lick of Taiwanese, he should be at my side 24-7, but that wouldn't just drain him, it would drain *me* as well. In a perverted sort of way, I'm glad I'm the only American on my team; if there were another, I'd feel obligated to hang out with him. To me, the old saying "familiarity breeds contempt" may be a bit strong, but I definitely agree with it. Because of my nomadic/loner nature, being around the same person or people for a long stretch of time makes me feel extremely claustrophobic, so I'm glad I'm by myself. I know, sick, right?

Today's practice was a morning one, and I actually prefer an early work-out to a late one during spring training. It's rough getting up at 6:45 AM, but we were finished and on the bus back to Taichung by 1:45 PM. Now, the rest of the day is free. For the first time since I've been here, my body felt great, almost 100%. It's funny, but when your body's hurting, either from injury or general soreness, you feel like you can't do ***anything*** on the field, but once it goes away, you feel like you can conquer the world. I was zipping the ball across the infield and swinging the bat—I even hit a homerun at our spacious practice field—almost like it was the middle of summer, and it was a great feeling. I told Mr. Wu that I would be ready for our scrimmage on Wednesday, but I don't think he's quite sold yet. I hope that another good practice tomorrow will convince him otherwise.

I wanted to finish today's entry by offering further evidence to my tal-ent vs. hard work theory that I postulated in one of my Baseball America website entries from early January. If you've ever seen Asian-style baseball, you've noticed how eerily similar the batters' swings are. I asked Mr. Wu why this is, and he said in his limited, broken English that basically, the Asians have accepted their physical shortcomings—lack of blazing speed or tremendous power—and have become masters of the fundamentals. Certainly, there are exceptions to the rule: our 6'4" first baseman has AA or AAA power and our right fielder hit 15 homeruns in 50 games last year. But for the most part, the Asians understand their general lack of size and strength as a people, and apparently from Day One, baseball players are taught to hit with the same basic technique.

Now, it's pretty much common knowledge that Asians are an extremely hard-working and disciplined people. Do you see where I'm going with this yet? So, here's my question: if everyone is taught to hit the same way and almost everyone has a solid work ethic and good practice habits, what separates those who peak out at the high school level and those who lead the TML in homeruns? The answer is talent. Some guys can hit, and some

guys can't. Period. I have heard the saying, "He's got the hitter's genes."
One big league hitting coach indelicately calls it having "hitter's sperm."
Whatever you want to call it, some people have that natural ability "to put
the bat on the ball." When Hank Aaron was a kid, he would hit bottle
caps with a broom handle. Talk about developing eye-hand coordination!
Other players have been "hitters" since they first picked up a bat in Little
League. I played with a guy who was one of those types of hitters, and he
and I would snicker while watching some less-than-talented guys take batting practice. The unfortunate *coup de grace* of baseball, though, is that
these guys could take BP for eight hours a day and lift weights until the
cows come home and *still* not have the bat speed, bat quickness, pitch
recognition, and eye-hand coordination of my ex-teammate, the same one
I mentioned in the introduction. This guy can "flat-out hit," and he
always could, and other players will never come close to that type of ability. As I said in that BA article, it's one of those sad but true facts of the
sports world. Sorry, people, but chalk up another victory for talent. Out.

Wednesday, March 7, 2001 (6:15 PM)
Taichung

I played in my first game today, a seven-inning scrimmage against
Luka. We pretty much got our asses kicked, but it was fun to get out there
and play in a game situation. I had a typical Bo Durkac day: 1 for 3, with
a walk, a run scored and an RBI. I scored my run from first base on a two-
out double, and I just barely beat the throw to the plate. When I returned
to the dugout, one of our catchers said, "Bo, good speed!" I didn't want to
burst his bubble by telling him that in the USA, my foot speed is generally
compared to that of a three-toed sloth. I felt pretty good at the plate,
meaning I saw the ball well and took some decent swings considering it
was my first live pitching since last fall. Defensively, I had one routine
groundball that I fielded cleanly and one hot smash down the line that I
dove for, but it just nicked off my glove. My legs still feel a little bit

"heavy" from all the conditioning, but I'm hoping that by the end of the month, I'll get that "light on my feet" feeling that I'm waiting for. Now for the off the field, interesting stuff.

On Monday evening, after not having seen a single English-speaking woman in about five days, I met a Canadian, Lara, and a South African, Tania. Like most English-speaking people here, they're teachers, and they're both friendly and seem to be a lot of fun. Tania invited me to come visit her and her roommate, Carol (another South African), that night, and since they live only four floors below me in the same building, I went. We basically just talked and had some coffee, and I must say it was refreshing to speak English with someone. I stayed for a couple of hours, and then I went back upstairs because we had an early morning on Tuesday.

Yesterday, after an uneventful practice, I ran into Lara at about 9:00 PM, and we sat and talked for about 45 minutes or so outside her apartment building, which is in the same complex as mine. She's from the Toronto area, and she lives with another Canadian couple, Ryan and Shane (no, Shane is a girl). She was interesting to talk to, and we went over some of the ropes for getting around Taichung, places to go and places *not* to go. She is dating an American here in Taichung, but I told her that maybe this weekend, we can have a "foreigners' night" out on the town, and she seemed to think it was a good idea, so we'll see. Oh, before I saw Lara, I had just come from a dinner with Carol, her New Zealander friend Simon, and about four or five other Taiwanese teachers. We went to a little restaurant around the corner, and I had to sit on the floor and eat. Talk about painful. Since I'm about as flexible as a slab of marble, it is very uncomfortable for me to eat under such conditions, but I did enjoy the food, the drink, and the company, so I didn't complain. One of the Taiwanese teachers, Jasmine, was born in Taiwan but had been living in Canada until about one year ago, so as I told the group last night, we had just about every part of the erstwhile British empire covered.

Everyday, it seems I find another little difference about the Taiwanese culture (and baseball style), and each one is interesting. The other day at practice, our 19-year-old, strong-armed shortstop missed three ground-balls in a row, and after the third one, Mr. Wu called him over. Mr. Wu then told "Yon-sen" to remove his cap, whereupon Mr. Wu gently rapped on the head with the knob of his fungo bat. I was laughing my ass off. Then, at the end of the defensive drills, Yon-sen and another infielder, who also wasn't fielding as well as Mr. Wu had hoped, had to go out to the centerfield warning track and scream their names and numbers at the top of their lungs ten times. "My name is Yon-sen, and I am Number Eleven!" Once again, I was roaring.

During the game today, there was food in our dugout. They have these tasty little biscuit-type egg rolls (think Waffle House meets Wok 'N Roll), and they're fair game during the scrimmage. As you can imagine, I ate quite a few, maybe six over the course of the game. Pitchers, after completing their halves of the inning, sometimes stand on the side and throw while we're hitting. In America, the only time I ever see that is when a pitcher is forced to wait more than 20 minutes or so between innings, but these guys do it *all the time*. Also, as I mentioned before, I think every single player on the team fired up a cigarette at one time or another during the game. I just don't get it.

After the game today, we had another two-team dinner. When we arrived at the restaurant, each table had a huge wok full of beef, cabbage, mushrooms, lettuce, and fish balls (no, not *those* kind of balls; I asked Kevin what they were and when he told he, I asked myself first if fish do indeed have balls but then figured that even if they do, they certainly couldn't be as big as what was in the wok—I thought I was in for a Pacific Rim version of Rocky Mountain oysters). Once again, I devoured the stuff, but in doing so, I realized that if I don't figure out how to use those infernal chopsticks soon, I might become the first player to be placed on the Disabled List for carpal tunnel syndrome.

Also, joining us at our table for a few minutes was Hishanobu Watanabe, who pitched very successfully in the Japanese Major Leagues for about 15 years, and you don't have to be fluent in Japanese to recognize his charisma. He smoked like a Western Pennsylvania steel mill and drank like an Irishman on St. Patrick's Day, and the guys at our table were carrying on with him with equal parts admiration and good-natured humor.

Tomorrow is a day off, with the exception of a light weightlifting session at 8:00 PM, and I'm looking forward to the rest. I find it interesting that during our spring training, we actually have days off mixed in. In America, the only time you get a day off during spring training is when it rains, and even then you end up lifting weights or hitting balls in a batting cage. For a culture so hell-bent on hard work, to get a day of rest seems a bit hypocritical, but hey, I'm not complaining. If they want to pay me for sleeping and surfing the Internet, so be it. Out.

Friday, March 9, 2001 (6:00 PM)
Taichung

With *Footloose* on the TV in the background—does Kevin Bacon have good hair in *any* movie?—I figured I could crank out another entry. Yesterday, after spending the day, well, sleeping and surfing the Internet, I visited the South Africans on the way up from our weight lifting session, and we chatted for about 3 hours. It's interesting to hear their views on relationships, racism in South Africa, and living here in Taiwan. I like to hear what makes people tick, especially those who aren't from where I'm from. I learned a little bit about the country, about how the Dutch and English influence is being smothered by the immense black population there (according to them, roughly 8 million whites vs. 30 million blacks). Carol told me that because of censorship, she was basically unaware of all the apartheid issues that the rest of the world saw on TV from time to time. I couldn't believe it. Can you imagine such censorship occurring in America? Yes, the good ol' USA may have its problems, but I'll take our government over any other one in the history of civilization—without a doubt. The next time you're bitchin' and moanin' about Uncle Sam's policies, hey, by all means, pack your bags and move to South

Africa or Taiwan or anywhere else; within a year, I guarantee you'll be begging for a one-way ticket home.

The other day, I decided that if I'm going to be here, I might as well indulge in my vices. Anyone who knows me knows of my love of iced tea, so I bought some tea bags at the local supermarket. I don't know how much cooking I am going to do, but I can only drink so much water. One of my other vices is chewing gum, be it just walking the streets or on the ball field.

I brought several packs of my beloved "Bubble Gum-flavored Extra Sugar-Free" gum, but I've also been introduced to a Taiwanese version of chewing tobacco, called the "bitternut." It's a green little nugget about the size of small Tootsie Roll that when you initially bite on it, the juices just gush out of it. They were telling me not to swallow the juices in the first few seconds, but then after that, it's okay. So, I tried it, and I honestly, I don't see what the big deal is. All the Taiwanese guys love them, but I felt like a two-legged ruminant chomping on the stuff. I'll stick to the gum and the sunflower seeds.

One thing I forgot to mention the other night is that on the way home from dinner, the guys in the back of the bus were "karaokeing" (is that spelled right?) over the bus speakers. Now, that's something that would **never** happen on an American baseball bus, with the possible exception of returning from winning a championship. Doing so would imply that 1) you think the other players want to hear you sing and 2) you, as an individual, are more important than the other players; neither attitude is acceptable in American baseball. Hell, if you want to listen to music, you have to use headphones. In fact, after each song, everyone on the bus applauded. Are you kidding me? By the end of the trip, my head was ringing, but these guys acted like a bunch of drunk, Japanese businessmen after five rounds of sake.

Today's practice was held at our home field for the first time. Unlike the field in Jia-yi, this one has a grass infield and very reachable fences. I can see why Abai, the guy who led the league in homeruns last year, did so well here. He and our first baseman ought to have terrific power numbers this summer, and maybe even yours truly might reach double-digits for the first time in the HR category. Also, it was considerably cooler today, and I think it's just because we've had a bit of a cool spell here. Everyone keeps saying that the middle of summer here is borderline unbearable, but, for now, I'll take the coolness during spring training.

It's Friday night, but it doesn't seem that way. Maybe it's just because it's spring training, when even in America all the days seem to run together. I don't have any plans on going out tonight, but we'll see. Tomorrow, the Canucks invited me to go out with them, and I accepted. I'm curious to see what this city has to offer. I keep hearing of a little strip of bars and dance clubs downtown to which all the foreigners tend to gravitate on the weekends, but someone was saying that a typical cover charge can be as much as $15 U.S. If that's the case, I'll either stay home or request that we go elsewhere. Dancing, to me, is about as much fun as pancreatic cancer, so I'd much prefer a little hole-in-the-wall bar with a couple of pool tables, a jukebox, and less expensive drinks. Fortunately, the Canadians, from what Lara told me, feel the same way, and she told me about a few places that fit the description. All I know is that I refuse to sit at home on consecutive Saturday nights; that's for married people—booooooooooooring. Out.

Sunday, March 11, 2001 (5:30 PM)
Taichung

Well, I did it. I went out on the town last night, and I had a very good time. Lara and I took a cab to meet the other Canucks at a little restaurant/bar called *Napoli's*. It was definitely my kind of place: pool table, well lit, and reasonably affordable. We "visited" for a while, and then the persistent clacking of the pool balls turned into an intoxicating Siren song, and I just had to go play. As I was playing, the Canadians were dancing on the diminutive dance floor. We stayed out until about 2:30 AM and then took cabs back to the apartment.

On Saturday, we played a team from Mainland China. Evidently, they are trying to start an amateur league there, and the team we played is from a city near Beijing. They were pretty good, with some good players, but we finally won our first "game," 4-3. All of the pitchers we faced were left-handed, which means that I had to hit right-handed. One of the first questions I ask before every game is about the starting pitcher and with which hand he throws. I then pattern my pre-game batting routine accordingly. Well, yesterday, I asked Mr. Wu if this team has any lefties, and through a series of physical gyrations, he told me no. Therefore, I didn't practice my right-handed swing at all, only to find that I would bat righty four times. To complicate things further, the first lefty was throwing very hard, or at least it seemed that way. One of the rarest things in baseball is a hard-throwing, left-handed pitcher, and because of this, when you face one, your hitting "instincts" are not as prepared as they normally would be against other types of pitchers. My first three at-bats were exercises in futility, but I felt a little bit better when I saw that the big guns on our team were struggling against him and it wasn't just my own ineptitude. Each of my at-bats, though, was progressively better, culminating in a sharp, line drive single to leftfield in my last at-bat.

Now, Kevin tells me that there are only two lefties in our whole league, which poses a bit of a problem for me: how much should I practice my right-handed swing? Over the course of my career, I have been a better hitter left-handed, but last year, I felt as good about my right-handed swing as I had in a long time. If I spend very little time in practice working from the right side, I may find myself ill prepared when the situation presents itself in a game. On the other hand, if I'm only going to get a few swings everyday, I should probably use those swings to hone my left-handed swing, which I will be using probably 90% of the time. It's definitely a fine line to walk, and I'll just have to determine how to allot my swings as the season progresses.

From an adjustment standpoint, I am starting to crave certain things. For example, I would pay a king's ransom for the 1-½ hours of "Seinfeld" and "The Simpsons" that was on TV each weeknight in Chico. Now, I'm not a huge fan of "South Park," but it is on TV here in Taichung every so often. Instead of subtitles, however, they simply overdub the English-speaking voices with Taiwanese voices. Therefore, the show is about as useful to me as a driver's license is to Stevie Wonder. And, yes, for those of you who are familiar with the show, you don't have to be fluent in Taiwanese to see that Cartman is still the foul-mouthed, obnoxious kid here that he is in America. Also, lamentably, I have yet to see a chocolate chip cookie or a fudge brownie. I don't have a huge sweet tooth, but every once in a while, the urge for large quantities of chocolate arises, and it would be nice to indulge said tooth. Finally, the portions of food here are rather small, as you would imagine. I went to a local coffee shop for a hot cappuccino, and not only do they offer just one size, but the size itself is very average. When I want to eat or drink, I want it *now* and *lots* of it, but such accommodations are rare in Taiwan—maybe that's why Asians, as a people, tend to be less obese than Americans. In the meantime, my chameleonic nature should allow me to continue to adapt to the surroundings without incurring feelings of homesickness or frustration. Hey, whatever doesn't kill you only makes you stronger, right? Out.

Friday, March 16, 2001 (10:00 AM)
Taichung

It's been a few days since my last entry, partly because there isn't a whole lot to say and partly because I've partaken in another love of mine—shooting pool. In the summer of 1984, my dad and three of his brothers, none of whom were smaller than 6'3", 220 lbs., moved an eight-foot, ¾ inch slate pool table into our basement. From that day on, I was hooked. When I was in junior high and high school, during the summers, I'd have friends come over, and we'd play until 2:00 or 3:00 AM. When I read that Gregg

Jefferies, who burst onto the big league scene in 1988 like a ball of fire, said that he shot pool everyday when he was growing up to increase his eye-hand coordination, I did the same for a few months. And when I'd come home from college, when Brandi, my little sister, was still in high school, I would make her play with me to stave off the ennui that generally comes with Christmas vacation. It's funny, but to this day, whenever we get together, we always make a point to shoot a few games before we go our separate ways. I have often wondered if I'm "normal" because I don't have many traditional "hobbies," like playing golf, or hunting, or fishing, or hiking, or camping, or mountain biking, or whatever else, but playing pool is definitely my *numero uno*.

Monday night, Si-von, our chunky catcher, was shooting pool by himself on one of the pool tables in the apartment complex when I wandered by. I asked him if I could play, and he agreed. I would say he beat me pretty handily, and sensing that it would be more competitive and more fun on a better table, I flagged down Kevin to ask him if there were any pool halls around. Si-von and I then agreed to go to a pool hall, which turned out to be immaculate, on Wednesday night. We "wagered" that whoever lost had to pay the hourly rate for the table. I knew that Si-von is better than I am, but I also knew that the grand total would amount to barely $5.00 US; I figured it was worth it. It turned out that I beat him 11-7, so I made out quite well.

Last night, we went again, and as soon as I walked in the door, Si-von pointed to the main pool table—complete with a video camera so people can watch in other parts of the hall—and racked up the balls. Much to my surprise, the lady whom I've observed on TV here playing 9-ball ambles over for a game or two. Evidently, she is the number one-ranked women's 9-ball player in Taiwan, and I wasn't sure how many games we were going to play, but I knew I better bring my "A" game. Unfortunately, my game, on my best day, is about a "Q" compared to hers, and, basically, she eviscerated me. We ended up playing a race to 7 games, and while the final tally was 7-3, it wasn't even that close. The only games I won were where luck intervened, and, even so, it wasn't as though she were playing a high-quality opponent who would force her to make every shot count. What I'm getting at is that if she wanted to, she probably could have won every game. There was one stretch where I missed on the six-ball in one game and I didn't even get to shoot until the seven-ball—*three games later*!! I have never so thoroughly enjoyed getting waxed; it was a pleasure to watch her play. Later, Si-von and I played, and this time he beat me, so I had to pay. It only amounted to $4.00 US, and if that's the case, I have a feeling we'll be going quite a bit.

One thing I have constantly neglected to mention is the overwhelming odor on the streets of Taichung. Now, I have smelled some pungent aromas in my time; spreading cow manure on the farm, driving past a paper mill in southeast Virginia, and my own breath in the morning after a rough night out on the town all come to mind. But I have smelled nothing as nauseating as the tofu stands along the street outside of our apartment complex. I don't know what they do to the unfortunate soybeans, but it has to be pretty painful. In fact, the stench from the tofu stands *far* supersedes the omnipresent reek of the sewage system, and that's saying a lot.

As for baseball, we had Monday off followed by practices the last three days. The Tuesday and Wednesday practices were held here in Taichung and were relatively uneventful; Thursday's, however, was unbearable. When Julius Caesar was warned a few years back about the ides of March, perhaps the old man was speaking of the heat and humidity of Jia-yi, Taiwan. To borrow a phrase from my sports-literature hero, *Sports Illustrated*'s Rick Reilly, it was "hot enough to melt concrete." I can't remember the last time I sweated so much, but I think it was the first time I saw Anna Kournikova on a tennis court. By the end of the workout, I had sweated through two shirts and every single stitch of my uniform. Even my shoes were soaked, almost to the point that they felt like I had been wearing them while inner-tubing down a creek in the middle of summer.

As I write this, we are on our way to Lo-Don for an exhibition game, but the game itself isn't until tomorrow, due to the fact that Lo-Don is five hours away. Obviously, the Taiwanese believe in being properly rested for their unofficial games; in America, for our *regular season* games, we would sometimes leave at 7:00 AM, drive for six or seven hours, check into the hotel, and then go to the park for our normal batting practice routine at about 4:00 PM. Yes, it makes for a long day, but so goes life in the minors. The biggest reason that minor league teams operate like this is cost. It's simply too expensive, and apparently unnecessary, for the team to spend an extra night in a hotel. In the Taiwan Major League, though, where the middle word is indeed "Major," cost is less of an issue, so it appears we will operate more in tune to the needs of the players.

We have today off—other than the travel—and we play tomorrow, followed by two consecutive off days. Now *that's* my kind of schedule. I am at the point where all the BP and groundballs aren't going to do me any good: I need to *play*. We're just about at the halfway point of spring training, and after perusing our schedule, the second half consists of several more games than did the first half, which is good. It will alleviate the boredom and repetition that accompanies any spring training while allowing me to fine-tune my hitting and fielding without any major repercussions for substandard performances. My knee, with the help of a Taiwanese version of Alleve, has been holding up well, and I've been participating in all of our conditioning drills. They don't outwardly express it, but the coaches and Mr. Wu seem to appreciate and to respect it.

Finally, I pulled a classic "vet move" yesterday. A vet move, short for "veteran move," is when an older, usually more savvy player, does what everyone else is doing but in a way to reduce his own personal anguish. For example, when it's time to loosen up your arm, a veteran will position himself to throw with the wind while in turn forcing his partner to throw into the wind, the result being less stress on the vet's arm. Our conditioning yesterday involved pairing up with another player and jogging along the warning track from one foul pole to the other ten times. Well, I grabbed Si-von, my pool buddy and the only other guy on the team less-equipped than I am to enter a triathlon. That way, since I was already dragging ass due to standing in all that heat for three hours, I could be the leader in my pair rather than the follower and thus appear that I am hustling. Every little bit helps, right? Out.

Saturday, March 17, 2001 (10:30 PM)
On the bus

We are on the bus home from Lo-don, and having just watched *The Perfect Storm*, I figured I could take the time for another journal entry. By the way, I had gotten mixed reviews on the movie, but I enjoyed it; with all the tearjerker movies out there, I was actually surprised by the ending. Now, *Shaft*, starring Samuel L. Jackson, is playing, so I'll keep one eye on the TV screen and one on my laptop screen.

We played the Taipei Gida (gida means "sun" in English) in a "real" exhibition game. Yes, that sounds a bit oxymoronic, but the game, despite being an unofficial one, had a regular season feel to it. I'm telling you, you have to see the atmosphere of the games here. These fans are the most interactive fans I've ever seen. First of all, there is a man who continuously bangs on a drum during the whole game, and the fans follow in unison by banging together plastic cones. Since Gida's uniform is predominately red, their fans had red cones while our fans' were blue. I mean they keep up the banging for the whole freakin' game! I suppose if you've ever seen highlights of a World Cup soccer match, you know what I'm talking about. All the noise can be somewhat disconcerting in the beginning, but after a while, I didn't even notice it.

The game itself, in spite of being just an exhibition game, was a lot of fun to be a part of. We jumped to a 4-0 lead after six innings, but in the bottom of the 7th, our ace pitcher ran into some control problems and ended up allowing six runs. Gida tacked on another one in the eighth for a 7-4 lead, but we rallied in the top of the ninth for three runs, knotting the score at seven. Gida failed to score in the bottom of ninth, so the game ended in a 7-7 tie. Many times, a spring training game will end as a tie because the managers carefully walk the delicate tightrope of getting a pitcher a proper workout and not throwing so many pitches as to tire him out for the season. So, when a game goes into extra innings, it would force the managers to use pitchers who weren't scheduled to pitch; therefore, the game ends after the predetermined number of innings—usually between seven and ten—has been reached.

I started and played six innings, and although I felt great, both in the field and at the plate, I had a sub par game. I made an error on a relatively routine grounder and went 0-2 with a walk and a strikeout, but my legs felt strong and my knee didn't even bother me remotely. Baseball's funny that way. Sometimes, like today, I feel awesome, and I stink up the joint; other days, whether it's playing on no sleep or having had a bit too much to drink the night before or playing a little "banged up," I had some of my best games. My mom likes the story when I, as an eighth-grader, got my braces tightened for the first time, and, subsequently, I couldn't eat my typical gargantuan lunch. She said I was so pissed off that I took it out on the other basketball team to the tune of 22 points and 12 rebounds. Anyway, today I felt good, and that to me is most important at this point.

Now, I have eaten three meals as part of all three of our intra-league spring training games, and all three of them have been remarkably similar. Therefore, I want to talk about the Taiwanese eating experience. Last night, both teams gathered at a restaurant in Lo-Don for dinner, and I want to describe, from a cultural standpoint, how different it is. First of all, ten of us sat at a table that in America would probably seat only six. I've heard sociologists talk about how "personal space" can vary among cultures, and here in Taiwan, this space is significantly smaller than in the USA. Maybe it's just me, but I hate being or feeling crowded, especially when I'm eating. Oh, well. Secondly, the bowls, plates, and cups are small—*very* small. Also, from an etiquette standpoint, things are different. Since I've rarely seen knives and forks, it considered acceptable to grab a piece of meat in the chopsticks, bite off half of it, and return the rest of said morsel to your plate. In America, of course, 100% of whatever is lifted off your plate is supposed to enter your mouth, something I learned at a young age; my dad didn't think too highly of my biting half of a sausage link off my fork rather than having cut it in half, whereupon his right hand found the back of my head.

Furthermore, Americans generally use serving spoons to transfer a sample of food from a large bowl or dish into your own smaller one. Here, however, if there is something on a centralized plate that you would like to eat, you simply grab it with your chopsticks, the spread of germs be damned. I don't have a problem with that kind of serving, but I can see where some people might.

In closing, let me say that I am enjoying myself thus far, despite such cultural differences, and I'm sure that as we start playing more games, I'll enjoy it even more. This week, we have one practice, one travel day (which is basically a day off), and three games. I like that. I read a few years ago how Robin Yount, the Hall of Fame shortstop/centerfielder of the Milwaukee Brewers, said that he chose baseball over football because he "didn't like the idea of one game for every four practices." I couldn't agree more. Out.

Monday, March 19, 2001 (9:30 PM)
Taichung

A few years ago, Mark Twain, arguably our greatest American novelist and veritable fountain of quotable quotes, theorized, "Sometimes, it is better to keep your mouth shut and appear stupid than to open it and remove all doubt." Well, I'd like to add a corollary to his theory, and it is this: "When in a foreign country, 'tis far better to keep your mouth shut and appear aloof and indifferent than to open it and feel stupid and inadequate." That's how I feel sometimes, and it's frustrating. I find myself on the elevator quite often with my teammates, but since I can't carry on a

conversation with them, I just stand there. I have tried, believe me, to ges-
ticulate in order to communicate with them, but they end up looking at
me the way a dog tilts its head when it hears an odd sound. I think they
understand my language problems, and they therefore, as far as I know,
don't consider me to be arrogant.

Furthermore, when I want to order food from a restaurant and Kevin
isn't around, I either have to go to KFC or McDonald's—which I refuse to
do regularly in order to avoid gaining unwanted pounds—or to another
establishment that I have frequented in the past. The people in the two or
three places who know my face generally know what I like to order, but
sometimes questions arise, and I have to go through a series of gyrations to
make known my intentions. I think every racist American should be
forced to live overseas for a little while in order to appreciate these kinds of
difficulties facing *our* immigrants, who, whether you like it or not,
founded our magnificent nation. Recently, I saw a documentary on
Roberto Clemente, the Hall-of-Fame outfielder of the Pittsburgh Pirates
and the first great Latin American ballplayer. Some of the interviewees
claimed that Clemente was originally thought of as "dumb" because he
couldn't speak English properly and that when reporters quoted him, they
would print how he *sounded*, rather than what he meant. For example, he
would say, "I heet the ball…" and they wrote it just like that, poking fun
at Clemente's Spanish pronunciation of the letter "i." How arrogant,
racist, and ethnocentric can you be?! If you're one of those people who
thinks that the world ends at the Canadian and Mexican borders and at
the Atlantic and Pacific oceans, well, I sincerely feel sorry for you.

Today was an off day, so I spent it relaxing, as I said I would. I got in a
light weight-lifting workout, and Si-von and I shot some more pool. He
provided the transportation, the stick, and since I won this time, the cost
of the table. I feel as though I used him, but he didn't seem too upset with
the outcome; what happened when he got back to his wife and newborn is
a different story. Evidently, I also missed a team-conditioning workout,
which was held at about 5:00 PM, but Kevin didn't tell me a thing about

it before he got off the bus in Taipei. I actually would have gone, I think, but once again, I look like the lazy American because I honestly had no idea about it. To me, an off day is an off day, meaning *no* mandatory work of any kind, but apparently there was also a weight training session tonight that I "skipped" because I had already lifted earlier. God, I wonder what they must think of me! Oh well, I guess I better play some damn good baseball to earn my keep around here.

It's funny how "hands-on" the coaches are on our team; it's almost like being back in college again, where some form of instruction greets every mistake. For example, our elder statesman, whom I have nicknamed "Ah-gohn" (grandfather), made a baserunning mistake late in our game the other day, and one of our coaches immediately approached him. The conversation appeared to be amicable, but that is something that would never happen outside of Class A ball in the USA. Look, mistakes, both mental and physical, are going to happen, even when you're a 35-year-old, but you just try to keep them to a minimum. "Ah-gohn" knew he screwed up, so why exacerbate it by questioning his "Baseball IQ?" At least, that's the American attitude; the fans, the coaches, the teammates, and the opposition all knew he had a brain cramp, so just leave him alone and let him put it behind him.

Also, in America, you are left on your own to keep yourself physically fit and ready to play everyday. No one tells you when to lift. If you don't want to lift, then don't lift, but don't come crying when your performance suffers. I suppose that prevailing attitude comes from the "every-man-for-himself" principle upon which our great country was founded. In other words, no work = no food. Here, though, just about everything is micro-managed. I have been playing professionally for seven years now, and I know what I need to do to get Bo Durkac ready to play, from proper rest, to diet, to stretching, and everywhere in between. I can't speak for my current teammates, but obviously the coaching staff can or else they wouldn't make our 30+-year-olds lift weights along with everyone else. Again, I'm not putting the Taiwanese way down; I'm just pointing out the differences.

It has been posited that sports is a reflection of society, and after two weeks here on the "ROC" (a nickname which comes from Taiwan, Republic of China, the country's official name), I'll buy that now more than ever. Out.

Thursday, March 22, 2001 (4:15 PM
Kaoshiung's *Ambassador Hotel*

There is a law of science that says, "For every action, there is an equal and opposite reaction." Well, in the Taiwanese Major League, "For every logical action, there is an equally illogical action." Therefore, I want to spend today's entry dealing with the paradoxes that I notice here everyday as a member of the TML. First of all, I have to remind myself constantly that we are, in fact, big leaguers; the talent level of the players here is nowhere near American Major League talent, but in Taiwan, there is no higher level. Consequently, we receive some "big league" treatment: a very comfortable and spacious bus, a beautiful hotel on road trips, and, of course, the salaries. The hotel in which I am sitting right now is immaculate, and I'll give you one simple indication of how nice it is: there is a phone in the bathroom. Now, unlike all of you world-travelers and high-powered business executives out there, this is new to me. Certainly, I'm aware that such creature comforts exist, but I don't know if I've ever stayed in a hotel on a baseball road trip that featured such an amenity. The room also offers "WebTV," which once again, I am aware of, but I have no idea how to use it or how much it costs. The only "webs" I'd ever seen in a hotel room were the cobwebs in the ceiling corners.

But, some other things that go on negate all of these "luxuries". For example, after last night's game, which ended at roughly 5:00 PM, I was told by Kevin that the laundry would not be ready for the next day and that I was supposed to have brought extras of everything. Well, I wonder if he understands the term *ex post facto*. Or, for all you non-Latin speakers, as Adam Sandler's character Robbie said in *The Wedding Singer* when his fiancé left him jilted at the altar, "That was something that could have been brought to my attention ***yesterday!***" After our game, which was played in as hot and humid conditions as I could ever recall, I came back to the hotel and washed my pants—both pairs—in the sink. That's right, in the sink. I also had to hang dry the three tee-shirts, two pairs of sliding shorts, and four pairs of socks that I had sweated completely through. You can imagine what I must have smelled like when I put that uniform on today, but outhouses on a tuna boat undoubtedly smell better. To make matters worse, my pants weren't completely dry when I put them on for the game, and that's not a pleasant feeling. The other guys had brought extras, so they were all wearing fresh clothes, but since I was "misinformed," to put it gently, I had to be uncomfortable.

To go off on a bit of a tangent, a situation like the one above brings up the term "opportunity cost" and how that is the basis of all of life's decisions. Every decision you make is directly or indirectly related to the following question: is what I'm about to do worth the inherent consequences? Should I get married to Mr. Right Now or should I wait for Mr. Right? Should I eat that big piece of pie knowing that I struggle to maintain my weight? Are the headaches involved with playing baseball in Taiwan superseded by the amount of money they're paying me? I don't know about the first two questions, but the answer to the third one is a resounding yes. If I were earning, say, half of what I'm making now, then I don't think that I'd stick it out, but the money keeps me going.

It's not that bad, though. So I had to wash my pants in a sink once. So I had to wear stinky shirts and shorts for a meaningless spring training game that no one attended. So what? It's not as if I were playing Game 7 of the World Series on national TV or attending an awards ceremony smelling like Boris Yeltsin's breath. Everything is being washed properly tonight, so I'll be clean as a whistle for Saturday's game.

Now, I am very inquisitive by nature—I was told last night by some local females that I have a "curious face" after unloading a barrage of questions upon them—but the reins of the language barrier have slowed down that runaway carriage considerably. In other words, I can't very well go to our equipment manager, Abai, and ask him why in Sam Hill they can't have the uniforms washed and dried in 14 hours. It's not as though our game ended at 1:30 AM and we then had a practice at 7:00 AM; we're talking about 14 hours here, people. But, I kept quiet. It is extremely hard for me *not* to comment on something that I don't understand, but I did.

Furthermore, we haven't showered after our games here in Kaoshiung, and here's a particularly revolting image for you: I was so dripping with sweat after the game today that as I was eating the post game meal on the bus back to the hotel, sweat was dripping of my face and into the food. Gross. But when you don't get to shower after a game, and when you sweat like Mike Tyson at a beauty pageant, that stuff happens. Now, I've been in some pretty cramped and stuffy and dirty clubhouses in the minors, but I can count on one hand the number of times I've had to shower in the hotel or had to wash parts of my own uniform (never). Do you see what I mean about the contrasts? You already know about the conditioning freak/chain smoker dichotomy that exists, but what do you think about this stuff? It's definitely a "learn-on-the-job-and-keep-your-mouth-shut" experience that never provides a dull moment. But, as I said, the headaches are nowhere *near* strong enough to make me consider leaving, so I'll continue to pull an REO Speedwagon and "Ride the Storm Out."

I'm running out of time now, so I'll recap the baseball stuff in an all-encompassing entry over the weekend, probably on the way home after the game on Saturday. Stay tuned. Out.

CHAPTER 2

▼

FEARING THE WORST

Saturday, March 24, 2001 (2:30 PM)
Taichung

As promised, I will now discuss the baseball part of our three-game, four-day road trip to Kaohshiung. First, however, let me preface it by saying that my feelings are very ephemeral when it comes to writing about or discussing baseball, inasmuch that when I am doing well, I can write/speak *ad nauseum*, but when things are going lousy, I tend to be quite curt. Even with mom and dad, if I were in a slump, I couldn't stand to talk about baseball. Heck, during an awful stretch in my junior year of college, when my batting average was at its nadir, I was so unpleasant to be around that I broke up with my girlfriend at the time to spare her the torture of my company.

Well, I am basically stinking up the joint at the plate right now. I haven't really smoked a ball since I've been here, and the hits that I have gotten have been choppers through the infield. I am not sure what the problem is, but it is undoubtedly in my approach. Briefly, an "approach" is your own personal plan of attack that you develop over your career, and it is usually predicated upon what pitches you handle well and what pitches you handle poorly. For example, many big league hitters, believe it or not, struggle hitting certain pitches, and if a pitcher can throw that pitch consistently, that big leaguer will find himself on the bench quite often. That same hitter, though, has a certain part of the strike zone that when the pitcher throws it *there*, the hitter murders it. A lot of big league hitters have had long and successful careers with that type of an approach.

My personal approach, over the past two years, has been just like that, and it's really quite simple: if the pitcher throws it where he wants it, I'm most likely going to be out, but if he throws it where I want it, I'm going to hit it hard somewhere. Certainly, it's a lot more involved than that, but that is the essence of my "approach." As a .330 hitter over the last two years, I can't remember throwing my helmet or breaking anything out of frustration due to excessive failure at the plate because my approach has been so ingrained. Basically, if the pitcher got me out, he simply threw the ball where I didn't like it. But the reason that I would rarely be outwardly frustrated is that I know that no independent league pitcher, for any considerable time, can consistently throw the ball to those spots, and I know that eventually he is going to give a pitch that I *do* like. Then, I enjoy the success.

Here, though, my approach is a little bit off, and I'm not quite sure how to fix it. I am "seeing the ball" well, the generic baseball term that means a hitter is recognizing what the pitch is and where it's going just after the pitcher has released it, and I'm not swinging at bad pitches. For some reason, however, the pitches that I normally hit hard, I'm hitting weakly. I have no problem "tipping my cap" to a pitcher and conceding that in that certain at-bat or on that certain day, he was simply better than

I was; what burns my ass is when he throws me a pitch that I like and I shank it. I've made my living the last two years on those types of pitches, and I can't afford to miss them. Right now, I *am* missing them, and if I don't figure out what the hell is going on, I may soon find myself in a Chico Heat uniform.

The upside to the situation, if there is one, is that Mr. Wu has been playing me everyday and batting me fifth in the order, which means that he is tolerating my struggles thus far. I suspect that he understands the transitional problems that we "whiteys" can have and how our baseball can suffer from them. I just hope that he gives me ample opportunity, like maybe a full month of games, before he decides my fate. Hell, at this point, I'm about ready to tell him that if he still thinks I'm horseshit at the end of April, then send my sorry ass home, but please give me one month to prove my worth. Another positive right now is that we still have two weeks of spring training left, with probably 8-10 more games involved, so if Mr. Wu keeps putting me out there, everything should work out fine. Finally, our cleanup hitter, Abai, the guy who led the league in homeruns last year, will undoubtedly receive better pitches to hit with my hitting fifth, and let me explain why. Although I have never struck the fear of God into American pitchers with my lack of raw power, the fact that I am 1) an American third baseman, 2) size-wise capable of hitting the long ball (even though I rarely do) and 3) going to be batting left-handed most of the time (like Abai) will cause the opposing pitcher to throw strikes to Abai lest they walk him to face me. I think Mr. Wu understands that, and hopefully he'll take that into consideration.

On a lighter note, let's move on to the off-the-field stuff. I haven't mentioned it yet for some reason, but we picked up an American pitcher about a week ago. His name is Richard Bell, and he pitched for the St. Paul Saints of the Northern League over the last two summers. He was also on the Intercontinental Cup team, the one that went to Sydney, with me in November of 1999, so we knew each other, however briefly, from there. He's a lefty with a good fastball and a good slider, and he's set to be our closer. So far, despite having the same problems with adjusting to our rigorous conditioning as I did, he has thrown very well, and I see him being a dominating pitcher in our league. He's also a good guy, quite talkative, and very unpretentious. That makes for a good combination for me since he's going to be my road roommate; if I *have* to talk to someone, I'm glad it's a guy like that.

So, Rich and I went out on Wednesday night to a place called Graffiti's, which I was told about by a former TML'er from the USA, because all the Taiwanese women working there speak English. It's a little pub that doesn't actually serve food but can have food delivered there, and that's what Rich and I did. I had a bacon cheeseburger, my first non-McDonald's Western food, and it was, shall we say, different. I don't know what kind of meat it was (horse, kangaroo?), but it certainly didn't taste like an American hamburger. Nevertheless, I devoured it, an order of fries, a bowl of French-onion soup, and Rich's cream of broccoli soup that he didn't have room for. Now, if the burger was sub par, then the two soups were garbage, considering what I'm used to.

You see, every time I was ever at my paternal grandparents' house growing up, I was practically force-fed soup, ranging from chicken soup to beef soup to maybe the single greatest food ever to pass between my lips, *paprikash*—a Hungarian-style, triple-bypass special, cream of chicken-type concoction. My dad's mom introduced the dish to me at probably the age of four (when Lance, my little brother, and I used to call it "puppyguts"), and from that day on, whenever we'd visit, Lance and I would almost simultaneously ask, "Where's the puppyguts?" Anyway, my mom learned from Grandma Durkac the tricks of the trade to making a good bowl of soup, and if it weren't blasphemous to say so about a Jewish woman, I'd bestow the Seinfeldian moniker of "Soup Nazi" upon her for her acumen with the creations. The problem now is that most restaurant bowls of soup just don't quite measure up, kind of like dating Cindy Crawford only to end up marrying Roseanne.

The next night featured the same thing, but, this time, the three Americans on the Kaohsiung team dropped in, and we sat and yakked it up for a while. Ted Silva pitched for Kaohsiung for three months last year, Erik Bennett pitched for Chico last year with me, and Freddie Diaz played shortstop for the Zion Pioneerzz in the WBL for the last two years. The five of us talked about our off-the-field situations, with Erik lamenting about how it took three weeks to get his phone hooked up. After hearing about their living accommodations, which really don't sound *that* bad, I was feeling pretty lucky about what I have here in Taichung. We also discussed our game schedule for the season, and it goes like this: each team plays either Wednesday and Thursday night or Friday, Saturday, and Sunday night. That is going to be weird. Like Ted said, he has an advantage because as a starting pitcher, he would pitch only once a week anyway, so now he simply gets an extra day or two between starts, which shouldn't bother him. For the rest of us, however, playing so sporadically is not a good thing. In any sport, a player needs to "stay sharp," meaning he needs to play often enough to keep his skills from atrophying, but with this schedule, we may find it hard to do so. We shall see.

Last night I had a "date," if you will, with a Taiwanese woman who speaks excellent English and whom I met the night before. She actually used to own her own restaurant/bar in Kaohsiung, and she is friends with the other English-speaking employees of Graffiti's. She and I went to a restaurant called *The Brass Rail*, which features a nice selection of Western food, and I ordered a Philly cheese steak. Simply put, it was awesome! I told Juliette, the owner of the place, that on the West Coast of America, it's often difficult to find a good cheese steak, but at her restaurant, 10,000 miles from The City of Brotherly Love, I had one to die for. Needless to say, she appreciated the compliment. Speaking of Pennsylvania cities, it was neat to see a Pittsburgh Steelers pennant and bumper sticker on the wall of the establishment. Evidently, certain soccer-crazy Europeans had brought scarves of their favorite teams to adorn the walls of *The Brass Rail*, so a native of Pittsburgh, where there is also a restaurant/bar called *The*

Brass Rail, wanted to match their spirit. He therefore presented the para-
phernalia to Juliette as kind of a "West meets East" kind of thing. Small
world, huh? As for what happened at the end of the "date," let's just say
that I didn't get a whole lot of sleep (grin). Out.

Monday, March 26, 2001 (8:45 PM)
Taichung

I want to talk about humidity, and, more specifically, the effect it has
on the human body. First of all, and I'm serious about this question, does
extreme humidity make your hair hold better or make it go flat? Feel free
to e-mail me the correct response. At the risk of sounding horribly vain-
glorious, I noticed the other day in Kaohsiung that when I styled my hair
before going out one of the nights, it was very flat. Maybe it was due to
harder or softer water, but I'm not sure. A more pressing concern of mine,
though, is how humidity is making me sweat like Tammy Fay Bakker at
the Revlon counter. Like today, for example, we practiced in Taichung,
and it was probably between 75° F and 80° F today and overcast—with a
few sprinkles mixed in as well. But, by the end of practice, every single
stitch of my clothing was soaked all the way through, including my cleats.
I mean, I can understand sweating profusely if it's 90° F and sunny with
some humidity, like it is in Jia-yi most of the time; today, however,
appeared to be a normal temperature day. Hell, halfway through practice,
I had trouble throwing the ball accurately across the infield because my
hand was drenched, and I didn't have a spot on my uniform to wipe it off.
Now, I've played baseball in upstate New York in the summer where it can
get unbelievably uncomfortable, but it wasn't like that *every day*. Here,
there is just no letting up.

To make matters worse today, I was all set to leave the apartment at
9:10 AM to go get some breakfast before our 9:30 AM scheduled departure when Rich met me as I got off the elevator. He was on his way to tell
me that the bus time had been moved up to 9:10 AM, and apparently, he

was told that yesterday and was supposed to relay the message to me. Well, he didn't. So, having been greeted with this startling revelation, I had to make a choice: do I say screw the bus time and go eat since it wasn't my fault that I was late, or do I bite the bullet and go to the bus sans breakfast? Not wanting to "rock the boat," I opted for the latter. Needless to say, I was thoroughly pissed off, though not necessarily at Rich because I could see myself doing the same thing. I was just ticked that I wasn't going to be able to eat until after practice. I don't think I said ten words during the whole practice because when I'm excessively hungry or tired, especially due to someone else's negligence, I am about as friendly as a trapped wolverine. (On a side note, my grandma had a little sign in her house that said, "It's easy to be pleasant when life goes by singing a happy song, but the man worthwhile is the man who can smile when everything around him goes wrong." Well, if that's true, I must be the most worthless man who ever lived).

The reason why the bus time had been moved up 20 minutes is that we were going to have a brief meeting with the mayor of Taichung. So, we went to the courthouse, and, typical of a politician, he arrived about 10 minutes late. He was up there yapping about this, that, and the other thing, and all I could think about is how in Sam Hill I'm going to make it through practice without dying. I was about ready to eat the damn table we were sitting at. Anyway, we finally got to the field, and on the street, vendors were selling some kind of muffin. I figured this was my only chance to avoid hypoglycemia, so I bought two of them and wolfed them down in about three minutes. It was very unsatisfying, but beggars can't be choosers, right?

Practice itself went as normal, but by the end, I was starting to feel a little light-headed and weak. I made it, though, even through all the conditioning, and when I got on the bus, I ate two of those rice boxes, much to the amazement/amusement of some of the guys. I guess they just don't get it: I *have* to eat. I don't understand how people can skip breakfast, or, for that matter, any meal. If you do it to lose weight, well, you're barking up the wrong tree; any nutritionist in the world will tell you that's the last thing you should be doing. Some people choose to skip breakfast for whatever reason, but, like I said, I just don't understand it. Actually, I don't think I felt better, both nutritionally and socially, until about 4:00 PM today. I think the fact that I had 27 e-mails waiting to be read lightened my spirits. Have I ever mentioned how much I love the Internet?

We are heading to Kaohsiung again tomorrow after our practice because we have another exhibition game with Fala (lightning) on Wednesday. I'll probably write another entry on the way home after the game. In the meantime, stay tuned. Out.

Wednesday, March 28, 2001
Bus from Kaoshiung to Taichung

I thought this journal entry would cover the game we would have just played, but we got "humiditied out," if you will. In other words, we didn't play because the field didn't dry sufficiently following two days of rain. Instead, we did some running and some hitting in the batting cage. I mean, how the hell do you expect water to evaporate into an atmosphere that is already saturated? I know I keep harping on this blasted humidity, but I'm telling you, it is ungodly. If there is a place in America that is as humid day-in and day-out as this island, please tell me where it is because I'd have to feel it to believe it. I mentioned the other day how revolting it is to have sweat drip into your food, but I have a new one for today.

First, though, I remember my one of my dad's brothers once telling me about working in a steel mill when he was younger, and he apparently had the unenviable task of throwing coal into the blast furnace. He said that at the end of the day, he could pour sweat out of his work boots. Well, today, I actually poured sweat out of my shoes at the end of practice. That's right, I poured about a ½ cup of sweat out of each shoe. I did it right in front of our trainer, Vivian, and a couple of players, and they looked at me as if I were a horrible genetic mutation. And the worst part of it all is that it wasn't even that hot out, maybe 70° F. Some of the guys weren't even that sweaty, but I was sweating like Bill Clinton during a polygraph. I don't know what my problem is. Granted, I've always perspired more than normal—a good friend of mine from college says that I'd sweat in the shower—but this is getting out of control. I had to beg out of the last half of conditioning because my pants, socks, and shoes were so sweat-laden that the extra weight was hurting my knee. I don't think I'm exaggerating when I say that I lose an average of 12 pounds of water-weight per practice. One of these days, I'm going to find out for sure.

Okay, enough about the human cooling system. Now, it's time to discuss our thrice-altered schedule. I already told you about Monday's snafu and how miserable I was, but similar, last minute changes occurred again yesterday and today. In American pro baseball, I don't know if I have ever seen a schedule change, certainly not within three or four days before a scheduled event. Maybe it's due to meticulous planning, but I doubt it. I think it's due to, once again, the individuality of American pro athletes. When you sign a pro contract, you are supposed to be responsible enough to get to where you have to be on time. It's not like college where everything is micromanaged for you, from study hall to breakfast to hotel check-out. Every manager I've ever played for—and I'm certain every manager, period—has basically three rules: 1) Be on time, 2) Play hard, and 3) See rules #1 and #2. Just as managers expect us to be punctual, we expect them to give us schedules that are set in stone (or least give us ample warning if there's to be a change), and that is generally the case.

Here, however, we've had three schedule changes in the last three days. Now, let's say that I had made plans to do something on Tuesday afternoon before leaving to Kaohsiung. Well, practice was moved back this time, from 9:00 AM to 11:00 AM, and I was notified by a knock on my door at 8:30 AM. Obviously, it cost me a couple of hours of sleep, but had I wanted to go somewhere between the end of practice and our departure, I would not have been able to. Today's change was a more understandable one in that the inclement weather forced us to leave an hour later than expected. A change like this could happen anywhere, so it doesn't really count. But I think the reason why eleventh hour changes are made here is because you are supposed to be at baseball's beckincall 24-7.

Look, in America, we love baseball as much as any baseball-playing people in the world, but we also have lives outside of baseball, too. I'm not sure if that's a good or a bad thing. It certainly is a different thing, though. After four weeks, I think I'm starting to understand the Asian way, and it goes like this: They operate under the quixotic notion that all their maniacal training and their turning over their lives to baseball will make them significantly better players. Maybe it's a good idea that I don't share my talent vs. work ethic theory with them. For example, the other day, Kevin, Coji Mudo (our Japanese pitcher), and I were discussing Sadaharu Oh, "The Babe Ruth of Japan." He hit 868 homeruns in his career, 113 more than Hank Aaron's American record, so I wanted to see what Kevin thought about Oh's skill with the bat. I asked him why Oh was so successful, and even though I knew what Kevin's response was going to be, I let him say, "Well, he work(ed) very hard." Immediately, I said, "Every Japanese player works very hard, right?" Kevin then added, "Well, he had a gift." I wanted to say, "No shit, Sherlock!" but I didn't think he'd quite understand that.

Don't get me wrong; their exemplary practice and training habits will undoubtedly make them less injury-prone, and that's certainly important. I just don't see why *they* don't see how important the talent factor is in determining a player's progress. Then again, few American athletes lend any credence to my theory, so why should the Taiwanese be any different? Another example is regarding our infield-outfield practice, which apparently will occur every day during the season. Briefly, that is when each player, except for the pitchers, goes to his own position and the coach or manager hits balls to him, whereupon he throws the ball to the designated base. In America, infield-outfield is going the way of the dodo bird, especially at the big league level. Even in Chico, we would average taking it maybe twice a week because there is very little point in doing so; hell, we view it as an unwelcome interruption of our card playing and eating time. The way we look at it, if you haven't figured out how to catch the ball by 5:45 PM, you ain't gonna catch it at 7:05 PM. Evidently, Asia begs to differ. Out.

Saturday, March 31, 2001 (1:00 PM)
Bus from Taichung to Kaohsiung

I think every day when I wake up, I'm going to blast *Led Zeppelin*'s "Communication Breakdown" as a harbinger of the day's events. Today, we were on our way to our "Opening Ceremonies" in Kaohsiung, and all the players were to be in full uniform. Yesterday, I was told that we are wearing our blue shirts for the event, but wouldn't you know that as soon as I got on the bus, I saw everyone was in his white shirt. Rich, who was already on the bus, had just gotten back from going to get *his* white shirt, as they neglected to tell him, too. It was 12:25 PM when I first got on the bus, and when I returned, it was 12:32 PM, which means technically I could be considered late. Certainly, there were extenuating circumstances, and, therefore, no one—including Mr. Wu—appeared to be upset, but that's irrelevant. I don't like being late for anything baseball team-related because it makes you look as though you're bigger than the team.

I haven't figured out how the Taiwanese react to such a player, but in America, if you really want to ruffle some feathers, act like you're above the team. A player who is continuously late—I've explained to you the importance of being on time—will soon draw the ire of every player on his squad. I was introduced to the term "O.F.P." in 1996 with Visalia when one of my teammates was late for a road trip, and, boy, the other players let him have it. O.F.P. is an acronym for "Own F—in' Program," meaning that the player is on his own schedule with little or no regard for his teammates' feelings. You see, baseball players have very fragile egos, so anyone who intentionally or unintentionally makes himself appear to be more important than the other players is not looked upon too highly. Once, in 1997 with High Desert, my roommate and I were 15 minutes late for a trip from Bakersfield to San Jose because we didn't receive a wake-up call from the front desk. It didn't matter to my team-mates *why* I was late, and I got a little razzing from them. My manager, Chris Speier, burned a hole through me with the ice-cold stare of his pale, blue eyes and then levied a $25 fine on me. It simply is unacceptable to be tardy.

But the ultimate example of incurring the animosity of one's teammates occurred a few years ago (names will be omitted to protect the identities). A player and his roommate were 30 minutes late for a bus trip for what-ever reason, and as they were walking from the hotel to the bus with their baggage in plain view of our team, I could hear the mumbling beginning. This player was having a monster year for us, which in the minors auto-matically breeds jealousy—remember what I said about delicate egos?— and instead of picking up his pace to show his teammates that he was sorry for his oversight, his leisurely gait suggested that he was 30 minutes *early*. Well, when he got on the bus, the players really let him have it, brutally sarcastic stuff like, "Hey, whenever you're ready" and "Don't worry about us; we'll wait for you." We could see in the roommate's facial expression that he was sincerely sorry, and, later, he admitted as such, but the player himself, in the wake of all the chirping, uttered the most unforgettable line I have ever heard. He said to no one in particular, "Hey, don't bite the hand that feeds you." We were flabbergasted. Most of the players agreed that his comment was the most blatantly disrespectful quote they had ever heard. Let's just say that this particular player had a very difficult time socializing with his teammates for the rest of the year.

Now, I personally feel that camaraderie and chemistry receive far too much credit for a team's success in sports. That may sound blasphemous to some people, but former Pittsburgh Pirates manager Jim Leyland, gen-erally considered to be one among the best in baseball, made a similar statement. He said that he had managed teams where everyone loved one another and the team stunk, and he had managed teams where everyone hated each other and the team was outstanding. Good players, not good chemistry or good managers, make for good teams. If that weren't the case, Joe Torre, not Alex Rodriguez, would be earning $25,000,000 per year. I actually had a discussion about that subject recently with a female inter-collegiate athlete friend of mine, who claimed that when she and her teammates pull for one another, it helps the players perform better. At the risk of sounding sexist, this line of thinking is a decidedly female thing, and I feel I can honestly comment on such a topic without any repercussions because I have been around sports my whole life. But I don't think any male would agree with her. The way we look at it, as Alpha-males to the *nth* degree, if you need someone rooting you on from the sideline to enhance your performance, you need to be hosing down lettuce at Safeway, not being paid to play a sport. Yes, you cheer for your teammates and congratulate them when they make a nice play, but I personally don't give a rat's ass if the guys on the bench are offering me encouragement or aren't saying a damn word; all the rah-rah crap in the world isn't going to help me hit the freakin' baseball.

The reason I bring all this up is because language barrier or not, I don't want to be viewed as an O.F.P.-type guy. I've learned through my years of baseball that when you are of ordinary ability like I am, you must control all the things that you *can* control. You can't change the fact that you're slower than a seven-year itch or that you can't hit a baseball into orbit; you can, however, control things like hustle and being accessible to the fans and media and how your manager and teammates perceive you.

Every little bit helps in the manager's determining whether he is going to keep you or release you. Especially in independent leagues, where winning is the bottom line, you can't have a "cancer"—someone who's always late or causing problems—in the clubhouse. The only time a "cancer" is on a team, at any level in any sport, is when he possesses extraordinary skill, a guy like a Dennis Rodman or a Gary Sheffield. These guys will always have jobs because the general managers of the sports world think that their obnoxious behavior in the clubhouse will be negated by what they do on the court and field. But average players need to keep their noses clean and do the little things to earn their keep. The bottom line is that I would hate to be released from Taiwan, or anywhere else, because the manager thought I was a disruptive influence.

On a side note, let's discuss the hypocrisy of sports. A few years ago, I read a book by Joe Garagiola, and one chapter of the book deals with hypocrisy. Perhaps the most tangible example I can offer is the monologue by Crash Davis in *Bull Durham* when he finds fungus on Nuke LaLoosh's shower shoes: "If you win 20 games in The Show, and you have fungus on your shower shoes, the press will call you colorful. But until you win twenty games in The Show, it means you're a slob." Another example would be a pitcher who jumps around and yells at himself and outwardly psyches himself up and wins 17 games a year versus the exact same type of pitcher who instead wins only five games a year. Basically, the baseball "intelligentsia," and I use that term loosely, would call the former pitcher a "competitor" and the latter a "hothead." That line of thinking is so common in sports today; the bottom line is that if you can produce for your team, you will be granted a little latitude in what you do while you're away from it.

In closing let me briefly discuss the extravaganza known as Opening Night. We arrived at the stadium and then proceeded to sit around for 45 minutes, at which time we had a brief autograph session. Then, the four teams were all led onto the field for the Taiwanese national anthem. The national anthem, though, was preceded by a dance routine set to a rousing rendition of "I'm Your Man" by the now defunct, 80's pop group *Wham*. If that wasn't odd enough, the dancers were the Kaohsiung version of *Hooter's* girls. That's right, the girls were dressed in the exact same attire as you would find on any American *Hooter's* waitress. But there was one problem, and I'll bet you know what it is: let's just say that this particular *Hooter's* might want to make sure it has a good attorney to handle any false advertising claims. In fact, we Americans and the Ozzies suggested that the establishment might want to consider renaming itself *Hoot's* in light of their, um, physical shortcomings.

All in all, it was good to see an amped-up crowd, complete with the never-ending cacophony of whistles, drums and chants. After four weeks of monotonous spring training, I'm ready for some of that. We stuck around to watch the first inning of the game between Fala and Gida, and then we left. I had heard originally that we were going to watch four or five innings, and I was dreading that; I'd rather be a towel boy in a Turkish prison than go to the ballpark to watch a baseball game. On the surface, when you consider we drove seven round-trip hours for a two-hour ceremony, the whole day could be viewed as a waste of time, but we did it for the fans. In the wake of the gambling scandal of a few years ago, baseball is on very precarious ground here in Taiwan. Fortunately, both leagues are making a concerted effort to recapture the adoration of the fans. Also, Taiwan's amateur team just won the Asian championship, toppling not only baseball neophytes such as The Philippines, Malaysia and India, but traditional powerhouses Japan and Korea as well. Apparently, "baseball fever" is on its way back here on the ROC, and it is our collective job as players to resuscitate it completely. After all, more fans means more money, and everyone—white, black, red, yellow, or purple—understands that. Out.

Tuesday, April 3, 2001 (6:30 PM)
Taichung apartment

One of the biggest issues in the world right now is the "foot and mouth" disease that is running rampant in Europe. Little mention has been made, however, of another foot-related affliction that's taking place on the island of Taiwan. Apparently, several American baseball players are suffering from "soaked shoe syndrome." Yes, folks, this alliterative ailment is the result of the horrible humidity on the island combined with the slight portliness of the American ballplayers. According to sources, these infected players have been unable to complete some of their practices due to severe water loss and subsequent saturation of their footwear. Although no deaths have been reported, the Americans have been advised to hydrate properly themselves, abstain from mass alcohol consumption, and shed the extra weight they're carrying to avoid any further complications.

Chalk this next part up in the weekly "What in Sam Hill is going on here?" column. On Sunday and Monday, we practiced at a field that most American high schools would scoff at. When I say it is dilapidated, I don't just mean the stadium itself; our cow pasture on "Midnight Achers" (our farm in Kittanning) would provide a better surface than this field. We were doing our pre-practice running drills, and all I could think about was how to avoid spraining my ankle. The infield surface was marginal at best, yet I couldn't figure out why we were there in the first place. I mentioned before about how I have to remind myself consistently that we are "big leaguers," but stuff like this makes me wonder. I can see why perhaps on Sunday we practiced there because we were originally supposed to be off that day, and therefore a local amateur team might have scheduled a game on our regular field, but why Monday? That's like telling the Pittsburgh Pirates, "Hey, guys, sorry but you are going to have to practice at Westinghouse High School today." I never did find out why we had to forfeit our field, but I find it hard to believe that we would defer to an amateur team. One of life's mysteries, I guess.

Other than that, there's not a whole lot to say about the past three days. We had the three workouts, each one less physically taxing than the previous one—outstanding!! Today, at the end of practice, Mr. Wu announced that since tomorrow is our first game, he wants us all to concentrate very hard. A comment like that would draw snickers from any professional baseball player. To me, the definition of a professional ballplayer is someone who respects the team rules, respects his managers and coaches, respects his teammates, respects the fans and media, and above all, respects *the game* itself. You have to take it upon yourself to be at your peak, both mentally and physically, for every single minute that you're on the field. In other words, you shouldn't have to be told to "concentrate" or "focus" or "get your rest" or "get to the park early for extra work" if you're struggling. You, as a pro, have to be mature and, well, professional enough to do all these things yourself without being told.

I honestly feel that I always have done this (and still do) and thus my distaste for over-coaching and excessive rules—like curfews, for example, which are stringently enforced here. As I mentioned before, I know what I need to do to get Bo Durkac ready to play and play well for an entire professional season, and, therefore, I don't need anyone to "get me fired up" or remind me to get proper sleep. That was what I loved about playing for Bill Plummer for my first two years in Chico. We never had curfews, and despite my excessive night-owling, I always got my 9-10 hours of sleep. He also offered optional extra hitting before every home game, and for the second half of 1998 and all of 1999, I was there everyday. Most importantly, though, he simply let me play. Other than working on my hitting technique with me or repositioning me at third base during games, he never said anything to me. It wasn't as though he literally never said a word to me; he just treated me like a professional baseball player, and I loved that.

Here, however, we have a lot of rookies on our team, and Mr. Wu evidently feels the need to get them mentally ready to play at the professional level. It appears that he is, in fact, targeting the younger players with such instruction, and even if he could speak English well, I don't think he'd say anything like that to me because he doesn't say anything like that directly to our older players. Hell, he himself, as a 40-year-old, played second base last year for Luka, and I have to believe that if someone told him to "concentrate" and "focus," he'd probably laugh, too. Ah, but you gotta love it; it feels like Instructional League again.

Finally, every single game that is played in the TML this year is supposed to be televised, both live and then as a replay of the game at about 11:00 PM. I was watching some of the Fala-Gida games that were played over the weekend, and I must admit that I am looking forward to being on

TV. Other than a few clips from news highlights, I've never actually seen what I look like playing baseball. It should be quite interesting. Out.

Wednesday, April 4, 2001 (11:45 PM)
Kaohsiung Hotel

Let's get right to the point: after a 45-minute rain delay, we won our season opener tonight, 2-1. When I say rain, I mean *rain*. At about 5:10 PM, three-quarters of the way thru our batting practice, the rain came down in buckets. In the amount of time it took Mr. Wu to hit me a short pop fly behind third base during BP, it went from a few drops to a mild monsoon. At first, it didn't appear as though we would play, but the combination of a field built to handle such downpours and a diligent grounds crew made the field sufficiently playable by 6:45 PM.

Our Japanese pitcher, Coji Mudo, a.k.a. Mudo-san, threw one helluva game, scattering seven hits over seven innings and making some quality pitches when he had to. Rich came in to pitch the eighth and ninth innings, and other than two walks, he threw really well, striking out two hitters and yielding no hits. Offensively, we had only four hits but managed to eke out the two runs with the help of a big two-out, RBI single by our DH, Han-chi (which actually means "sweet potato" in Chinese) and two wild pitches which allowed Yon-sen to score our second run. Fala's starting pitcher actually had a no-hitter going for 4 2/3 innings when Si-von, who took over behind the plate after Ah-how took a foul tip off his forearm, reached first. (One thing I've neglected to mention is the Chinese nickname, remembering of course that in Chinese, the family name comes first, e.g. the "last name" of the famous Chinese statesman, Chou En-lai is, in fact, Chou. Just as we Americans would call someone with the last name Scott "Scotty" or Brown "Brownie," the Chinese often take a last name, add the sound "Ah" to the front of it, and then accent the second syllable. For example, we have guys nicknamed Ah-HOW, Ah-HUI, Ah-CHOU, Ah-CHUN, and Ah-HUN on our team). Han Chi promptly followed with his single up the middle. In spite of having only four hits, we hit several balls sharply that went for outs, *i.e.,* "at'em" balls.

Yours truly had an okay game at best. In order, I struck out, hit a rocket right at the first baseman, flew out to centerfield, and grounded out to shortstop. The first at-bat requires a little bit of a description, so bear with me. In America, there are two basic schools of pitching technique—the "tall and fall" and the "drop and drive." An example of the former would be Randy Johnson, someone who, at 6'10", rises up "tall" with his leg kick and then uses gravity via a "falling" motion to propel the pitch to the plate. Pitchers like this generally feature a fastball that travels on a downward plane due to the angle created by the height of the pitcher and the pitching mound itself. I would guess that the majority of American pitchers fall into that category. An example of the second style would be Tom Seaver, who, if you remember, was famous for having a dirt stain on his right kneecap, the result of "dropping" down low and "driving" with his powerful legs. Because of a lower release point, Seaver's fastball would be "flatter" than Johnson's, meaning that it didn't have nearly the downward angle.

One of the first things that Erik Bennett mentioned to me when we first met up a couple of weeks ago was the Taiwanese pitchers' propensity to "drop and drive." Obviously, when you aren't very tall, you can't create much of a natural angle with your release point, so there is almost no advantage to being a "tall and fall" pitcher. Couple that with the fact that the pitching mounds here are comparatively much lower and flatter than American mounds, and you get a league chock full of "drop and drivers." The reason I bring this up is because that is why I struck out in my first at-bat.

No doubt, hitting is a very difficult skill, and according to some, the most difficult task in all of sports. In order to become a good hitter, you have to play as many games as you possibly can from the time you first pick up a bat, so you can develop the instincts that you need to survive. Well, my instincts are used to seeing a ball that, when released from a certain point, travels ever so slightly downward until it is below the bottom edge of the strike zone. The pitch that struck me out today was that type of pitch. I thought that when he released it, it was going to end up about 8 inches below my knees, but, unfortunately, due to the "flat" plane that the "drop and drive" pitchers employ, the ball never traveled down like I'm used to seeing. Therefore, the ball crossed the plate at about the top of my knees and right down the middle, an easy "strike three" call for the umpire, and I just stood there with the bat on my shoulder. Ouch. I wanted to tell Mr. Wu what exactly had happened and why my instincts had deceived me, but *you* try explaining this paragraph to a Chinese-speaking manager. I could have tried to do so through Kevin, but, like the old saying goes, "The world doesn't care about labor pains; it just wants to see the baby."

Defensively, I had two chances, the first one being a nice play, meaning I guess it was a notch above "routine" on the difficulty scale. There were two outs and a runner on first when the batter hit a three-hopper down the line. I went over, backhanded it cleanly, and threw a strike to first. Like I said, not a highlight reel play, but you have almost no room for error on a play like that. The other one was an easier play on paper, but it was sort of a "clutch" play. Two outs, runner on third, sixth inning, 2-1 lead. The batter hit a little squibber in front of me that I had to charge in on and flip to first. The toughest part of the play was trying to toss a wet ball across the infield, but I threw it early enough—normally I time my release on a routine play to nab the runner by about a step—that if it were a bit off line, Ah-hui, the first baseman, would have had time to catch it and then touch the bag. Fortunately, though, the throw was perfect.

All in all it was a successful game both for the team and for me. Pitchers, I feel, have the advantage in the early part of the season because we hitters are still trying to get our timing down, and that may explain the fact why the two teams combined for only 11 hits. Therefore, I'm not going to get too bent out of shape for going 0-4 because no one else, for either team, really had a great game offensively. I hit one ball very well, and in my other at-bats, I saw all of the pitchers' repertoires. Early in the season, that in itself is a good thing. The bottom line, though, is that we won.

Now, it's time to discuss major league baseball, Taiwanese-style. We got to the park at about 3:45 PM, and we started our pre-game routine at about 4:00 PM. We did our running and stretching, the *sine qua non* of every practice or game, until about 4:20 PM, and then we loosened up our arms. As I was throwing, I was watching Fala take their BP, and I saw something I had never seen before: the 1st base umpire for tonight's game was at first base watching throws from the infielders to the first baseman, getting into proper position, and then signaling either out or safe. Never have I seen that before. Speaking of umpires, each game in the TML will feature six—that's right, *six*—umpires, one for each base and one for each foul line. Normally, in the WBL, we would have only two or three.

The fans, though sparse in number, easily filled the cavernous stadium with their endless hooting and hollering, especially with their plastic cones that they bang together in unison. If you've ever been to a rock concert or nightclub and have stood next to a speaker while the music is blaring, then you know how your body feels once the music stops. It's as if someone draws the life essence out of you. It was like that here for the first few innings tonight, but after a while, I hardly noticed the noise. The stadium seats probably 20,000 people, though tonight I'm guessing only 1,500 showed up. It also features a Diamond-Vision scoreboard, the kind you would find in American AA or AAA ballparks. The scoreboard didn't actually show replays, like most big league scoreboards do, but it was quite a spectacle to behold, considering that I've never actually played on a field with a scoreboard like that.

You see, stuff like that is so "big league" while other stuff is so "college." Once again, the dichotomy never ceases to amaze me. For example, we again didn't shower after the game; we simply rode the bus back to the hotel and showered in our rooms. Can you see the members of the New York Yankees walking through their team hotel in Seattle dressed in their entire uniforms? Not bloody likely. Also, I find it hard to believe that a stadium this nice does not have adequate laundry and locker facilities so we can leave our equipment at the stadium rather than lugging it back to the hotel with us. Even Reno, Nevada's, Moana Field clubhouse, which was about as warm and spacious as the solitary confinement cell in the Shawshank Federal Penitentiary, at least provided us shower and storage facilities, as well as a clubhouse attendant to clean our uniforms. Here, not wanting a repeat of the last clothing fiasco, I brought two, and in some cases four, of everything. According to Kevin, they will wash our uniforms, but they may not be ready for the game tomorrow. That makes about as much sense as the lyrics to a *Talking Heads* song. Either you wash them and have them ready by the time BP starts the next day, or you don't wash them at all.

Finally, I want to make certain that you, the reader, understand that I am not "Taiwan bashing" when I make these observations. Every culture has it's own way of doing things, and what is commonplace in one society may be completely abstract in another. It is these differences that make people want to travel in the first place, isn't it? If people were identical everywhere on Earth, other than seeing nature itself, what would be the point of traveling? Hey, I love America as much as anyone, but like I mentioned before, I am not that ethnocentric to think that the American way is the only way. When you, as an American, sign to play here, you also sign on to the whole Taiwanese way. Certainly, you don't forsake everything American, but out of respect to the country and your teammates, you should try to assimilate the best you can. If you're not ready to be a "team player" in every sense of the word, you can always go back to the USA. I am honestly happy being here and would like to play here for the whole season. In spite of all the cultural differences, I am enjoying it; I just can't wait until I start playing some good baseball. Out.

Thursday, April 5, 2001 (10:00 PM)
Bus from Kaoshiung to Taichung

Well, do you want the good news or bad news first? OK, the bad news. I got the collar again, meaning I had another game without any hits. We faced a lefty today, so therefore I had to bat right-handed. I hadn't faced a lefty in a game situation since a scrimmage about three weeks ago, but I had a good round of batting practice and felt comfortable at the plate. Unfortunately, this pitcher fed me a steady diet of forkballs, a pitch that breaks sharply downward just before it reaches home plate. He wasn't throwing very hard, and I just couldn't wait for the ball to get to me. Thus far, that's my biggest problem from a hitting standpoint. In America, pitchers like to throw their fastballs—it's definitely an ego thing. They challenge hitters more there, in part because a lot of American pitchers have good fastballs, and by "good," I mean 88 MPH or better. Here, though, it is rare to see a fastball at 88 MPH, and that's why Taiwanese pitchers rely more on deception than sheer power to get hitters out. If I don't make some adjustments, I may be facing American pitching rather soon.

Anyway, I struck out my first two times—both on forkballs—and after fouling off several of them in my third at-bat, I grounded to shortstop. In my final at-bat, I faced Ted Silva, and I grounded out to second base. Once again, against Silva, I was "early," the baseball term that means I didn't allow the ball to travel far enough before I swung at it. Granted, Ted's an American, but he too relies on control and deception to get hitters out. I've always been a "dead red" hitter, and the continuous supply of junk that I see at the plate is undoubtedly the reason why I'm struggling. I've come to realize that the problem is not in my swing because I'm really starting to hit the ball well in BP, and that usually means that I'll start hitting well in games. For some reason, however, I have been unable to adapt to the pitching. As I said, it had better happen soon because the Taiwanese powers-that-be traditionally don't have a lot of patience with the imports.

The good news is that we won again, 4-3. We got off to a good start as Ah-Hui launched a thunderous two-run homer in the first. Fala answered with two of their own in the bottom of the first on a series of singles and walks. We added one more in about the fifth, and, like last night, Rich came in to start the eighth. For the first time since we've been here, he got hit a little bit. They scored an unearned run off him to tie the game at 3-3, but Si-von put us ahead to stay with a solo homerun in the top of the ninth. Rich then closed the game out in the bottom of the inning, inducing a 4-6-3 double play to end the game.

One of the reasons I think runs will be at a premium in this league is because of the anti-expansion effect, "contraction" if you will. You see, perhaps the biggest culprit in the homerun derby that takes place seemingly on a nightly basis at the big league level is the fact that there are so many more teams now than in the past. Let's do some math. In the mid-1970's, when I believe the last pre-1990's expansion occurred, the total number of big league teams was 26. In 1993, the Florida Marlins and the Colorado Rockies were added. Then, in 1998, the Arizona Diamondbacks and Tampa Bay Devil Rays were also added. Now, let's say an average big league team features 10 pitchers, running the total number of big league pitchers in 1992 to 260 pitchers. In 1998, that total was increased to 300, meaning there were now 40 pitchers in the major leagues who would have normally been in the minors.

There's an age-old baseball saying that says, "Good pitching stops good hitting," and that will always be true. If a superstar big league pitcher has his best stuff on a given day, the team that he is facing is in deep trouble. Yes, one or two guys may get a few hits off him, but for the most part, he is going to stymie the opposition's offense. Take Game 5 of the 2000 American League Championship Series, for example, when the Yankees' Roger Clemens decimated the Seattle Mariners offensive attack. The combination of pinpoint control of his 95-MPH fastball and a virtually unhittable split-fingered fastball gave the Mariners basically no chance—on that day. Certainly, no pitcher can have his "A" game every time he takes the mound, but, that day, Clemens did, and Seattle's hitters could have taken California Redwoods to the plate and had the same results.

Contrary to what the layman sports fan may tell you, good hitters make their livings off the average and below average pitchers. I mention this, in fact, in my hitting manual. Jeff Bagwell, 1994 NL MVP, has been positively anemic in his last two postseason appearances (both against the Atlanta Braves), but if he had to face the Braves' pitching staff, arguably the best pitching staff ever, everyday for 162 games, he'd never approach the MVP-type numbers that he puts up every year. I even heard Kirby Puckett, former Minnesota Twins centerfielder say, "Hell, take your 0 for 4 or your 0 for 3 with a walk against the aces, be happy with it, and come out the next day ready to beat up on a lesser pitcher." Speaking from personal experience, against a typical 10-man pitching staff in the WBL, I can figure that the 1-2-3 starters, the set-up man, and the closer will give me trouble while the other five pitchers I can do my damage against. It varies, of course, from team to team, but the point is that you can't be expected to put up good numbers if you have to face quality pitching every night.

Here, though, due to "contraction," that is exactly the case. Traditionally, Asian pitchers throw a lot more pitches, number-wise, than their American counterparts. That's just the way they operate. I think they feel that throwing more frequently will allow them to keep their arms stronger and healthier, and while this indeed may be true, the theory is not conducive to career longevity. Because they can throw so many pitches, they need fewer pitchers, and with only two or three games a week, you need only six or seven pitchers per team. Therefore, there are going to be no "weak links," pitchers against whom you can expect to get a lot of hits. In our two games, for example, we brought in Rich to pitch the last two innings of each game, something an American closer would *never* do, but since we only had the two games, Mr. Wu could afford to do that. In fact, we used exactly three pitchers for those two games; I can't remember ever seeing such blatant disregard of a team's relief pitching. Once again, though, with fewer games, such is the nature of the beast. The bottom line is that I think this league will be an extremely low-scoring league, and the hitters' numbers across the board are going to be significantly lower than what I'm used to seeing. It's just a prediction, but we'll see.

We have Friday and Saturday off and will resume workouts on Sunday. Since I've been doing so lousy, I asked Kevin to see if I could get someone to go to a field—any field—in Taichung and throw me some BP. Hitting off a tee or hitting some "soft-toss" drills, which a lot of the younger players will do on Saturday, will do me absolutely no good. I need to see game-style pitching. Kevin said that this would be highly unlikely at best. It's just another paradox to add to the list: I want to do extra work on my own time, but I can't find anyone in this hard-working culture to oblige me. Like yesterday, when I wanted to go the field early to knock some of the rust off my right-handed swing, Kevin said no one had ever made such a request before. He said doing things together as team is the most important thing, *i.e.*, riding the bus to the field together, warming up together, and hitting together. *Then*, if there's time, I could get in my extra hitting. I told him the whole idea of a team is to win games, and to win games, you need to have each player performing to the best of his ability, and if team camaraderie and chemistry have to take a back seat to reach that end, so be it. He looked at me as if I had just told him that 2 + 2 = -6.8. Under the Plummer regime in Chico, if I wanted to take BP on an off day, you bet your ass that he'd find someone, if not himself, to pitch to me. Baffling, simply baffling. Out.

CHAPTER 3

▼

COMING HOME EMPTY-HANDED
TO AN UNFAITHFUL WIFE

Sunday, April 8, 2001
Bus from Taichung to Chiang Kai-shek Int'l Airport

Well, the day of reckoning came today, as I heard the dreaded "knock on the door" at about 12:30 PM. Practice was scheduled for 1:00 PM, and I had just finished eating and was starting to get dressed. Kevin and Mr. Sun, our fanatical conditioning coach, came to the door and gave me the bad news. Apparently, Mr. Wu was unable to lower the boom himself because he was hung up in traffic, so he delegated Mr. Sun as the bearer of bad tidings. I had this funny feeling about being released, not so much because my hitting was so lousy, but more so by the way the players and coaches were interacting with me.

When I first got here, Mr. Wu was constantly joking with me and teaching me a daily "word," if you know what I mean. After about the third simulation game, though, he became more distant. I kept telling him (and myself), "Mr. Wu, one more game and I'm ready to go," but evidently he grew tired of watching feeble at-bat after feeble at-bat. I can't say that I blame him, either; hell, if I had a third baseman, of any race, who was hitting the ball like Calista Flockhart, I'd release him, too.

Being released, like living out of your car and having no financial stability, is just part of playing baseball for a living, and you never know how it's going to happen. It usually occurs in one of three ways: 1) a clubhouse attendant saying, "Hey, so-and-so wants to talk to you," with so-and-so being that particular organization's Grim Reaper (a la in *Bull Durham*); 2) someone showing up at your hotel door with everything you had in your locker in the clubhouse and a plane ticket home—they do this so the player won't steal anything from the clubhouse or make a scene (as a former Atlanta Braves minor leaguer told me); or 3) someone stopping you in the middle of a practice and just saying, "Sorry, but you've been released (many organizations). I don't know if any of these qualify as "humane," but the idea is for the player to get the hell out of there with as little player contact as possible.

I wish I could figure out why I did so poorly here. Maybe it's the fact that I'm on foreign soil. I did some figuring the other day, and I would guess that my combined batting average of Australia (3 for 12), Colombia (about 1 for 15), and here (counting the simulation games, probably 3 for 27) is approximately .130. That's obviously a far cry from the .337 and .331 I batted over the previous two summers. Like I said, I have no idea why I stunk so badly, but the bottom line is that I did. I knew it, the coaches and players knew it, and I therefore understand the decision.

What's particularly galling to me is the fact that the whole Taiwanese experience went exactly opposite of how I would have predicted. I figured that I would struggle with the off-the-field stuff and that the baseball part would go smoothly. I'm not saying that I expected to come here and become a superstar; I just hoped to do well enough to make it through the whole season. As it turned out, of course, the non-baseball stuff went surprisingly well, all things considered, but my hitting was simply lousy.

Anyway, I got the news at 12:30 PM and therefore spent the next five hours closing up shop, as the bus I am currently on was scheduled to leave at 5:30 PM. I gave some stuff—tea bags, sugar, and chocolate—to the South African girls and left the rest for Rich, if he wanted anything. My plane to San Francisco leaves Taipei at 10:00 PM and will land at 6:30 PM. (The whole time zone thing reminds me of a story about former ABA player and super-flake Marvin Barnes, who was once informed that his flight was going to leave at 6:45 PM and land at 6:40 PM. He then responded, "I ain't getting' in no damn time machine!") I am looking forward to getting back to my friends and family of the USA, but, as I said a few entries back, I sincerely wanted to stay here for the duration of the season. Unfortunately, like the mother of a good childhood friend of mine used to say, "Yeah, well, people in Hell want ice water."

I suppose now I will contact the Heat again, hoping to hear that they haven't signed a third baseman as of yet. Assuming they will have me back, spring training will start in about three weeks, and it will be nice to have a little bit of a head start and not have to deal with the general aches and pains of the preseason. This journal, which began as an exclusively Taiwanese recount, will now become a season-long compilation. Whether it has the same appeal or not remains to be seen, but I would sincerely like to thank all of the people who corresponded with me during my 40 days on the R.O.C. It really meant a lot to me. I have been thinking about how to entitle my journal at the end of the summer, and one extremely apropos title consistently seems to jump to the forefront of my mind. You ready? *2001: A Baseball Odyssey*. Out.

Monday, April 16, 2001 (11:00 PM)
Chico, CA

After an eight-day hiatus, I have decided to resume my journal even though I am in the midst of some dead time. I called the Chico Heat last Monday morning to find out my status with the team, and I was told that they had given "my" position to another player. I say "my" because I had played third base for the Heat for the previous three years, and had I not gone to Taiwan, it would have been four. Apparently, WBL regulations prevent a team from inviting more than 30 players to spring training, and the Heat had "maxed out" its roster. Therefore, the front office offered to move me basically to the team of my choice. Since the Heat still owned the rights to me and I was not technically a free agent, I would have to either be traded or sold to another team. I thought immediately of the Solano Steelheads and the Sonoma County Crushers as perhaps the two most appealing options, so I checked out their websites to e-mail their GM's and to check out their third baseman situations. I also e-mailed the other three teams in the league, as well as the Atlantic and Northern Leagues, to notify them of my availability. As it turned out, Sonoma County's third baseman from last year, whom I thought was really solid, decided to retire, leaving them with a hole at the hot corner, so I was a perfect fit. After a little bit of haggling with their field manager, I agreed to the terms that he offered me. I could have held out and pursued the other teams and leagues I had contacted, but I figured that it would be in my best interests to sign with someone as soon as possible. The Crushers then had to work out compensation with the Heat, and, within an hour, I was unofficially a Crusher.

I must admit that I was a tad miffed at how little effort the Heat made to keep me. I understand that the salary cap severely limits what a team can do player-wise, but three years of dutiful, productive service should have warranted a little more effort on their part. I have always been very self-deprecating about my baseball ability, in part because I spent the better part of my youth telling everyone how wonderful I was, but there comes a time when you have to look at the numbers. No, I don't have homerun power nor do I have base-stealing speed, but I'd like to think that my offensive and defensive numbers are solid. I also was somewhat active in the community, have never been in any kind of trouble with the law, and tirelessly signed autographs after every home game, win or lose. In fact, the clip about my move that appeared in the local newspaper here said that I was "one of the Heat's most popular players." Again, I understand the handcuffing effect of the salary cap, but if they *really* wanted to make room for me, something tells me that they could have.

Oh well. I'm not going to bitch and moan about the whole ordeal because that won't make matters any better. I have nothing but good things to say about the fans and the community of Chico, and, for the most part, the Heat as an organization, and those are the memories that I will take with me. I can't say for sure what will happen after the season and where I'll go—maybe I should worry about making the Crushers team first—but I will probably end up back here again. I really like the area and the people here, and the fact that I will have played for the archrival shouldn't have too much of an impact. It will definitely be weird playing against the Heat, though, that's for sure.

(It bears noting at this point that Greg Ball, a Chico *Enterprise-Record* reporter, wrote an article that quoted manager Charley Kerfeld as saying that he considered me to be a "cancer" to the team. He added that even had I not gone to Taiwan, he would have most likely traded me to another team. Apparently, he felt that my "me-first" attitude easily negated my solid performance on the field and that the Chico Heat would be a better team without me. I wrote a response to Charley's accusations for the *Enterprise-Record*, and even though the newspaper didn't print it, I excerpted part of it for this journal. The contents can be found in the June 10 entry.)

Spring training starts on May 3 in Sonoma County, and, in the meantime, I will be working out here in Chico with the Heat players who are currently in town. I haven't done anything physically since I left Taiwan, but I had enough baseball there that it should only take a short amount of time to regain what I had developed. I have just returned my contract to the Crushers and am waiting to find out my host family situation there; I would like to know my new mailing address and phone number as soon as possible. A new start is just around the corner, and I really am anxious to get going. I've never been a big fan of maintaining the *status quo*, so this may turn out to be a welcomed change. After all, a rolling stone gathers no moss, right? Out.

CHAPTER 4

▼

SLEEPING WITH THE ENEMY

Wednesday, May 2, 2001 (4:45 PM)
Rohnert Park

It's been over two weeks since my last entry, but I promise that this will be the last hiatus, barring any unforeseen circumstances. One of the main reasons—hell, the *only* reason—that I haven't written anything is because there has been nothing to write about. I spent the last three weeks or so in Chico, where I was working out in preparation for my move to the Sonoma County Crushers. It was good to see some of the guys from last year's team again, but the thought of playing against them is a bit weird. There is no animosity that I know of between them and me, and it's not like football, where you're a teammate with someone one season and trying to decapitate him the next. Like Cal Ripken said a few years ago, "Baseball is not an enemy sport." Yes, pitchers have to pitch inside and baserunners have to break up double plays and occasionally bowl over a catcher, but beyond that, there really is no physical contact involved. You can be friends with your opponent and still try to kick his ass; it's not a mutually exclusive relationship.

From the bitterness standpoint, well, that's pretty much all gone. As I said, initially I was miffed, but now, I have come to realize that it was a baseball decision and nothing else. Take the Brooklyn Dodgers' Jackie Robinson, for example. He may have been the most important player in baseball history, yet he was traded to the hated Giants after nearly a decade with Brooklyn (he, of course, refused the trade and retired). Evidently, the GM of the Dodgers at the time felt that Robinson's services were no longer desired, but the Giants obviously didn't feel that way. Apparently, however, Robinson felt that the bad blood between the two teams was far too intense to become a Benedict Arnold. In the WBL, the Chico-Sonoma County rivalry is well known within the league, but it's nowhere near great enough for me to feel like I'm "selling out" Chico. After all, it was the Heat's decision, not mine. I'm sure people and newspaper reporters are going to ask me if I'm going to play with a chip on my shoulder against the Heat, but I won't consider them any different than anyone else in the league. I've always felt that you owe it to your teammates, your manager, your owner, the fans, and the game itself to go 100% all the time, from the time you arrive at the park until the time you leave, so saying you're going to "step it up" against one particular opponent means that you're giving a less than full effort against another. To me, that's entirely unacceptable.

I arrived here in Rohnert Park (a pretty valley town of 40,000 people about 40 miles north of San Francisco Bay between Petaluma and Santa Rosa on CA Rte. 101, for all you geography buffs out there) on Monday night. We have our first official workout tomorrow, but I wanted to come down a few days early to get set up with my host family, the Jones, and to become acclimated to the area. Today, I went to the stadium for a light workout and to meet some of my new teammates, many of whom I have played against in this league. The Crushers had a tough year last summer with a lot of turnover, so there are only about 6-8 guys returning from last year's team. I'm not exactly sure how many guys will be in spring training, but I should find out tomorrow.

It's always interesting—and somewhat exciting—to meet new players. The introduction always seems to follow the same course: a handshake, an exchange of names, and a "So, where did you play last year?" (if he's new to the league) or an "oh yeah, I remember you." Along these lines, one theory I have concocted in my six-plus years of pro ball is that a player's natural ability to play baseball is inversely proportional to the following three things: the ability/desire to learn Spanish, the ability to explain why you are successful at what you do, and the ability to remember names of previous opponents. Certainly, this isn't true all the time, but far more often than not. I always think of Philadelphia Phillies 1st baseman Travis Lee, a former teammate of mine with the High Desert Mavericks in 1997. To give you an idea of his "natural ability," he received a $10,000,000 signing bonus in the fall of 1996, which at the time was a record. To this day, he is the best all around baseball player I've ever played with, bar none. Travis didn't know a lick of Spanish. After striking out, I'd ask him how he could have possibly hit that same dirty changeup into the next county, looking for a response like, "Well, he threw it to me two at-bats ago" or "I saw him tipping it by digging for it in his glove," in other words an answer that someone like me would give. Well, he'd say, "I had it in the back of my mind that he'd throw it." In other words, he had no idea how to hit; he just did it. Finally, we had a pitcher named Jeff Sobkoviak, and one month into the season, Travis had no idea how to spell his name or how to pronounce it—and this was his own teammate! I just shook my head.

Anyway, I met roughly two-thirds of the guys who were invited to spring training, and we all did some throwing and some hitting in the batting cages. I still haven't met the manager, Tim Ireland, though he has quite a track record and the reputation as a fiery guy. Also, it was confirmed that Kevin Mitchell, 1989 NL MVP with the San Francisco Giants and player/coach last year with the Crushers, will be the hitting coach this year. From what I read about him last year and from what I heard from the players, he is a great guy in the clubhouse, and someone who is sincerely interested in helping players improve. In fact, a man of his wealth and stature could have flown to St. George, UT, last year rather than take the 12- hour bus trip, but he didn't, stating that he was no different than any other player on the team. I wish the snot-nosed, bonus-baby punks of the baseball world would take note of *that*. I look forward to meeting him and discussing hitting with him. There is one problem, though: he wore my beloved #7 last year. Something tells me that when it comes time to choose uniform numbers—a situation where seniority and merit mean everything—my two years of service in Class A doesn't quite measure up to being a former NL MVP. Looks like this chunky third baseman might have to consider a new number. Rats. Out.

Saturday, May 5, 2001 (5:15 PM)
Rohnert Park

Today is "Cinco de Mayo," which, whether you're of Mexican ancestry or not, means it's time to *fiesta*. I have become a bit of a homebody since I've been here, as I have yet to go out on the town. I can't remember the last time I stayed at home five nights in a row during baseball season; maybe I'm ready for marriage........on second thought, scratch that. Being new in town, I have to find this team's "go out guru," the guy who always seems to know where the action is on a given night. In Chico, I suppose I was pretty good in that capacity, having played there for three years, but I need some guidance here. There's a place called *The Cantina*—obviously a Mexican place—where most of the guys are heading tonight, and I shall join them. I'll keep you informed.

I actually wrote an entry on Thursday, but my word processing package was acting up, and, unfortunately, it has "disappeared." To summarize what I wrote, we went through the standard introductions, where Tim

Ireland, the manager, introduced himself, pitching coach Dolf Hes, and then the front office staff. Bob Fletcher, the owner/GM, said that he felt as though on paper, this is the best team he has ever started with. After three days, I feel the same. I am especially impressed with our pitching. We have maybe four or five guys whom I've never seen throw before, but of the ones I have, I like our chances. There are four or five relief pitchers that could be closers for most teams in this league, but here, they will have to settle for being set-up men/middle relievers. The closer job will undoubtedly go to Tim Scott, a 34-year-old who has about 5-6 years of big league experience with the Florida Marlins, Montreal Expos, and San Francisco Giants. He started 2000 with Solano but was signed by Cincinnati at the midway point of the season. Thank God he's on our team because he is as close to unhittable as any pitcher in this league. In other words, with our relief corps, if we can take a lead into the fifth inning, we should be in good shape.

Our three workouts thus far have followed the same basic pattern: stretch, loosen up the arms, hit in the batting cages, hit "live BP" from the pitchers, and then do our running. The running part has been interesting and is definitely a reflection of our manager. Ireland believes, as do I, that we won't have much firepower at the plate this year, and we'll therefore have to rely on "manufacturing" runs, which means we'll do a lot of bunting, stealing, hit-and-running, and generally putting pressure on the opposition's defense. Evidently, he has always managed this way, and his track record speaks for itself. Usually, a spring training, post-practice conditioning session involves running some sprints in the outfield grass or doing a light, long-distance jog. Our conditioning, though, has been on the basepaths, where Ireland is a stickler on good leads, explosive jumps, and proper angles, the thought being that these three things can score a team perhaps 2-3 more runs per week and translate into maybe 5-7 more wins over a 90-game season. He understands that any little bit helps. We haven't done an enormous amount of running; rather, we've focused on the techniques he has been teaching. Most of us older guys haven't done anything like this since our affiliated baseball days, so it's good that he's reacclimatizing us to the finer points of baserunning.

Yesterday's practice involved team bunt defenses, one of those dreadful yet necessary parts of any spring training. We went over the signs and responsibilities of the pitcher, the catcher, and every infielder, though not without incident. We had one pitcher who was receiving one sign and performing a completely different task, prompting Tim to ask, to no one in particular, if we needed to change the signs. He said, "We can use hieroglyphics, Morse code, whatever, but we got to get this right." The whole team broke up over that one. A lot of managers might have become a little upset at such a mental error, so it's good to see that he has a sense of humor.

To the AWOL category, we can officially add Kevin Mitchell. I was looking forward to playing with him on a daily basis, but, due to his diabetes, he will be simply the hitting coach. He also is a "great guy in the clubhouse," a general sports label bestowed upon an older, well-traveled player who is playing several levels beneath where he used to play. In other words, he never "big-leagued" anyone and was sincere about helping the younger players improve. Now, you may be wondering, "Why does a former MVP want to play in a small time independent league for next to nothing?" Well, I'll answer that. The next time you listen to a major athlete's retirement speech, I'll bet the ranch he'll say that of all the things he'll miss, he'll miss his teammates the most. Mitchell, in fact, said something along those lines last year in one of the newspapers—that he simply loves being around the guys. It doesn't have to be a situation where you're around familiar teammates, guys with whom you've played for a number of years; just laughing and joking and going out with and playing cards with "the guys" is enough.

Baseball is funny like that: during the summer, you can be thick as thieves with a guy, but if one of you doesn't come back the next year, you probably never talk to the guy again. It's not a rudeness or standoffishness thing; it's just the nature of the game. Certainly, you'll meet one or two guys per team with whom you'll keep in touch over the winter, but as for the rest, it's "Hey, great playing with you; see you next spring." It sounds cold, but, really, it's very commonplace.

Anyway, Mitchell was due in town yesterday, but someone said he is trying to sell his truck, or something like that, in San Diego and will arrive soon. I have played with a few guys who had some big league time, but certainly not someone who has a decade of experience and an MVP on his résumé. It will be interesting to hear some stories of his time in "the show," as well as some of his theories on hitting. This summer may be an especially nostalgic one for him because 15 years ago, he was a member of the world champion New York Mets. In fact, in the epic Game Six against the Boston Red Sox of that World Series, the game in which the game-winning ground ball rolled through Bill Buckner's legs, Mitchell was the second of four consecutive Mets hitters to reach base with two outs, and he later scored the tying run. Being the baseball trivia connoisseur that I am, you can bet your ass that I'm going to grill him on *that* game. Out.

Sunday, May 7, 2001 (6:00 PM)
Rohnert Park

First off, let me just say that "Cinco de Mayo" didn't disappoint. I met three of our pitchers at *The Cantina* as planned, but we decided not to stay there. For one, they had a cover charge, and, secondly, the line constituted probably a 20-minute wait, so we decided to go to a little hole in the wall joint called the *Cotati Yacht Club*. Two of the pitchers had been there the night before, and they kept telling the other pitcher and me how cool it is. So, the two of us—the skeptics—got there about five minutes before the other two, and the place was next to dead, prompting us to meet our *compadres en crimen* in the parking lot in order to question the decision. They assured us that it would start filling up at about 10:30 PM, as it had apparently done the night before, so we entered. Sure enough, by 10:45 PM, the population had doubled, and by 11:30 PM, it was packed.

Needless to say, the skeptics' doubts were erased, and the four of us had a great time. It turned out to be absolutely my kind of place: two pool tables, a jukebox, reasonable prices, and no young kids spilling beer all over me. Something tells me that I'll be there again.

One thing that I discussed in the "lost" entry from Thursday is the incredible ethnicity of our team. Let's see, we have two Dominican Republic natives (Compres and Valera), a Mexican-American (Garcia), a Native American (Neboyia, a.k.a. Chief), two Japanese-Americans (Takahashi and Kishita), a Japanese guy (Yoshimoto), three African-Americans, and fifteen white boys. Jeez, even our trainer is black, which is a first for me. Maybe it would be best if we didn't have a radio at all in our club with this motley crew.

On the field, we had another typical spring training practice. Once again, Tim incorporated one more baserunning station—reading the ball off the bat from second base. The more I think about it, the more I realize how important "small ball" is going to be to us. Hell, we may end up looking like a damn college team with all the little things we'll undoubtedly do. On paper, we have no power. Sure, shortstop James Lofton and outfielder Chris Powell each hit around 10 homeruns last year, but they aren't threats to hit the long ball. We do have an outfielder, Jeff Depew, who came into the WBL last year right out of college and showed some pretty impressive power, but he seems a bit inconsistent right now. Perhaps in a few years he may develop some consistency, but on this team, we don't have one guy who can be counted on for 15 or more homeruns. Then again, it doesn't matter how you score, just that you score.

I do, however, like our defense. Lofton and Valera appear to be a solid keystone combination while Powell is a solid centerfielder. I obviously don't know how Tim sees things in the outfield, but he should have a few nice options from which to choose. You know, you can basically divide up a team into three major categories: pitching, defense, and offense. Yes, pitching and defense generally go hand in hand, and some baseball people will say that it constitutes "90%" of the game, but if you have, say, a bunch of "groundball" pitchers, well, you better have some damn good infielders, or it's all for naught. If a given team has two of those three on a nightly basis, it's going to be pretty successful, and if it is fortunate enough to have all three, like we did in my three years in Chico, it will be almost unbeatable, as we were. Here, though, we may only have two of the three, but the two we seem to have are indeed the best two to have.

As I said, today was a pretty ordinary day, so I'll close. We start our exhibition game schedule at the end of the week, and I'm anxious to see what we look like as a team. In the meantime, I'll continue to work out the kinks and crank out the entries; by opening day, I want to be playing like Willie Mays and writing like Willie Shakespeare. Out.

Monday, May 7, 2001 (8:45 PM)
Rohnert Park

Like today's practice, this entry will be short and to the point. For some reason, we worked out at 3:00 PM today, much to the chagrin of several players. I felt as if I were in Taiwan again with this last-minute change (it had originally been scheduled for 11:00 AM). Some guys weren't able to get out to the golf course as scheduled, and one guy, Takahashi, was unable to make it to Pac Bell Stadium for tonight's Giants-Expos game. Apparently, he is a good friend of Russ Ortiz, the Giants starting pitcher, and Ortiz was leaving some complimentary tickets for him. For me, however, the later start meant some extra sleep, and that's always a good thing.

Today was the first day that we took BP from Tim and Dolf, as opposed to live BP from the pitchers, so we all finally had a chance to get some good quality swings during BP. Before we took BP, though, Tim announced the starting lineup for our exhibition game in Solano tomorrow—that's right, I was misinformed and therefore misled you. This is how it went: "Lofton, you'll lead off. Then Powell, Valera, and Bo, you'll hit cleanup. Have you ever hit cleanup before?" Flabbergasted, I said, "No." Then he asked, "Will that bother you?" Again, I said, "No."

You see, a lot of players have preferences of where they'd like to hit in the batting order, and most of these reasons are rooted in selfishness. So-and-so wants to hit second so he can score a lot of runs, or so-and-so wants to hit fifth so he can drive in a lot of runs. I never saw the point in complaining about where I am in the order. The only time I'll say anything is if I think I can improve the team. For example, about halfway through my senior year of college, we were struggling a bit offensively as a team, mostly due to our inability to find an adequate leadoff hitter. I was batting third, but my on-base percentage was over .500, so I asked Coach Hartman if I would be more beneficial to our team as a leadoff hitter. I knew that my RBI totals would fall dramatically—which they did—but I was more concerned about winning games. As it turned out, we immediately started scoring more runs and finished the season strongly. Last season, I led the League in on-base percentage, yet I was either sixth or seventh in the order for the entire year. I realize that I will never be confused with a jackrabbit, but I *know* it's a lot tougher to get from home to first than it is from first to home. Not wanting to add further strain to an already frictional relationship between Charley and me, I didn't say anything, but I still thought I would have been more beneficial to the team batting third.

If I am in fact our cleanup hitter at least for a while, I'm not going to try to alter my approach to hit like a "cleanup hitter." I've already told you how short of power we are on this team, and that's just the way it's going to be. I shall therefore refer to myself as "the fourth hitter in the lineup" so I don't give anyone the wrong idea. To me, the whole argument of where you should be hitting in the order is stupid because you hit according to the game situation, not where you are in the order. Yes, hitting in certain parts of the order will offer more opportunities to steal more bases or score more runs or drive in more runs, but this is a team game, in theory, so stats shouldn't matter. For example, if you're a non-homerun-hitting, five-hole (fifth in the order) hitter, and you're leading off the ninth inning with your team trailing by a run, your job becomes that of a leadoff hitter, *i.e.*, to get on base.

Nevertheless, I joked to Lofton that we may be in serious trouble if I'm hitting cleanup, but then I pointed out that it's not how you score them but rather that you *are* scoring them. If we need 15 hits to score six runs while the opposition scores five runs on eight hits, guess what? We win. That's the bottom line, isn't it? I'm sure Tim will tinker with the lineup during spring training and quite possibly into the first part of the regular season; I just hope that the players react professionally to such changes. From what I can tell, it shouldn't be too much of a problem.

Finally, I'll end with your seemingly daily "They Said It" quote. It was the end of practice, and the entire team had gathered around the pitcher's mound to go over the signs for tomorrow's game. We discussed the defense-related signs that the pitchers and infielders have to know well, and then we went over the offensive signs, which are as about as useful to the pitchers as wives were to Henry VIII. When we finished, Tim dismissed us, but Kishita, the *de facto* interpreter for our Japanese import, chimed in with, "Wait a minute. Yoshi doesn't understand shit. I don't understand shit either." We all got a good laugh out of that one. Out.

Wednesday, May 9, 2001 (9:15 PM)
Rohnert Park

I apologize for my failure yesterday to recap our first exhibition game. I shall therefore do it now. We went to Solano, where it was hotter than Britney Spears, and since they were repairing the visitor's dugout, we all had to sit in the blazing sun. The final score was 5-3 in Solano's favor, but that is basically irrelevant. Eight of our pitchers threw an inning apiece, and all our position players got at least one at-bat, and that sharing of the wealth is what really matters.

Personally, I got two at-bats and one chance—an easy popup—in the field. My first at-bat came against Jason Olsen, the reigning WBL Pitcher of the Year, and it resulted in a groundball up the middle that the short-stop fielded easily and retired me at first. The first official at-bat of spring training is tough enough as it is, let alone when you're facing a pitcher of Olsen's caliber. He has a decent fastball velocity-wise, but he keeps it down in the zone well. He also features perhaps the best right-handed changeup in the league. Knowing this, I wanted to make sure I saw as many pitches as I could to determine how well I was "seeing the ball." Remember, "seeing the ball" is when you are determining as quickly as possible what the pitch is and where it's going. I saw two fastballs and two changeups from him, so I would consider that to be a successful at-bat, in spite of my inability to hit a rocket off him. The other at-bat came against a lefty, Darold Brown, which meant that I had to bat righty. He's a typical lefty in that he usually throws—to me, at least—a fastball on the outer part of the plate, a changeup, and an occasional curveball. After taking the first pitch for a strike, I hit the second one off the end of my bat for a broken-bat single to left. Part of being a mature hitter is recognizing the difference between the two at-bats and although my second one resulted in a hit, I actually felt better about the first one.

We also implemented Tim's "track meet," if you will, resulting in four stolen bases. As I mentioned earlier, what we lack in thunder I hope will be compensated for with lightning. Tim understands the importance of planting an early seed in the other teams' heads about how we are going to be an extremely aggressive team, and, in doing so, he may be able to score us a few extra runs on reputation alone. It's funny, but while we receiving some more of our baserunning education in practice today, he mentioned to us that he was the "winningest manager in the world during the 1990's." I don't know if he has managed this way with every team he's had, but he understands a ubiquitous truth of any successful coach in any sport: you don't force players into "your" system; you install a system to maximize the talents of the players you've been given. Let me elaborate.

Don Shula, who holds the all-time record for victories by an NFL head coach, was known and lauded for his ability to adapt to the changing of both the athlete as a person and the theories of the game itself. From the time he broke in as a head coach in the 1960's to when he finally retired after the 1995 season, he had used countless players and numerous systems to win his record number of games. The prime example is how he won three AFC Championships in the 1970's with a powerful running attack featuring Jim Kiick, Mercury Morris, and Larry Csonka. In the 1980's, of course, he won—though not quite as much—with a passing game that utilized the prodigious talents of Dan Marino.

Now, let me offer an example of how *not* to do things. I have documented in this journal about my "approach" to hitting, and while it may not be sexy, it is somewhat successful. My "approach" involves taking a lot of pitches until I get the one I like, even if it means taking a walk in an RBI situation. As a result, I may not always drive in the run that others might. If I were to try, not only would I probably not drive in that run, but also I may not even get on base to score a run later. Ted Williams, arguably the greatest hitter of all-time, used to say, "A hitter gains no advantage by doing something on Tuesday that he wouldn't do on Friday." In other words, you stick with your "approach" come Hell or high water. The situation is no different than asking a guy like Sammy Sosa, who is as likely to swing and miss a fastball right down the middle as he is to hit a homerun on a pitch over his head, to take a lot of pitches in order to find one that he really likes. When I was in Taiwan, I was batting fifth in the order, and, at one point, I asked our hitting coach if he saw anything I was doing wrong. He told me that he thought I was taking too many pitches and that "I shouldn't be looking for a walk" as a five-hole hitter. Well, that really bothered me. First of all, I wasn't "looking for a walk;" a walk is just a result, sometimes good and sometimes bad, of my approach. Secondly, Ah-hui, our free-swinging, power hitting first baseman was hitting third, yet he had all the attributes of a classic fifth hitter. Instead of asking me to change my approach, perhaps Mr. Wu should have simply flip-flopped our places in the order to incorporate better our hitting styles.

Getting back to Tim, I would find it hard to believe that he has had a team with less power than this one, so running (and running and running) will be *the* major part of our offensive attack. How well we institute his system and how well the opposition adjusts will be a huge factor in our team's success. We should definitely be exciting to watch if nothing else.

Finally, after practice today, I went golfing with some of the guys. Until last season, I had played maybe six rounds my entire life, but I am really starting to enjoy it. Naturally, the better I play, the more I like the game because there are times when I agree with Mark Twain's quote, "Golf is a good walk spoiled." I struck the ball well, which for me is a gargantuan accomplishment; normally, I'm good for 10-15 shanks per round, but today, I think I only duffed two or three. I'm also starting to get a better feel with my short irons, though I'm a long, *long* way from ever shooting in the 80's. I shot a "by the book" 102 this afternoon, only three strokes short of my career best 99. I asked Brian Grant, one of the foursome, why I can't drive the ball low and straight like he can, and he replied, "That's because you have a baseball swing." I guess that's better than being a baseball player with a golf swing. Out.

Friday, May 11, 2001 (5:15 PM)
Rohnert Park

The Heat came to town yesterday for our exhibition game, and it was good to see some of the guys from last year whom I hadn't seen in my preseason workouts. They won the game, 9-5, but once again, who cares? They scored five runs in the 7th inning, with four of them coming off our closer Tim Scott. Hell, I'd bet that Scottie didn't give up four runs all of last year as the closer for Solano, and trust me when I say that he is the least of our concerns; like I said, he is as close to unhittable as there is in this league. I had to play first base because Yoshimoto has a bad ankle, so I got to chat with the Heat players quite a bit. They actually found it amusing that I, with my whopping four homeruns last year, am the cleanup hitter, and after seeing them hit three homeruns and two doubles, I asked them if they would mind lending us some power.

Personally, I didn't hit too well, even though I felt good at the plate. Reece Borges, who developed into the ace of our staff last year, got me out on a couple of quality changeups. Later, in my third left-handed at-bat, I grounded out to shortstop. In my final at-bat, this one righty, I flew out to centerfield. Starting on Monday, I am going to try to take as much "early BP" as I can. I did a lot of that in Chico, and it undoubtedly helped me to improve as a hitter, but now, I don't know how much I can actually improve. I'd like to think, however, that I am at the stage of my career when early BP will help me get off to a good start and to maintain my stroke.

Today, we had our first spring training casualty. Mike Hymes, who came straight to the Crushers last year from UCLA, was told by Tim that he wouldn't be a starter, at least right away, so Mike, knowing how important it is for a young player to play everyday, decided to try his luck elsewhere. He was one of four rookies that the Crushers had playing up the middle last year, and the "young pups," as Dolf calls them, had a unique bond with one another. The remaining "canines," if you will, were obviously sad to see him go. He is a good kid with pretty decent speed and UCLA on his resume, so I'm sure he'll catch on with someone soon. It just stinks to be the "odd man out" in a numbers crunch; maybe I'll form an independent league players' union to request, among other things, severance pay.

Finally, I had an epiphany today. A few of us—actually, about 20 of us—went out to the unofficial watering hole of the Crushers, *The Cotati Yacht Club*, sometimes referred to as "The Office." Well, the Crushers monopolized the place, much to the dismay of the other males in the establishment, and we all had a helluva time. Unfortunately, the drinking got a little out of hand for most of us, yours truly included, and I felt really lousy today at practice. But then I realized why my legs felt so crappy: standing. Let me explain. There is no simulation for standing for nine innings, no off-season program for an infielder to simulate getting in the "ready" position for 200 pitches. That's why spring training is so tough. The running drills can hurt the legs, yes, but the real culprit for the aches and pains associated with spring training is the standing and crouching. We as players always joke about trying to get into midseason form, be it pitching, hitting or drinking, as quickly as possible, but maybe I should come up with a winter program to prepare us for all the standing around. On second thought, if I were at the gym just standing there, getting into the ready position, and "adjusting myself" for three hours, I may get some strange looks. Out.

Sunday, May 13, 2001 (10:45 PM)
Rohnert Park

This journal entry will encompass the past two games. Chico came to town again on Friday and obliterated us by a score of 7-1. Their pitchers were actually throwing a no-hitter against us until about the sixth inning, which should give you an idea of how impotent our offensive attack was that day. Seeing our futility at the plate, I asked myself if a no-hitter has ever been thrown in spring training at any level. I doubt it, but you never know. As far as I know, no one, not even the stat rats at Elias Sports Bureau, keep track of statistics for spring training. Had the no-hitter occurred, though, we would have gone down in some kind of infamy. One of our catchers, mammoth-sized Travis Oglesby, whom I've unofficially nicknamed "Ogre," hit a homerun in the seventh inning to avoid the shutout. We also played poorly defensively as a team, making three errors and showing all the hustle, determination, and enthusiasm of Cistercian Monks, which prompted Tim to give out the first "wakeup call" of the young season.

After the game, rather than dismissing us as usual, Tim gathered us together and told us that our performance was the worst he had ever seen from any team he has managed, and if not the worst, certainly in the top five. He said there would be no more lollygagging on and off the field, meaning that we had 15 seconds to get to our positions and 15 seconds to get from our positions to the bench. To illustrate his point, he actually had us run to our positions and back three times, all the while timing us with his stopwatch. Then, he made us throw the ball around the infield after a strikeout three times because he wasn't happy with the way we did that either. Finally, all the position players lined up at home plate to run sprints to first base due to our not doing so in the games. Keep in mind that we did all this not only in front of the Heat players, some of whom gave me "What in Sam Hill are you guys doing?" looks as they left the field, but also in front of some of the home crowd that stuck around after the game had ended. I now feel an extreme urge to offer a commentary on this ordeal.

We are not college baseball players. In college, bad play often results in extra conditioning or something involving physical agony. While sometimes it may work, most of the time it doesn't, yet coaches believe that somehow torturing players will make them play better. If that were the case, then the Tampa Bay Devil Rays would have a team full of triathletes. I have never seen, let alone heard of, a manager utilizing such means to get his team to play better, but let me tell you this: embarrassment can be a damn powerful motivator. Look, part of being a professional, as I've said, is respecting the game, and that means you run hard both on and off the field and on the bases. It means that you throw the ball around the infield with some pep, and you give the general impression that you in fact *do* want to be on the field. Now, I'm not going to say that I have never loafed on a groundball or failed to run hard on a weak fly ball, but I'll bet I can count on one hand the number of times it did happen. I think that's part of the reason—along with not chewing out umpires and graciously signing autographs—that I've been well received by the fans in every one of my baseball stops.

Today, though, it's not cool to hustle; players see guys named Griffey and Bonds jake it to first base, so they think they can, too. While I will never condone not hustling, it is a tad different when you're making $11 million a year as opposed to $1100 a month. I don't think fans should ever boo a minor leaguer, but the exception is when a player offers little or no hustle, bringing to mind the quote, "Hustling requires no talent."

Incidentally, I talked to Bo Dodson, Solano's manager, before the game today, and he told me that as a player under Tim in the AA Texas League in the mid 1990's, Tim had his players do basically the same thing after a lousy performance. Boy, I can see doing it in an independent league, but doing it in affiliated ball? I didn't ask Bo what he thought about it, but he did say that he enjoyed playing for Tim and that if you play hard every day, he won't say two words to you. Sounds quite similar to the comments I made about Bill Plummer, doesn't it?

In today's game, we played markedly better. I've said it before and I'll say it again: you're going to have bad games. There are going to be times when your pitchers can't stop walking guys and can't keep the ball in the park. There will be times when the hitters appear to be swinging Wiffle Ball bats at home plate. We are human beings, and we are going to make mistakes, but if mistakes are made aggressively and are met with a steely resolve to make good on the next play, then no one will ever get on you. But when players start hanging their heads after an error or "taking their at-bats to the field," then professionalism has gone right out the window, and it's reality check time. We finally broke out of our team-wide hitting funk, and even though we only scored three runs, we had a lot of hard-hit outs. I even got my first extra-base hit of 2001, a two-out, RBI double over the centerfielder's head. Granted, it was a little wind-aided, but, at this point, I'll take anything. Nevertheless, it was nice to actually drive a ball for once. We played solid defense, with our lone error coming at the hands (or should I say off the hands) of Lofton on a routine groundball. Like Tim Scott, however, James is the least of our defensive worries, inasmuch as he is a heckuva shortstop, both offensively and defensively, and perhaps one of the top five all-around players in the league. So, in spite of the loss, our spirits were noticeably lighter afterwards, and Tim gave us the old, "Nice job, guys. Bus leaves tomorrow at 12:00. See you then."

In closing, I found something to chalk up in the "Now that's something you don't see everyday" category. First, however, let me offer an explanation. When I approach a groundball down the third-base line, I can't hesitate to hear (or not hear, if it's fair) the umpire's ruling, so I treat every ball as if it will be fair. Otherwise, if I hesitate for a split-second while awaiting the call, my throw may be late to first. In the Chico game, I had not one, not two, but *three* groundballs down the line that I had to play as if they were fair even though they were eventually called foul, and on all three of them (the last one would have been *really* close), I made a clean enough play and strong enough throw to get the runners at first. That type of play—when I have to make the throw because it's too close to call—happens maybe five times a year, but I'm glad they happened because it gave me a chance to show not only Tim but the other guys what kind of defensive player I am. Normally, groundballs down the line are very difficult plays and offer little margin for error, and any slight bobble or slightly offline throw results in the runner's being safe. In fact, after the game today, in which I made a nice play on a tricky grounder with a fast runner, as well as two or three routine ones, some of the pitchers joked that I may be using up all my highlight reel plays in spring training. I then had to explain to them that it's in my contract that I have to catch it and hit it because they sure as hell ain't payin' me to run. Out.

Tuesday, May 15, 2001 (4:45 PM)
Rohnert Park

Well, today's entry will begin with a good news/bad news situation regarding our exhibition game in Chico yesterday. I'll give you the good news first: we scored 10 runs. The bad news: they scored 15. Therefore, our preseason exhibition record finished at 0-5. I sure hope this isn't a harbinger of things to come for the season. Chico hit the absolute crap out of the ball, pounding a solo homerun, two three-run homeruns, and a grand slam. Ouch. We took a brief, one-run lead after I hit a two-out, two-run double in the third inning, but Chico responded with nine runs of their own in the bottom of the fourth. Man, those guys can hit. At this point, I don't see a real weakness in their lineup. Hopefully, though, once we get our pitching staff arranged, I think we'll do okay against them.

On our side, we scored our 10 runs on 13 hits, with three coming from Lofton and two from Powell. I mentioned my double, but I also picked up two more RBI's on groundouts, one of which could have gone for another double down the first base line if not for a highlight reel play by first baseman Jon Macalutas. Personally, I felt as good yesterday as I had all spring training, and since we don't have any more games until Opening Night, I hope that feeling remains until then.

From a team standpoint, however, I think we're still swinging at too many first pitches. It's one thing to smoke a first-pitch fastball over the heart of the plate or an off-speed pitch if you're anticipating it; our guys, unfortunately, have been swinging at the first pitch and hitting weak fly balls and grounders. It has gotten so bad that even Keith, our *trainer*, has noticed. I talked to Lofton and Powell about our impatience over the past two games because statistically, they and I are the only proven hitters on the team. Valera seems to have a pretty good idea at the plate, but I haven't seen his numbers to know what he's done over the last couple of years. Lofton and Powell both agree with me, and if it keeps up into the second week of the season or so, we may have to address it. That's the tricky part.

The key to discussing a facet of someone's game is to do it as positively and professionally as possible. Think of it this way: if an unattractive man makes a pass at a lady in a bar and she's not interested, she can say 1) "You are the most revolting thing I've ever laid eyes on—get out of here" or 2) "No, thank you. I'm not interested." Such is the nature of a hitting discussion. You can't question a player's ability, but done properly, you can question what he's doing at the time. Furthermore, there is no one "right" way to hit; some people hit, and some don't. Period. If you have to stand on your head, swing a conductor's baton, and let the count go to 0-2 every at-bat in order to produce runs for your team, then, by all means, do it. Some guys are patient hitters. Some are aggressive hitters. Some are fastball hitters. Some are off-speed hitters. It's really irrelevant what type of hitter you are as long as you produce runs. That's one of the reasons why it's so difficult to teach hitting.

Take the 1998-2000 New York Yankees, winners of the last three World Series. They were known as a team that "took a lot of pitches" and "went deep into the count." They made the starting pitchers throw more pitches than any team in baseball, and any baseball guy will tell you that perhaps the biggest key to scoring a lot of runs is to get the starting pitcher out of the game as soon as possible so you can beat up on the middle relievers. There was an exception on that team, though: Derek Jeter. He was completely opposite in his approach, as he swung at a lot of first and second pitches. Sure, the Yankees would have wanted him to hit deeper into the count, but Jeter, who was hitting second in the order most of the time, was getting hits and getting on base and, most importantly, scoring runs. The point is that although Jeter went against the grain in his hitting, he nevertheless was successful at his job, and "If it ain't broke, don't fix it."

In fairness to some of our guys, a lot of them are young, and a lot of them don't have their jobs secured as yet. Therefore, they are pressing a little bit perhaps, causing them subconsciously to alter their approaches in hopes of impressing Tim and winning a job. That's the baseball paradox for you. It's not like football, where a coach can get in your face and scream at you and berate you so much that you're ready to bulldoze your own grandmother; in baseball, the ultimate game of skill and precision, usually the more wound up you get, the worse you do.

We have three more workouts before Friday's opener, and they should be light ones. We may have a simulated game to give the pitchers and hitters one more, game-type situation on Wednesday, but I haven't heard for sure yet. I do know that the rosters have to be set by Wednesday night, and that day is never a pleasant one. I wrote in my *Baseball America* journal last year about the intimacy of independent league spring training versus the watch-your-back nature of affiliated spring training. For almost two weeks, the 26 of us have been working out, going out, and hanging out together, but unfortunately, we can't keep everyone. It's really a shame, too, because we have a great group of guys here. Once again, though, such is the nature of the beast. Out.

Wednesday, May 16, 2001
Rohnert Park

"Ask not upon whom the guillotine falls; too often, it falls upon thee." Yes, today was roster-trimming day. According the WBL, the final, 22-man roster must be turned in to the league office tonight, so there were a lot of heavy hearts around the clubhouse. God, I hate this time of year. The WBL has a rule regarding the number and, more importantly, "types" of players you must have on your roster. *Type 1*: the Rookie. If a hitter has never had a professional season in which he had 100 or more at-bats, he is a "rookie." The one glitch is that the WBL waives your first year of independent league baseball, which means that if you go to the WBL (or any other independent league) right from college and get anywhere from one to 1,000,000 at-bats, it doesn't count against your status. For pitchers, everything else is the same except that the measuring stick is 50 innings pitched. *Type 2*: the Limited Service (LS) player. Any player who is not a rookie and who has not played a full season of at least Double A baseball—by full season, I believe it means once again 100 at-bats or 50 IP—then you have LS status. *Type 3*: the Veteran. Basically, a full season in Double A makes you a veteran.

Now here's the tricky part. Each team must carry a minimum of four rookies and a maximum of eight veterans, at least three of whom are hitters. Whatever is left is comprised of LS guys. Obviously, a team will max out its veteran part because that's usually where the talent lies. The tough part for a veteran is that he must perform and perform well since he is taking up valuable roster space. In other words, "Be good or be gone." The rookies are in a precarious situation in that if they do well, they will meet their AB or IP requirements, rendering them LS guys the following year. I know for a fact that some players in this league have maintained rookie status by intentionally stopping short of the markers. You would too if it meant jeopardizing your chance of playing the subsequent season. I'm fortunate in that I am an LS guy, which means there exists no added, undue pressure on me to perform because LS guys are a dime a dozen. Think of the LS guys as "fillers" on a new CD. Some songs the band insists on, and some the producer insists on. What's left are the fillers.

The frustration comes when a player loses his job simply because of his status. How would you like to be told that you've been fired due to some screwy quota requirement, especially when you are better than the other guy? Like I said, this has never happened to me, but I can see how unfair it is. Such is the way of the WBL. I guess it's a good policy in that it prevents any one team from stockpiling a bunch of veterans and cheap rookies, but it's bad in that it can keep a guy from winning a job that he deserves. Maybe it's good that I never played past A-ball. I can't believe I just wrote that.

Anyway, we have our roster set now. I forgot to mention the Japanese outfielder we picked up about a week ago. His name is Makoto Sasaki, and he was a nine-time All-Star in the Japanese Major Leagues. He's 35 now, and he came to the USA for spring training in hopes of catching on with a big league team. Unfortunately, he didn't, and before returning to Japan, he received a call from Tim about coming here. A quote from a Japanese sportswriter in a recent newspaper article stated, "He was the first Ichiro [Suzuki]." He looks to be a damn good hitter and a solid outfielder, but we'll see. We also picked up a left-handed pitcher, an outfielder, and a catcher over the last two days. I haven't seen the lefty throw, but his eight years and AAA experience in the Pirates' organization lends him some credibility. The two new hitters look like solid ballplayers, one of whom, Josh McAffee, is a former Diamondbacks farmhand, and we remember each other. The other one is a native of Colombia, and we vaguely remember each other from my winter league excursion in 1999.

This entry is the last one until opening night, which is Friday. I can't guarantee that I will print one that evening, as I will be in a mad rush to make it to The Office as early as possible. If, however, I am unable to make it there with a decent amount of time to spare, then I will crank out a summary of that first game. Really, what's more important? Too many Friday nights at home leads to domestication, which leads to marriage. Need I say more? Out.

CHAPTER 5

▼

CONSTANT TURMOIL

Saturday, May 19, 2001 (3:00 PM)
Vans from Rohnert Park to Solano

Let's get to the point: Crushers 13, Solano 8. That's thirteen runs on twenty-two hits. I joked that we had more runs and more hits last night than in our first four exhibition games combined. It was unbelievable. Jason Olsen, the reigning Pitcher of the Year in the WBL, started for the Steelheads, and we hit him around pretty well. I don't know if it was our hitting skill or Olsen's failure to throw as he normally does. Normally, when a team hits like we did last night, it's a combination of the two; however, you can't expect to beat up a pitcher of Olsen's caliber very often. Something tells me that will see a different pitcher—most likely, the 2000 version—the next time we see him.

When I was in Taiwan, I wrote how fleeting my writing of myself may be based on how I am doing on the field. I also mentioned that I prefer *not* to discuss baseball when things go lousy. It would be similar to being a salesman and you call home to talk to your parents: "Hi Mom and Dad. Well, not only did I not make any sales this week, but I also lost the two accounts and I had been given." Maybe I am too immature to handle the good and the bad of baseball with equal aplomb, but I've always been that way. Deal with it. Yesterday, though, I hit more balls hard in one game than I did in seven games in Taiwan, so I'll elaborate a little. I hit three doubles, driving in three runs and scoring three runs, and all three hits were rockets. The last one was one of the five hardest hit balls of my career, a two-hop rocket to the gap in right center field. I felt great at the plate, and, even better, I finally got some results.

Offensively, we had a nice combination of cheap hits, clutch hits and good, aggressive base running. It was really fun to watch. Unfortunately, you can't expect to perform like that every night. Some of the guys on the bench were jumping up and down like it was the first game of the play-offs—ah, the frivolities of youth—after we took a 7-0 lead in the top of the third inning. I wanted to tell some of them to relax a little bit, but I refrained. Sure enough, Solano answered with five of their own in the bottom of the fourth, but we countered them with two more in the sixth and four in the eighth.

From a pitching/defense standpoint, we were solid, if not spectacular. Kevin Pickford, the left-handed eleventh hour addition, started and pitched into the fourth inning. He was aided by one double play, the pitcher's best friend, in each of the first three innings. For the game, we turned four in all and narrowly missed a fifth, prompting Dolf only half-jokingly to claim that we surpassed all of last year's total. Our pitchers walked eight batters, a bit too high a total for anyone's liking, but in fairness to them, the game was basically a blowout. You never condone a sub-par performance, but pitchers have to pitch in the context of the game. When we're winning handily, our pitchers will pitch differently than in a nip-and-tuck game. Basically, a pitcher's job in this situation is to throw a lot of strikes and let the hitters get themselves out, but, in the back of his mind, he's thinking, "Okay. Don't walk this guy. Work ahead." So what's the first thing that happens? He gets tight and doesn't throw with the same carefree mindset that he normally has. I've been raving from Day One about our pitching staff, and despite the eight runs and eleven hits, I still say we have the best staff in the league.

Finally, for those of you who are interested in the off-the-field stuff, I did *not* make it to The Office last night. We are commuting to Solano and back since it's only an hour and fifteen-minute drive, and we got back last night at 1:00 AM. I suppose I could have made it there by 1:15 AM, but that would be borderline alcoholic/obsessive/pathetic, so I just went home and went to bed. In retrospect it was fortuitous timing because after Thursday night, I needed the sleep. Needed the sleep? Yeah, yeah I know what you're thinking: "Bo, why on Earth would you stay out drinking 'til 3:30 AM the night before your opening game?" Well, contrary to what all you goody-goodies think, I am able—hell, I *have* been able—to live such a nocturnal lifestyle and still produce on the field (notice the three doubles). If I can eternally bitch and moan about the downsides of minor league baseball, you can bet the ranch that I'm going to indulge in the upsides. Once again, deal with it. Out.

Sunday, May 20, 2001 (3:00 PM)
Bus from Rohnert Park to Solano

First of all, we are on a *great* bus. John Thompson (JT), who endured a 32-hour bus trip from Tri-City to Yuma and back with no air conditioning last year, asked me to pinch him and wake him from his dream. Even for a quality organization like Chico, I was baffled by how bad the team bus situation is there. We had our own bus, complete with the team logo on it, and it was definitely nice to look at, but on the inside, it was awful: broken seats, nonworking TV's, and nose hair-curling stenches. The worst part was that the AC worked sporadically at best, but it never worked when we needed it, namely through the desert regions of California, Arizona and Nevada. Let me tell you that driving through that part of America in the middle of a summer day without AC can't be too far removed from entering the Seventh Circle of Hell.

On a lighter note: Crushers 9, Solano 7. I think we had only eight hits as a team—compared to fourteen or so for them—but we had two two-out, two-run doubles (compliments of McAffee and me) and a two-out, three-run homer by The Big Ogre. It reminded me of John Wooden's quote, "It's not how many points you score; it's when you score them." Some sports truths are universal, no? Obviously, we can't expect to average eleven runs a game this year, but at least we now know that we have the capability to put some runs on the board. Thus, in the event of a team-wide offensive funk, we won't have to push the panic button.

Now, a story from the payroll department. On Thursday, management asked several of us to restructure our contracts in order to sign some quality veteran players. It was basically a "push" financially because the restructuring amounted to receiving a lump sum, up-front payment followed by a reduced monthly salary. As I said, it was a "six one, half dozen the other" proposition, so I didn't mind. It's amazing how by-the-book Sonoma County is compared to some of the other teams in the league. In Chico, under the Plummer regime, I understood that there was some pork barrel politics going on, but as far I know or heard, nothing like that happened last year. Unfortunately, the same can't be said for a team like Solano, who, over the course of last season, had about six guys with big league time on its roster.

Al Davis, the renegade owner of the Oakland Raiders, said that violations of the NFL's salary cap should be met with the harshest of penalties because such transgressions tilt the competitive balance, and I wholeheartedly agree. Speaking of harsh penalties, look at what happened to the NBA's Minnesota Timberwolves, who were guilty of trying to pay forward Joe Smith illegally. Commissioner David Stern lowered the boom on the franchise, hitting it with a huge fine and crippling its future by taking away draft picks. Now, are you trying to tell me that someone with big league time is going to Vacaville Freakin' California to ride on buses and live with a host family for $1500/month? Not bloody likely. The problem is that you can't prove the illegal payments. One team in this league, a few years ago, gave a player a $7000 signing bonus under the guise that he was a "scout" as well, and the player simply had to recommend a few players to the organization for the payment to be justified. Where's Elliot Ness when you need him? Maybe we can nail these bandits for tax evasion or mail fraud. I mean, c'mon, everyone in the league knew what Solano was doing, and that was what made it especially sweet to knock them out of the playoffs last year.

We have a 6:05 PM game tonight followed by an eight-hour bus trip to Long Beach. I often wonder how guys who have spent the vast majority of their careers in Triple-A and the big leagues can handle all the nickel and dime stuff that goes on in this league. For example, after Friday night's game, we had no hot water in the showers. As the Church Lady would say, "How convieeeeeeeeeeeeenient!" Last night, all of a sudden, we had hot water, which leads me to believe that whoever is in charge over there makes Homer Simpson look like a Rhodes' scholar. I don't know how a guy like Tim Scott, our reigning senior citizen and only BLT (big league time) guy, puts up with it. Personally, having never made it out of A-ball, I don't know any better. No one has ever shined my shoes or carried my bags for me. I'm used to fast food, long bus trips, cold showers, and sardine-esque clubhouses, so such headaches roll off my back pretty easily. If ignorance is bliss, than un-worldliness is pure elation. Out.

Sunday, May 21, 2001 (11:15 PM)
Bus from Solano to Long Beach

I figure that I can write a brief entry while my sleeping pills are kicking in. Have I mentioned that I *love* this bus? JT and I don't know if we'll be able to get off it in Long Beach. Before I get too giddy, though, I have to see if it can handle the Kilimanjaro-like climb on I-5 South going into southern California without losing too much velocity or the AC.

The offensive juggernaut known as the Sonoma County Crushers came to a screeching halt today at the hands of Jason Brosnan. He's a top-notch WBL left-hander who uses a sneaky fastball, a slow curve, and a changeup to keep hitters off-balance, and facing him reminds me of a story I read about Eddie Lopat. Lopat, perhaps *the* classic lefty junkballer, pitched in the American League in the 1940's and was so good that Ted Williams put him on his Top 5 Toughest Pitchers list. Anyway, Lopat apparently became quite proficient at dismantling the thundering offensive attack of the New York Yankees, especially in Yankee Stadium. The story goes that after each win by the visiting Lopat, every adult male in the crowd would go down to the dugout looking to sign a contract; they simply couldn't believe that a "thumber" like Lopat could so easily baffle the Yanks. Another quick one: One day, Lopat started a game and gave up triples to the first two batters he faced. After that, he retired (I believe) 27 consecutive batters, throwing in essence a perfect game. During the post game interviews, the reporters asked him what had happened with the first two hitters, and Lopat responded, "Well, when I went out there, my arm felt great, so I thought I'd pump a few fastballs by them. After those first two guys, though, I figured I better just go back to my barnyard stuff."

Now, I can see how Joe Wannabe Probaseballplayer thinks he could be successful against this type of pitcher, a guy who doesn't throw that much harder than a good high school pitcher against whom you may have had some success fifteen years ago. But before you, a thirty-something, decide to cash in your 401K and rekindle your big league aspirations, let me poke two holes in your balloon. First, when you face "conventional" pitchers four or five days a week, a guy like Brosnan can really screw with your timing. Secondly, if he were *that* easy to hit, he and pitchers of his ilk wouldn't have jobs, so they must be doing something right.

I think we had only six hits as a team, a far cry from the previous two days. By the way, from here on, whenever you see team stats such as hits or runs or walks or strikeouts, they will not always be 100% accurate; I'm a journalist, not a beat writer. My road roommate, Tim Davidson (TD)— who just joked with me literally 30 seconds ago when he saw me writing, "Bo, are you gonna put 'And my roomie gave up the ass'?"—did just that: he gave up the ass. It's good to see that he hasn't gotten all bent out of shape over the poor outing. These things happen, and the important thing to remember is that a 90-game season is a marathon, not a sprint. TD's a helluva pitcher in this league, and he'll rebound.

Just to show you what I know about baseball, we have been impressive offensively and somewhat suspect from a pitching standpoint, exactly the opposite of what I had predicted. Again, it's a long season, and numbers don't lie: the track record of our pitchers is better than that of our hitters. While this weekend can probably be considered an aberration as to what will actually transpire during the season, the bottom line is that we took two of three on the road against a pretty good Solano team. I, and we, can live with that.

Finally, Mitch is in the house. That's right, Kevin Mitchell, our hitting coach, has arrived and at 5'10" tall and 250 (??) lbs., he's the closest thing I ever seen to a four-limbed, ambulatory tree stump. Due to some lingering unpleasantries between Sonoma County and Solano as a result of last year's, ESPN-appearing brawl, Mitch thought it would be best to "keep on the down-low," at least for the first two games. He was in uniform for today's game, though, and he and I discussed, among other things, how to approach a pitcher like Brosnan (incidentally, we were on the same page). I also grilled him on two rumors that I had heard about him. The first one was in regards to a story I read about him during his NL MVP season of 1989 and how he had learned to hit the curveball by playing Wiffle-ball with his grandmother. While he neither confirmed nor denied the grandmother thing, he did say that he played in Wiffle-ball tournaments in his mid-teens. Secondly, I had heard that Mitch was signed to his first

professional contract after a scout had seen him hitting a softball uncon-
scious distances. The scout obviously felt that if he could ever catch up to
a big league fastball, Mitch would be positively lethal. As it turned out,
Mitch did okay for himself. (It should be noted that he was signed by a
scout who had seen him, as a member of an American Legion-caliber amateur team, play well against San Diego State University's baseball team.)

Thus far, he is an extremely garrulous and likeable guy. Just the other
night, I asked Mitch, donning a bright red and orange Hawaiian shirt, if
he wanted to join us for some beers and some chicks at The Office. He
politely declined, citing his diabetes as the reason that he can't drink alcohol, so I suggested that he abstain from the former and engage in the latter. As we were walking to our cars, I was casually giving him directions to
The Office, and he quickly interjected, "Oh wait. I remember that place
from last year." He then said that he had seen a few motorcycles outside
the place, adding that it was not the kind of place for "a black man dressed
like this." I wanted to say, "Don't worry, Mitch; we got your back," but
then I realized that from what I've heard, he doesn't need a whole lot of
backup. Knowing that J-Lo (Lofton), Mookie (Terry Johnson), and Boat
(Marcel Longmire) were going to *Quincy's*, a feeble attempt at a dance club
but a dance club nevertheless, I asked Mitch if he'd rather try his luck
there. He said that he would, though I'm not sure if he actually did. I
asked him, "Mitch, you like those dancey places, don't you?" He let out a
laugh and said, "Oh yeah!" I then tried to picture him dancing with just
one girl, and it seemed if not preposterous then highly unlikely; it would
take at least two-and-a-half young ladies to get their arms around him.
Out.

Tuesday, May 22, 2001 (1:30 PM)
Long Beach

Right now, I am sitting in a Motel 6 within spitting distance of I-405.
Niiiiiiiiiiiiiiice! Yesterday, when we were pulling into the parking lot after

the game, John Thompson said, "Wait a minute. This isn't the Ritz-Carlton." We wish. The only Ritz-Carltons in the WBL are the crackers and the cigarettes, but, hey, it still beats working for a living, right? By the way, "JT" has taken an early lead as team jokester. He's funny as hell, and most of his jokes revolve around the daily comedy that is life in the WBL. A former AA pitcher with Seattle and the Chicago White Sox, he has a good fastball, a sharp curveball, and a solid changeup, and, like a lot of guys, he's a little bitter about being here. Unlike a lot of guys, however, he has a legitimate case.

Last night, we got our butts kicked by a bunch of rah-rah college kids. In looking at Long Beach's roster, we wondered where in Sam Hill these guys came from. I'm just guessing, but I'll bet only 6-8 guys on the team have *any* pro experience. In fact, their cleanup hitter, Jason Cly, was a *pitcher* for Division II Chico State University as recently as last year. I'm not trying to take anything away from their guys; it's just that it's pretty hard to come right out of college and perform well in this league. They have this deal in Southern California called the scout league, and from what I understand, it's for kids right out of college or younger players with a little bit of pro experience. Southern California may be *the* hotbed of baseball talent in the U.S., so a scout may indeed find some quality ballplayers who slipped through the cracks. Again, I don't where Long Beach found these guys, and although some of them look like they can play a little, across the board I don't see them doing too well. But hey, what do I know?

Anyway, we played in their home opener last night, and they stuck it to us pretty good, maybe 7-1. I liked their starting pitcher, Mike Saipe, who looked to me like an upper-tier pitcher in this league. No one seemed to know where he came from, but he obviously has been around for a while. I think I read that he's 29, but other than that, he's unknown to most of us. It's funny how some guys can find one guy unhittable and another guy can absolutely rake him. I thought Saipe had quality stuff, at least last night. He showed me a big league-style curve that he threw for strikes—something I almost never see in this league—and a sneaky fastball that he moved around really well. Powell hit three rockets off him, so evidently he was seeing the ball well, but Saipe had my number.

You know, yesterday was one of those days that really frustrate you. I was 0-4 with two strikeouts and an error in the field. I suppose I could blame it on the long bus trip, bad sleep, and in general upsetting my normal schedule, but I have played in several "strap it on" days—when you arrive at the park about 1½ hours before the game and skip BP and infield/outfield—when I have hit the crap out of the ball. You just never know what's in store on a given day.

Today, though, we were back in our regular routine and the results showed. We kicked *their* asses, this time 10-1. Rafael Piña, our well-traveled (Taiwan, Mexico) starter, took the mound and threw six innings, giving up only one run on about six hits, none of which was hit very hard. Derek Fahs—Fozzie—came in for the seventh and eighth and struck out four guys, and he was followed by Tim Scott, who blew the doors off the lower part of their order in the ninth. The Big Ogre was our offensive thunder for the evening, driving in five runs on a clutch two-out, two-run single in the seventh and a two-out, bases loaded double in the eighth. He also flew out to the base of the wall in deep left-center field. You see a guy like Oglesby, who caught and played first base for the Diamondbacks in High Desert (Class A) last year, and you have to wonder how he's not with an organization. He's only 23-years-old, and I'm telling you, the kid has huge power. He has hit some absolute rockets this year, one of them a homerun to right field in Solano (and another one in spring training), and while he may be only average as a catcher, with his power potential, he could have a nice future as a first baseman. He has hit some balls this year that I could only dream of hitting, and I have told him that I would give my first-born son to hit just *once* a ball like he has.

Tomorrow is a "getaway day," which means that we have to check out of our rooms at noon—being the veteran, savvy player that I am, I just called to get an extension until 1:30 PM—but we don't take the bus to the field until 3:45 PM. Normally, the hotel gives a team four "getaway" rooms for us players to put our travel bags in while we wait. Talk about staving off ennui. Most players just hang out in one of the rooms, some play video games, and some just disappear until bus time. (For future reference, if you ever stay at a hotel and you see a bunch of young guys milling around, chances are that they're part of a baseball team.) Whatever the case, you have to entertain yourself for a few hours; thankfully, I have my trusty, absolutely-positively-can't-live-without-it laptop. Out.

Thursday, May 24, 2001 (1:30 AM)
Bus from Long Beach to Rohnert Park

After six games, the Crushers are 4-2. We beat Long Beach again last night (today is technically Thursday), 7-3. We got a second consecutive solid start, this one from Pickford, who gave up only two runs over six innings. We turned it over to Kirt Kishita, who gave up an unearned run in the seventh. Brian Grant (BG) and Tim Scott closed out the game with little trouble. Offensively, we started off slowly, as lefty Travis McCall pitched a perfect three innings. With one out in the fourth, however, CP hustled down the line on a high chopper and beat it out. I came up two batters later and hit an RBI single. That knotted the score at 1-1, and we added three runs in the 6th and three more in the seventh to close out our scoring. Through these six games, we've seen how good—and bad— pitching, hitting, and defense can be. If we can ever "click on all cylinders," we'll be tough to beat.

For the record, I am really enjoying Mitch. He's such an outgoing, funny, and talkative guy, and he never refuses an autograph request. He also takes his job very seriously. As I wrote the other day, we hit like crap on Sunday and Monday (before each game we didn't take our normal BP), and after the Monday game, I told Mitch, "Screw this no BP bullshit. I need BP everyday, and at home, I want early BP everyday to stay sharp." Mitch told me not to worry and that he'd take care of it. Sure enough, on

Tuesday, he arranged the BP schedule so I could get a lot of extra right-handed swings. It was the same on Wednesday, too, and it must have worked because I had back-to-back two-hit games. He told Tim that I was used to getting a lot of extra swings from my days in Chico, so Mitch is making sure I stay well tuned. Not only that, but he is out there throwing BP to us and hanging out around the batting cage, chirping like a cricket. He's part-instructor, part-motivator, and part-trash talker. Example:

Bo: "Hey, Mitch. I heard Randy Johnson took your wood (broke your bat)."

Mitch: "Shit. I told him to quit throwing me that damn slider and gimme the fastball."

Bo: "And?"

Mitch: "He did."

Bo: "And?"

Mitch: "I hit a double off the wall."

Later, we were eating at *Carl's Jr.* after the game, and Mitch was telling some of us about the money he made during his years in baseball (I won't say how much, but there are a lot of commas and zeroes involved). I told him that I wanted to make that type of money, and he said, "Not with a swing like that." Ouch. Truth hurts.

Today is an off day. Tim noticed that my knee has been bothering me a little, so he told me that, while admirable, my arduous pre-game fielding routine is not going to help ease the mild pain in my knee. I've always used BP and fungoes (groundballs) to both get a good sweat going and hone my skills. Especially in the fielding part, I practice a lot of range work—balls hit to the left and right of me. I never saw the point in practicing the easy groundballs; I can make those plays with my eyes closed. But there comes a time when I should realize that a healthy knee is more important than a maniacal pre-game workout. Furthermore, Tim told me to stay off my knee today. I was considering going golfing, but the double-whammy of a tender knee and a 7:00 AM ETA into Rohnert Park has pretty much shot that idea to pieces. I suppose the fact that I am going to spend the day relaxing has an upside: I'll be well rested for The Office. If tonight is as off-the-hook as the last two Thursdays, I may not get as much sleep as I'd like. Out.

Saturday, May 26, 2001 (12:00 PM)
Rohnert Park

"The coldest winter I ever spent was summer in San Francisco."

—*Mark Twain*

Last night was opening night at Rohnert Park Stadium, and it was cold. I could actually see my breath during the game. As a member of the Chico Heat, I played against the Crushers here for three years, but I don't remember it being this cold. It was almost as if I were back in Kittanning, playing amidst snow flurries. I was one of the few guys not to wear long sleeves under my jersey, drawing a few strange looks from teammates and fans, but I hate that constricted feeling that sleeves give me. Besides, it wasn't *that* cold. You know, with all my incessant complaining about kicking around in the minors, you have to wonder about there being an upside to it all. Well, my friends, not too many things can compare to a home opener. First of all, it was a packed house. I don't know what the actual attendance was, but I'm guessing about 3000 fans showed up last night, and the Crushers treated them to a closely fought 4-3 victory over the Yuma Bullfrogs. Secondly, the smoke emanating from the many barbecues made it onto the field, where the game was played in a haze of aromatic splendor. Lastly, I played a pretty good game, hitting a two-run homer and making a couple of nice plays in the field. Unlike the Long Beach opener, where I went 0-4 with two strikeouts and an error, I hope I gave the fans something positive to talk about. You know the phrase, "You never get a second chance to make a first impression?" Well, this was my first official home game as a Crusher, and it was very nice to get off on the right foot.

Throughout this journal, I have written about how easy it is to go from the penthouse to the outhouse in baseball. It's just the nature of the game and the nature of sports in general. Even if your last name is Jordan—while few and far between, even *he* had bad games—you cannot expect to be at your best every single game, especially in a long season like a pro baseball season. Think of it this way: give every minor leaguer a choice of trying to reach the big leagues the conventional way or via a shortcut. Now, the shortcut is such that the minor leaguer would get to play one game and have to get one hit and either score or drive in a run. If he succeeded, then he would go right to the big leagues. If he failed, he could never play pro baseball again. How does that sound? Well, I certainly can't speak for every minor leaguer, but I *know* I wouldn't opt for the shortcut. Baseball is just too unpredictable. The strength of my game is consistency over a full season, and there is no way that I would gamble my future on one game. The point I'm trying to make is that I was absolutely garbage in Long Beach's opener and pretty decent last night, and so goes the game.

For example, take my homerun. Yuma's pitcher, Jason Bond, is a lefty with a really good changeup. In that at-bat, he threw me a first-pitch changeup that I looked really bad on. Two pitches later, he threw me another changeup that I looked really, *really* bad on. So now the count is 1-2, and I am looking for the changeup up all the way. Well, he throws the changeup, and I hit a homerun. Basically, I gambled and won, and I'm the star of the game. Had he thrown a fastball anywhere for a strike, however, I would have either taken it for strike three or broken my bat into 138 toothpicks. Again, that's why in baseball you have to consider a season's worth of statistics, not just a few weeks or even a few months. The next time I face Bond, he may make me look like a Little Leaguer.

We have six games in our home stand, and three of them are day-games. I think I only played in one day-game in my three years in Chico, but they're quite common here. I have mixed emotions about day games. I like the fact that after the game is over, you have all evening to hang out and do stuff; for instance, if you meet a nice young lady and you want to go watch a movie or get some dinner, you can. The downside, though, is that if the day-game is on a Sunday, it severely hampers the nightlife on Saturday, like tonight. We have a 1:35 PM game tomorrow, so that means that I actually have to tone it down a bit this evening. God, this baseball thing is really putting a crimp in my carousing. Out.

Sunday, May 27, 2001 (7:00 PM)
Rohnert Park

Well, we just got the brooms out. We swept the Yuma Bullfrogs in three closely fought, exciting games, running our record to 7-2 after nine games. I'm not exactly sure of the league-wide standings, but I believe that Chico and we have the two best records thus far. The Crushers "won ugly" this weekend, and while we have to make some improvements, it's certainly light-years better than losing pretty. For those of you who may not be 100% sure of what the phrase "winning ugly" (not to be confused with the term "coyote ugly," which is used to describe waking up—usually with a raging hangover—next to someone whom you just met who is so unattractive that you'd rather chew your arm off than wake the person up by asking him/her to roll off your arm) means, it signifies one of three things: 1) your team, despite playing poorly, won because the other committed several mistakes, 2) your team committed several mistakes, but the opposition failed to capitalize on them) or 3) one particular phase of your game—pitching, defense, or offense—was horribly inept, yet one other facet was strong enough to counteract the putrescence. Today, we made four errors in the fourth inning, and Piña, who threw another great game, gave up three unearned runs to put Yuma up 3-2. We battled back to tie the game at 3-3, and it stayed that way until the bottom of the eighth, where *we* scored an unearned run to go up 4-3, and that's how it ended.

What I neglected to mention about the bottom of the eighth is that Tim basically won the game for us. Throughout the game, we had several runners in scoring position, but we just couldn't get that big breakout inning, and I would attribute it to Yuma's starter, Tom Bergan. He threw a helluva game, as did Jeff Sobkoviak yesterday (he took the tough-luck 3-0 loss), keeping us off-balance with his fastball, curve, slider and changeup. Both guys had successful stints in Chico when I was there—I even played third base behind Bergan when he threw a no-hitter in 1999—and they both pitched outstanding games this weekend. Anyway, The Big Ogre led off the bottom of the eighth with a walk, and after two consecutive outs, Tim gave him a modified steal sign. Without revealing too much, Tim incorporated a baserunning play that he introduced us to in spring training, and it results in either a bonehead-looking baserunning gaffe or a successful stolen base. Fortunately for us, it worked to perfection, and Oglesby made it to second safely. After advancing to third on a wild pitch, he scored on an error by Yuma's third baseman. He has used this play successfully a couple of other times this year, and we are starting to see why he proclaimed himself "the winningest manager in the world in the 1990's."

Tim's quite a character. He has been all over the world as a scout, coach, and manager, and he speaks "baseball" Spanish, Japanese, and Chinese. I'm not ready to concede that he is quadrilingual because I don't think he could carry on a conversation in those three languages, but he definitely knows how to convey his managerial strategies to his foreign players in their native tongues. He has run our team with the cold-blooded efficiency of a totalitarian dictator, signing and releasing guys left and right. As long as you're not one of the guys on the way out, you know it's going to be fun playing for him because he will win. I don't think we had as much in-season turnover in my three years in Chico as we had this May here in Rohnert Park. I could write a pretty fair book about the unfair and ruthless nature of baseball, and Tim has done a pretty fair job of staying the course in that regard. But he understands that good players, not good managers, make for good teams (gee, where have you heard *that* before?). John Wooden—here he is again—said, "Physical superiority negates all theory," and anyone who knows sports will totally agree. Tim may have the best game plan in the world, literally, of how to win baseball games, but if his players can't institute what he wants, then it is all for naught. He is egotistical enough to understand that what he has done in his career as a manager—from the psychology to the physical—has been successful, yet he is realistic enough to understand that his players win and lose the games for him. Today, though, with his stolen base gamble, he definitely should get credit for the win.

One other thing that needs discussing about the first three home games of the year is the weather. In my three years in Chico, we played in exactly one day-game, and that was only because it was a rescheduled game. It's just too hot there to draw fans for an afternoon game. Here, however, it is much cooler, and actually, the nights can be downright cold. Even the temperature of our game today could be described as brisk, which means that I was barely sweating. Now, you know of my proclivity to perspire, so if I'm not sweating, it must be pretty damn cool. Also, the way the sun is positioned in the sky and the way the wind blows during games—both day and night—call to mind Candlestick Park. The 'Stick was by far the least favorite outdoor stadium for big leaguers due to those two reasons. If you want to see a grown man look like a bumbling idiot, watch him try to catch an infield pop-up at about 2:00 PM on a cloudless day in the Bay Area. Hell, it happened to me today when I momentarily lost a pop-up in the sun, only to regain sight of it, only to find that the wind had pushed it quite a few feet off course. By the time the ball hit my glove and fell harmlessly to the ground. I looked as though I had just participated in the Dizzy Bat Race. Talk about embarrassing.

We have three more home games and an off day on Thursday before we head for Yuma on Friday. After last year's season-long debacle, the fans seem to be genuinely excited about this year's team. Everyone I talk to says how much more fun it is to go to a game. Starting off the first home stand of the campaign with a three-game sweep is a good thing, no? We have Solano coming to town tomorrow, and they have been positively lousy this year, maybe 3-6. We are playing well, and they evidently are not, which should mean good things for the Purple People Eaters, but as Forrest Gump said, baseball "is like a box of chocolates: you never know what you're gonna get." Out.

Wednesday, May 30, 2001 (6:30 PM)
Rohnert Park

Bad news: the Crushers just lost their first series. There's a phrase that's ubiquitous in baseball circles that says, "Good teams win series." What that means is that a team strives to win each series in which it plays, whether it's a two-, three-, four-, or five game series. Now, you're probably thinking, "Jeez, Bo, don't you try to win *every* game?" Well, of course you *try* to win, but that doesn't always happen. For example, yesterday we were getting blown out, so Derek Patterson, our second baseman, pitched part of the eighth and all of the ninth for us. When you have only a 22-man roster (as opposed to the standard 25-man), pitching is thin, so you have to use each pitcher sparingly. As much as you don't like to do it, you have to "concede" victory in certain games in order to give yourself a chance the next day. We won the first game, so after the blowout in the second one, we still had a chance to win the series today. Unfortunately, it didn't work out, but that's baseball.

You know, I'm continually amazed at how few people know about the attitude of the professional baseball player in regards to winning and losing. I got home to the Jones' house tonight, and they asked me how we did. After telling them that we lost, Richard, the 15-year-old son, said, "Damn. You guys lost last night, too, right?" I answered in the affirmative, and he said, "What's wrong with you guys?" Later, I called my mother to tell her we lost, and bless her heart, she said, "Hey, what's going on?" Naturally, I had to mildly scold her, telling her that having witnessed her son playing pro ball for the past six summers, she should know that he doesn't really give a damn that we lost. I realize that's a tough concept to grasp for the non-professional athlete out there, but it's the truth—from the independent leagues to Double A to the big leagues. Certainly, if your team is losing habitually, then the manager may have to address it, but for cryin' out loud, we had just won six in a row. Believe me, no one on our team is going to Rite-Aid to buy razor blades or nooses.

I was thinking about this the other day, how hit-or-miss (no pun intended) baseball can be. Look, your favorite team is going to lose and lose often. Your favorite team is going to lose at home and lose often. Your favorite team is going to play like crap and get blown out at home. Deal with it. It's unfair and shortsighted to stake the level of your fanaticism of your favorite team on one game. Furthermore, you may make it to only one game this year at your local stadium, and you may time your visit to see, say, Mark McGwire or Sammy Sosa or Ken Griffey, Jr. Each of these men is a MVP-caliber player, but on that one given day when you're at the stadium, that day you've been awaiting for months, each one of them is capable of going 0-4, striking out three times (once with the bases loaded), and making an error. So much for watching your hero, huh? Sorry, buddy, but that's baseball. Joe DiMaggio, when asked why he always gave 100% every time he set foot on the field, said, "Because someone may be watching me for the first time, and I owe him my best effort." True, this concept may seem quite antiquated to the new wave of professional athlete, but as much as I am a fan of the "old school" attitude, I still feel that the vast majority of athletes give 100% all the time. What I am trying to say is that even on that rare day when your favorite superstar looks like a superputz, he *is* trying—believe me, he's trying. You just can't expect him to be "the man" every single day.

On a lighter note, just before BP on Monday, Tim asked the pitchers who would be the most capable hitter and/or outfielder if we were put in a pinch. Now, if you want to see the unveiling of alpha-male alter ego in the professional pitcher, just ask this question. Guys that are low-key in their manners suddenly become Mr. Hyde, and any pitcher that ever did *anything* with a bat in his hands is ready to strut his stuff. The scene is similar to a sexy, long-legged blonde walking past a construction site full of heckling men: they all want a chance, but when given the opportunity, they're not quite sure what the hell they would do. I volunteered JT, who was actually drafted in the 45th round out of high school as a shortstop, and Tim said, "Yeah, you know the scout that drafted him is baling hay right now." We all got a good laugh out of that one. Apparently, Brian Grant hit a single in his only at-bat last year (though he conveniently neglects to mention that he was thrown out trying to stretch the single into a double), so he is the self-proclaimed "best hitting pitcher" on the team, and when no one could offer any substantial testimony to refute such a bold claim, Tim gave him the okay. Therefore, BG was granted exclusive opportunity to take BP with the hitters; as for his swing, well, in the spirit of the Fifth Amendment to our glorious Constitution, I shall say no more. BG is a left-handed reliever, a role that isn't necessarily glamorous but definitely an important one. A former Blue Jays farmhand, he will be called upon to get out the big left-handed hitters of the league late in the game.

We leave for Yuma in the morning and expect to arrive at about 11:00 PM. We are all big fans of that type of schedule, as it will allow us to get a good night's sleep before the game on Friday. Last year, we would leave at 8:00 PM or so and drive through the night, either to avoid the heat of the day (remember no AC?) or to avoid paying for an extra night of lodging. I'm not sure which was the case, but, regardless, I am much happier this way. We play Friday-Sunday in Yuma and then Monday-Wednesday in St. George, UT. As you may or may not know, when we play the St. George Pioneerzz, we actually stay in Mesquite, NV, and take the 45-minute commute to game each day. The team puts us in *The Oasis* resort/casino, and the latter part of that title really puts a smile on my face. I can't wait to camp out at the Blackjack tables and pound Coronas until 4:00 AM. Maybe this baseball thing isn't such a bad gig after all. Out.

Thursday, May 31, 2001 (3:00 PM)
Bus from Rohnert Park to Yuma

As I stare out of the window of this *fantastic* bus on I-5, the desolation along the highway is positively ugly. We are on that horrific stretch of never-ending sunshine and desert brush just south of Bakersfield but before entering LA. I figure I can jot down a few things.

First of all, we had a few roster changes over the past couple of days. Kishita, who apparently is going to Italy to play, and Jason (Mad Dog) McCarter were released—though I'm not quite sure what Tim is going to do about acquiring more pitching, as we were already thin in that area. Also, Lofton was just signed to a Double-A contract with Boston. Although his leaving will create a gaping hole both at shortstop and at the leadoff spot, everyone is genuinely happy for him. It's always nice to see someone from the coal-mining town get that full scholarship. J-Lo and I joined the WBL in 1998, and I've felt that he has been one of the top four or five players in the league over the past three-plus years. He's a low key, soft-spoken guy who gets along with everyone, and we'll miss him.

You know, a 14-hour bus ride offers many options to the traveling minor leaguer: sleeping, reading, writing, watching the movie, playing cards, playing video games, listening to music, and just general chit-chatting. Several of us—Patterson (Patty), Jeff Pritchard (Pritch), JT, Tim Scott (Scottie), TD, and I —were discussing a trip to Pac Bell Park yesterday by Scottie, JT, and Mitch. More specifically, we were discussing their foray into the Giants' clubhouse. Apparently, Mitch strolled into the room as if he were a former MVP or something. He raided the clubhouse for bats, batting gloves, batting helmets, and he also joked to Barry Bonds that he was going to kick his ass. How many independent league hitting coaches can jokingly threaten a three-time NL MVP? Mitch is definitely a character. He told me on Tuesday that he planned on getting for me two one-flap batting helmets (one for each side of the plate) since I looked like Kazoo in my current one. Upon arrival to the clubhouse, Mitch asked the clubbie, Mike Murphy, the same guy who has been there since the Giants arrived in San Fran in 1958, what he had in the way of helmets, and the best he could find is a 7 5/8 size, which Mitch gave to me today. Since I have a gigantic cranium and need a 7¾ size, I am giving it to CP, and Mitch says that he'll get me a bigger one the next time he goes down there again.

On the bright side, Mitch brought me a breand-spanking-new third baseman's mitt, compliments of current Giants' third sacker Russ Davis, with whom Mitch played in Seattle. I haven't had a new glove since 1996, when the Diamondbacks gave me a Mizuno—along with a plane ticket and a pair of cleats—as part of my "record-setting" signing bonus. I have used that glove for the past five years, and while I love it to death, it looks as though someone used it to play catch with a live grenade. I will continue to use the beater until I break in my new one, but the Mizuno definitely has one foot in the grave. The new one is a beautiful Rawlings PRO1000-6K with unbelievably soft leather. I could have it game-ready in as little as three weeks. Attababy Mitch!!

On a side note, here are of some of the topics of conversation on the trip: the 1985 NL Rookie of the Year (the consensus is Mariano Duncan, but I'm not quite sold); where the WBL falls in the independent league hierarchy (we resolved that the Frontier League is Rookie Ball, the Texas-Louisiana League is Class A, the WBL is Double-A, the Northern League is Triple-A, and the Atlantic League is the big leagues); why our bus driver has no idea how to get to Yuma (everyone with SoCal roots is offering his own two cents); and of course, flatulence (where 90% of bus conversations begin and end).

Finally, I was talking to J-Lo about how the big leagues is a snooty, uppity country club and that as an institution, it is quite discriminatory. I mentioned to him how black golfers like Lee Elder were at one time unable to play at prestigious southern golf courses like Augusta National in Georgia because of their skin color. Well, I proffered that the big leagues won't let me into its country club because of my paltry and equally unchangeable footspeed, power, and arm strength. That has to be some form of bigotry, doesn't it? Maybe I'll call the ACLU for some kind of retribution. If idle hands are the devil's workshop, then long, monotonous bus rides are the breeding grounds for some incredibly hair-brained schemes. Ah, but it still beats working for a living. Out.

Saturday, June 1, 2001 (12:00 AM)
Yuma

Bad news: Yuma 8, Crushers 5. We just lost our third in a row, dropping our record to 8-5. The afternoon heat in Yuma is well documented and quite lamented, and BP was borderline torturous. JT said he saw on The Weather Channel that Yuma was in the "white" region, as in white-hot. Yippee. Actually, the thin air, coupled with the "misters" around Desert Sun Stadium, made the game time temperature rather reasonable. My roommate, Tim Davidson, had another shaky outing, and I have to wonder what's going on with him. He's one of those rare guys in this league who hasn't played organizational ball but is still a top-notch player. He wasn't drafted out of Texas Tech in 1997, and he has been a career independent leaguer. Last year, he was fifth in the league in ERA, so he is a known and valued commodity throughout the league. Unfortunately, though, he hasn't pitched up to his billing this year, but like a proven hitter who can't quite find his stroke, we just have to ride the storm out with TD until he catches his groove.

Walking to the clubhouse after the game, Mitch told me that Tim was "hot" and was going to have his first meeting of the year. We made a couple of mental errors—missed cut-off men and poor communication—and Tim wasn't too happy. He told us that "80% of the games in this league are lost because of mental mistakes and errors," and I concur. We won six in a row mainly because our opponents made the errors, not us. Live by the sword, die by the sword, no? Anyway, Tim spoke for only about three minutes, ending with the proclamation that "no bats leave the clubhouse until game time." That means that during our allotted BP time tomorrow, we will due nothing but defensive work, both team and individual. We will undoubtedly do infield/outfield communication drills, pickoff plays, and rundowns. Once again, yippee. Nothing like running around in 100-degree temperature. Although the last time Tim gave us a wakeup call, we responded quite well. I hope that tomorrow's lesson will have the same impact.

Mitch—or, more accurately, stories of Mitch—had me rolling today. I was talking with JT and Scottie about their trip to the Giants clubhouse yesterday. For those of you who don't know, big league wood—the general term for the high-quality wood that big league players use to hit with—is a rare commodity in the minors and especially in independent leagues. The big league wood bats, believe it or not, can make a big difference in a hitter's success. Remember what I said about the "country club?" They get better bats, harder baseballs, better lighting, better travel, and on top of all that, better money. Someone get me Johnnie Cochran; I smell a lawsuit. Anyway, one of Mitch's reasons for going to the Giants' clubhouse was to get some big league wood for us Crushers. He asked Barry Bonds what he had, and Barry gave him a box of Pro Stock bats, basically the same type we use here. Mitch told him to quit jerking him around and give him some freakin' good bats. Later, he told Barry that he was going to "tackle" him, and according to reports, Barry immediately sat down in his chair. I was rolling. I told Mitch that he can't threaten a three-time MVP like that, and he replied, "Like hell, I can't."

As much as I have grown to like him, he definitely is not the type of guy you want to cross, or, as my high school football coach used to say, he's not the type of guy you want to meet in a dark alley in a bad mood. He was telling us one day about his youth and how he was in a gang in San Diego. Back then, they used to fight all the time, but they never used guns like the kids do nowadays. He also used to box. If you combine the gang mentality, the boxing background, and the fire hydrant build, you basically want to remain on his good side. But I absolutely love him so far. There's not a trace of "holier-than-thou because thou hasn't played in the big leagues and I have" attitude. He tirelessly signs autographs in Rohnert Park—where he is easily *the* fan favorite—and on the road. He jokes around with everyone, and he needles Keith Garnett, our trainer, endlessly. Today, he gave me a brand new pair of turf shoes and a brand new pair of cleats, both compliments of the Giants. Right now, I have so much nice stuff that I actually look somewhat decent in my uniform. (Well, maybe if I drop a few pounds first.) Hell, I feel like I'm on the Giants with all the gear I have. I told Mitch, who said several times today, "Damn, Bo! You look like a ballplayer now," about one of my favorite Andy Van Slyke quotes: "The toughest part of making the jump from AAA to the big leagues is figuring out how to spend $60 a day meal money." I told Mitch that the toughest part of my day is trying to figure out what glove and cleats to wear. Attababy Mitch! Out.

Monday, June 4, 2001 (2:45 AM)
Bus from Yuma to St. George

Let me explain to you, the non-professional baseball player, about the joy of driving through the Arizona/Nevada desert in the middle of the night while in the midst of a five-game losing streak. If you can't detect the sarcasm in my written word, then you are about as thickheaded as one of our bus drivers. I was under the impression that half of a bus driver's job is to find out how in the hell we're supposed to get to our destination (the other half, of course, is actually getting us there in one piece). Our Mario Andretti *du jour* has been meandering through these God-forsaken roads like a maniac, and some of us are wondering if we are in fact on Disneyland's Space Mountain. The only thing worse than driving through the desert is driving through the desert at night. At least in the daytime, you can marvel at the lovely crabgrass and weeds. At night, the "bussie" has to avoid coyotes while driving at breakneck speed, and the only scenery are the distant lights of every two-bit gambling town in southern Nevada. "These are the times that try men's souls...."

It gets better: The five-game losing streak. On Monday evening last week, we were 8-2, having won six in a row. This Monday morning, we're 8-7. We absolutely suck right now. When we were winning, it was because we were capitalizing on our opponents' mistakes. Recently, though...well, do I need to make another "penthouse to the outhouse" analogy? People often ask me what caliber of baseball we play here in the WBL. I honestly feel that when two top teams and two top pitchers are going at it, we are at a legitimate AA level. Unfortunately, we would have had trouble beating an Omaha-bound college team this weekend. I'm serious. I'll bet we had eight errors in the three games, and those errors didn't take into account our other little miscues that don't appear in the box score. For example, on Saturday night, McAffee and I had a communication breakdown on a routine infield pop-up, which fell harmlessly to the ground for a base hit. We, as a team, also flat-out dropped three other routine pop-ups. It was positively embarrassing. The Crushers taketh, and then a week later, the Crushers giveth away.

I finally realized what the biggest difference is between a typical AA game and a WBL game: defense. Look, we have some guys in this league who can pitch. We have some guys who can hit. We even have some guys who can run. But defense is the great separator. You just don't see the crisp defensive play in this league on a night-in, night-out basis. Certainly, the fielding situation is exacerbated by some rough infield surfaces, but still, it's just not there. Yes, if you took an all-defensive team from the WBL, it would be pretty solid, but when you look at the league as whole, it's below average. Most of the action in a given baseball game takes place in the infield, so lousy infield defense usually means a lousy team.

Now, I've said that we have an outstanding pitching staff, and even in our five-game skid, I'll stand by it. The problem, though, is that pitching is only as good as the defense behind it. Here's an example: Say you have a pitcher who is in the middle of a rough inning. He has walked a guy, hit a guy, struck out a guy on a lucky call from the umpire and given up an RBI single. He's struggling, he knows it, and the whole stadium knows it. So, he's already given up a run, and there are runners on first and second with one out. Up to the plate steps a good hitter who doesn't run particularly well. The pitcher is battling the hitter, and eventually the hitter hits a sharp groundball to shortstop. The shortstop fields the ball cleanly, but his throw to second is slightly errant, allowing the runner from first to inter-fere with the second baseman's pivot throw. That throw then pulls the first baseman off the bag, resulting in a "safe" call at first. For the inning, thus far, there is one run in, two outs, and runners on first and third. The pitcher now has to face one more batter, and this time, he hangs a slider, which is promptly deposited into the cheap seats. Because the rules of offi-cial scoring say that you can't charge an error during a double play, all four runs of the inning are earned. Everyone knows that the double play should have been turned, but when the stats come out the next day, the pitcher's stats will be artificially inflated. The point I'm making is that our pitchers' numbers, as a staff, aren't too impressive, but I've been around pro ball long enough to know a good staff from a bad one, and ours is good. If we can shore up our defense, I think we'll be okay.

Anyway, we lost the last two games 7-2 and 9-5. Sunday's game wasn't as close as the score would indicate, as we were trailing 9-2 going into the top of the ninth. After we scored three quick runs, Carlos Villalobos—a native Colombian with some AAA time who finally had his work visa cleared—was standing on second with two outs when Sasaki came to the plate. File what happened next under "Things at a baseball game that you will see once in a lifetime—at best," something like the time when one of our players (I won't say whom, but he was on another team in another league) was ejected from a game and returned wearing the mascot's costume so he could better yell at the umpire. Sasa took the first pitch for a strike on the inside corner, and unsure of what the call was from the umpire, he asked, "Strike?" The umpire nodded, and then Sasa bent over and grabbed some dirt from the inside part of the batter's box. Whether such an action is commonplace in Japan remains to be seen, but the home plate umpire definitely took exception to it. He thought that Sasa was questioning his call and therefore ejected him right there. No one in the stadium had any idea what had just happened, and when Tim left the third base coaching box to learn that his leftfielder had just been tossed, the s—— hit the fan. Tim launched into a tirade that would have made Earl Weaver proud and cursed out the umpire like the ump had just questioned Tim's ancestry. When the first base umpire intervened, Tim blew up at him, too. In a perverted kind of way, it was impressive. All the while, Sasa had a pained, deer-in-headlights look on his face, the kind of look you'd have on *your* face if a Tokyo store clerk had falsely accused you of shoplifting and was ranting and raving to a policeman. JT then finished out Sasa's at-bat by looking at strike two and swinging and missing strike three. Game over. Crushers swept. On a lighter note, all JT was concerned about was his at-bat and how his swing looked; he must have asked everyone on the team. Twice.

Right now, we are about an hour out of Mesquite, and I have just learned that Tim has canceled batting practice tomorrow. I don't know if that's a good or bad thing, but it's one of those decisions—during one of those funks—that a manager has to make. He could laugh off our losing streak, saying, "Ahhhh, the hell with it; it's just one of those things." Or he could say, "Screw these sorry-ass putzes. I'm gonna whip 'em into playing better." I don't know if there is a right answer. I do know that Mitch wasn't too happy with our defense-only pregame workout on Saturday. Mitch understands that even the best of teams will play in a foggy stupor from time to time and that all you can do is ride the storm out. I guess it's time for Tim to work some of his managerial magic. The hocus-pocus could come in the form of a mass releasing of players, a chew-us-out meeting, a hang-in-there guys meeting or by saying nothing at all. He's a tough guy to read, but I know he's just boiling inside. His job is to win, or more accurately, to get *us* to win. Good luck, skipper, with the way we've been playing. Out.

Thursday, June 7, 2001 (1:30 PM)
Rohnert Park

Where do I begin? I penned my last entry during our drive from Yuma to St. George, and I am cranking this one out minutes after returning from a 12-hour bus trip. Honestly, that's the only major downside to playing in this league, the bus trips. If we could only fly.... Damn, Bo, wake up!!

The good news is that we took two of three from St. George, so we're now 10-8 with the Chico Heat coming to town. I think they are in first place by a half-game over us, so it should be interesting. The Big Ogre, who Mitch calls "Milk" because, according to Mitch, he looks like a big, white, corn-fed, country boy, saved our asses on Monday night by hitting a thunderous three-run homer in the top of the ninth to put us up by two. If we don't score there, we lose six in a row. I'm telling you, this kid has gargantuan power. Last year with the Diamondbacks, he struck out a lot, but with his approach now, he's lethal. On Tuesday, we scored eight runs in the fourth, which helped to stake us to an 11-2 lead, but St. George clawed back to make it 11-10. Fortunately, Scottie shut the door for his league leading fifth save, and we won again. Last night, we were blown out 17-11 in a typical St. George game, *i.e.*, lots of cheap homeruns. Bruce Hurst Field in St. George is WBL's version of Coors Field in Denver. It's not that you have to beat the team as much as it is that you have to outlast it. Anyway, like Meat Loaf said a quarter century ago, "Two out of three ain't bad."

Mitch was killing me in the dugout the other day. He's definitely an equal-opportunity needler, meaning that it doesn't matter if you're Colombian, Japanese, black, white, red, green, or purple, he'll give it to you. In Yuma he was talking about his growing up in a gang, and unable to visualize what that would be like, I told him that I'm just a small-town white boy. He said, "I know. You were probably in the Klan, too." Nothing's sacred with Mitch. Anyway, he accused Keith, the trainer, of eating all the sunflower seeds that other people have bought, and Mitch was razzing him pretty good. At the end, he called Keith "Tennessee Tuxedo," and I was howling. We then had an in-game discussion regarding what cartoon Tennessee Tuxedo came from, and we decided that he had his own cartoon. Remember him, the penguin, and his buddy the walrus? Now, don't get all bent out of shape, thinking, "God, Bo, shouldn't you guys be paying attention to the game, not to cartoon characters?" It reminds me of a story from my senior year of college when we had to beat U. of Southern Mississippi three in a row in Blacksburg to win the regular season conference title. Well, we won the first two, and minutes before the third game, I had my teammates in stitches by telling them stories about my beloved dog, Butch. More to the point, I was telling them about things Butch ate—a bird, a rat, a groundhog, afterbirth, calf testicles, a dead deer, etc.—and everyone was rolling. My mother was appalled. We then proceeded to sweep the Eagles. A good team is a loose team, right?

Which brings me to my next topic: mutiny. This isn't mutiny in the Henry Hudson sense, but in the loss-of-respect sense for Tim. Most of the guys on the team are pretty much fed up with his constant tinkering with our roster. It's not as if anyone is going to leave all of a sudden, but a lot of guys aren't really happy. Tim's been bringing players in for two or three games at a time and then releasing them. For example, when J-Lo signed with Boston, we grabbed Garry Templeton, Jr. to replace him. Temp drove from San Diego to Yuma to play three games there, and then he followed us to St. George, the thought being that he would then follow us to

Rohnert Park. Well, Tim decided to release him after last night's game, so now Temp has to drive all the way back to San Diego. There are also rumors about Tim's possibly bringing in two or three Japanese pitchers, which means that he may have to release some of our current guys. If that happens, then some guys will be seriously pissed off. It's not the fact that they're Japanese; it's that he's never seen them pitch before, so they're unknown entities. The guys we have now are certainly adequate and will probably get better. A lot of the guys think that Tim is trying to get back to Japan to manage, and the constant influx of Japanese players is a foot in the door. I know one thing: Mitch ain't too happy. Apparently, Tim and Mitch had a mild argument the other day, and Mitch, like I said, is not someone I want to be at odds with.

Personally, the roster tampering doesn't bother me too much. As long as I'm doing well—and thus far, I have—I don't have too much to worry about. Yes, it bothers me when a guy I like, both on and off the field, gets the axe, but what can I say about it? No, it's not fair, and sometimes, it may not even be the right decision, but I just have to bite my tongue, lest the guillotine find my nape. I mentioned earlier in this journal that when you first sign a pro contract, being released comes with the territory, especially in independent leagues, where everyone has been released two or three times or more. It's not pleasant, but it's just the way it is. The best idea is to shut up and play. Furthermore, no matter what my numbers are (again, they're pretty damn good right now), I still consider myself to be maybe only slightly above average. I suppose that attitude comes from the inferiority complex of not having that one big league-caliber skill, that one tool that makes people say, "Boy, wait 'til you see Durkac ———." There is not one thing you can put in that blank that would make a true statement. Therefore, I always feel there is another third baseman who could easily take my spot, someone who runs better or throws better or has more power. That's why I don't chirp like some of the other players do, for fear of losing my job.

Finally, it's good to be home. Most of us felt as if we'd been on the road for a month, not a week. We have nine games in ten days at home followed by a three game series in Solano, which is a commute. So basically, we're home for almost two straight weeks. *Que bueno!* In spite of the losing streak, we're still doing well, and Chico will definitely be a good measuring stick. I just hope that we can get some stability around here to maintain the morale of the guys. If we can find ways to win, though, everyone will be happy; winning cures all ills. Out.

Sunday, June 10, 2001 (8:00 PM)
Rohnert Park

Well, the Heat indeed came to town and took two of three from the Crushers. They have a helluva team, leading the league in pitching and in hitting, and they beat the snot out of us the first two days. The first seven hitters in their lineup are hitting .330 or better, and they pounded us pretty good on Friday. On Saturday, we gave them three unearned runs in one inning, and that was basically the difference. Today, we spotted them two runs, then scored four runs in the fifth and eventually held on for a tough 4-3 win. Greg Ball, Chico's beat reporter, did an interview with me before Friday's game –the context of which will be discussed later—about the proposed weirdness of playing against my former mates. Honestly, it wasn't too much different from any other game, except that they have a helluva team (oh yeah, I already said that). Ray Brown, the WBL's leading hitter, nearly ended any of my future plans of having children by hitting an absolute rocket at me on Friday. Brad Gennaro, a former AA All-Star, is finally hitting like he's capable of, second in the league in hitting. They threw three quality starting pitchers at us. There was just no relief. The only thing weird was being a "have-not" after being a "have" for the previous three years.

As for the article, it was quite inflammatory and bears reading. Go to the following website if you're interested:

(*http://www.chicoer.com/display/inn_sports/sports2.txt*).
Having just read it only an hour ago, I wrote a response to it, but I don't
know if the *Chico Enterprise-Record* will print it. We shall see. As much as
a fan I am of Ted Williams, I am amazed at how eerily similar—albeit
shorter, of course—it is to his "My Turn At Bat." In his autobiography, he
devotes a great amount of print to his detractors, both the on- and off-the-
field versions. He was always under fire for being a "cancer" in the clubhouse because of his lack of desire to hang out with his teammates, once
saying, "I have to look at their mugs all day. Do I have to do it at night,
too?" On the field, he was criticized for not driving in enough runs when
the money was on the line, instead trusting his well-honed knowledge of
the strike zone and taking the walk. He refuted that notion by saying, "A
hitter gains no advantage by doing something on Tuesday that he would
do on Friday." In other words, if you occasionally blur that fine line
between a ball and strike when it's an RBI situation, then, eventually, the
line will become permanently blurred, ultimately rendering himself a less
effective hitter. Furthermore, every time he walked, he had a chance then
to score a run, and if you combine his career runs batted in *and* runs
scored totals, I'll take The Splendid Splinter as one of the top handful of
run producers in baseball history—as if he needs further validation.

Anyway, Chico's manager, Charley Kerfeld, made some pretty disparag-
ing comments about me in the paper, and a friend of mine from Chico e-
mailed me that several people had apparently called the *Enterprise-Record*
and complained about what he said about me. Whether that's true or not is
still in question. For once, though, I will *not* back down from this situation. I will give Charley credit for one thing: he has a lot of connections.
Several different players in this league have been tendered contracts by
organizations, especially the Houston Astros, on Charley's recommenda-
tion, and he has been able to get quality players to come to Chico, guys like
Buck McNabb and Ray Brown. As for on the field, well, I can say that I
have forgotten more about baseball than he'll ever know. Hell, last year, on
the first day of spring training, he had no idea how to set up a double-relay

from the outfield. Tim Cooper, our shortstop, had to take over. Nice start, huh? He never threw BP and never hit fungoes, preferring rather to sit in the dugout and BS with the opposing manager.

I suppose I will always compare him to Bill Plummer, my first manager in Chico and the guy who set the standard of excellence upon which Charley has now attached his coattails. Plum was out there every day throwing BP with a bad arm and hitting fungoes to his infielders. His rules, such as how he wanted to protect a one-run lead in the eighth inning and proper bunt coverages, were crystal-clear and set in stone; there was no ambiguity. Even last year, we players knew that we were winning in spite of Charley, not because of him. In fact, several of us were miffed that he was getting far too much credit for our success, not once mentioning, "Hey, I simply have a helluva team. I'm not doing anything."

The following is an excerpt from the article I just wrote for the Chico newspaper:

I was the subject of multiple confrontations between coaches and players and a rules violator. On any pro team, at any level, you can't expect everyone to be best friends with each other. There are far too many backgrounds, races, religions, and personalities for everyone to embrace everyone equally. Pro baseball teams are quite "cliquish," and players tend to hang out with players of common interest. I am not attesting that everyone loved me on the team, but I definitely wouldn't consider myself a "cancer." Certainly, my sometimes-abrasive nature may have rubbed a few of my teammates the wrong way, but I would be astounded—actually, horrified—to hear that the Bo-haters far outweighed the Bo-likers. Also, unlike a lot of players who would show up at 3:28 PM for a 3:30 PM stretch, I went to early optional BP almost daily and was diligent on my fielding practice during regular BP, even with an ailing knee. I have always been a hard worker who has produced on the field, and that in itself should put an end to any such nonsensical "cancer" talk. As for my rules violation, let me explain. We were playing, ironically enough, in Sonoma County last year, and I had made arrangements to stay with a friend after the game, something quite common for players to do while on a road trip. The next day, we had to be ready for our daily team stretch at 4:00 PM. The friend dropped me off at Rohnert Park Stadium at 3:40 PM, and I was easily ready at 4:00 PM. When I saw my name was not on the lineup card, I simply asked Charley why, and he said, "You weren't on the bus from the hotel, so you're not playing today." Well, not only had he never said he had a rule about that, but no professional ballplayer I've ever met had ever *heard* of such a rule. Not only was the rule nonexistent, it was inane. Plus, you don't bench a starting player as punishment because it hurts the team; you fine him—or at least that's what most managers do.

Anyway, I'm not sure what the long-term effects will be of this whole situation. I'm reminded of the quote, "Don't burn your bridges. You'd be surprised at how many times you have to cross the same river." I'd like to think that despite having never played at the AA or AAA level, which automatically brings a certain amount of validation, my numbers are good enough that I should be able to play professionally somewhere for as long as I choose. I don't think I have to worry about Charley's opinion of me. If I ever need a baseball reference, I'm sure Plummer or Tim would provide a more than adequate referral.

I've always followed John Wooden's saying, "Who's right isn't nearly as important as what's right." I've heard so many married men jokingly say that the most essential words in marriage are, "I'm sorry, dear. You were right." Every time I hear a husband say that, I want to vomit. If, after a sustained period of reflective thought, I realized that I was wrong about something, then I would definitely apologize to whomever I had wronged. On the other hand, though, if I feel I'm right, then I'll battle you tooth and nail. Whatever happens between Charley and me remains to be seen, but something tells me that it won't get any nicer. Out.

Monday, June 11, 2001 (12:00 AM)
Rohnert Park

I just wrote about an ongoing feud between a player and his former manager, so I wanted to drop a quick entry about something that happened today. After the game last night, Tim wrote on the message board that position players had to be at the field at 3:00 PM today and the pitchers at 3:45 PM. Tim's times this year have been pretty ambiguous—the old "be at the park at 2:00 PM," but we don't stretch until 3:30 PM type of thing a couple of times—so when he was ready to give us a refresher course on baserunning at 3:00 PM, several guys remained in the clubhouse. CP was the last guy to get out to the field, and here's roughly how the ensuing conversation went.

Tim (gruffly): "Why are you coming out to the field at 3:12 PM when the board said 3:00 PM?"

CP: "I didn't know we had to be on the field at 3:00 PM." (CP had actually been sitting in the clubhouse since about 2:15 PM).

Tim (to all of us): "Do you guys not understand that you are to be dressed and on the field at whatever time I put on the board?"

CP: "Well, it (the time on the board) changes every five minutes."

Tim: "Oh, don't give me that bullshit! You get your ass out here on time."

CP: "Whatever...."

Tim: "Don't blow me off like that!"

CP: "F— that."

Tim: "That's it. Get in my office right now!"

Tim and CP then went into Tim's office while we continued to stretch. Tim then returned to the field and met us at first base for our baserunning symposium. Before the instructional part of it, though, he said, "I realize that not everyone is going to like me, and that's okay. If you have a problem with me, let's go into my office, and we can arm wrestle or sumo. Whatever the problem is, just keep it private." CP then returned from the clubhouse, and everything was fine, as if nothing had happened, and Tim did his baserunning instruction.

You see, when grown men are around each other day after day for an entire summer, there are going to be some unpleasantries. It's inevitable. For all you "old school" people out there who believe that you should never argue with a coach or manager, well, that line of thought has gone the way of Kevin Costner's film career. While college coaches still have their kids on a pretty tight leash at times, it's especially true in the pro ranks. I certainly would never openly argue with a manager, but some guys have no problem with it. Again, it goes back to that fear of being released, and some guys are either too good to be released and they know it, a la CP, or too dumb to know that they could very well sign their release forms by such a defiance. I think that's what happened with Ramon Valera, the Dominican utility infielder who was released about one week into the season. He was apparently unhappy with his playing time, so he blew up at Tim, who promptly released him. For a guy who was hitting under .200, I guess that wasn't such a wise move.

Anyway, during the game, Tim seemed friendlier than normal, and I'm not sure why. Maybe the altercation had something to do with it, and maybe Tim was sensing that morale was low. I don't know. I do know that Tim and CP carried on during the game as if nothing had happened. Part of being a professional is knowing that you owe it to the team and the organization to let bygones be bygones if there is some friction. Certainly, if there are irreconcilable differences, then maybe the player and the manager shouldn't be on the same team, but that is rarely the case. In pro baseball, you don't have to be best friends with everyone—as I said, it's pretty much impossible to be.

Along these lines, I recently had a conversation with Valerie (my host mom) about camaraderie in baseball, and bless her heart, too, but she shares the opinion of nonprofessional baseball players everywhere. She said that on Richard's squad, they're "just not playing as a team." Rather than opening up a volatile can of snakes, I swallowed hard and said nothing. She's such a sweetheart, but she—and most people—just doesn't get it. In pro baseball, chemistry is such an overused term. I know, I know, I've said that 100 times, but I'm amazed at how many people, and even some players, don't buy it. Today, I was talking to Mac (Josh McAffee, our way-too-pretty-to-be-a-catcher catcher) about this very subject, and he still wants to buy into the notion that a well-bonded team will play better than a fractured one. We went back and forth about it, and then I just said, "Look, Josh, maybe I'm the exception, but I don't need guys cheering for me. All the clapping and rah-rah BS won't help me hit any better. If you need to be motivated by your teammates, then, in my opinion, you shouldn't be playing professional baseball." He heard me out, though I'm not sure he necessarily agreed with me. And, for the record, in light of my testimony about my own stubbornness, it was a very amicable conversation between two men who freely expressed their opinions and then proceeded to drive in two runs each as the Crushers beat the Breakers, 7-5. Out.

Wednesday, June 13, 2001 (11:00 PM)
Rohnert Park

First, before I forget, some clubhouse humor. I rolled into the clubhouse today, and a *Playboy* magazine was in circulation. It was a "Lingerie" edition, and unfortunately, there were no articles to read, much to the chagrin, I'm sure, of the players. Anyway, there was a section of former Playmates from 1975. Upon seeing the scantily clad women, I ventured over to CP (he of the ripe old age of 32) and asked him, "CP, wasn't this chick a senior when you were a freshman?" The whole back part of the clubhouse was rolling, and CP gave me a little snicker. Later, the talk turned to our introduction songs, the songs that the public address announcer plays as the hitters walk up to the plate and as pitchers enter the game from the bullpen. Well, Pritchard comes out to a music-only song from the *Boogie Nights* soundtrack, and it's basically the kind of music that is heard in a poorly made pornographic film—or so I've heard. I said, "Pritch, if you were a porn star, what would your name be?" Without hesitation, he said, "Bang Bang LaDesh." We were dying.

Pritch is an interesting character. He played in the Frontier League, a league predominately for kids one or two years out of college, last year, and he "doesn't really have a position." That's the baseball term for a guy who can either hit or run well but doesn't have a position that he plays well defensively. In Pritch's case, he was an outfielder in college, but he's caught, played second base, and played the outfield for us. He has a strong arm and is a switch-hitter, and Tim is amazed that no one has tried to make him a catcher. Pritch plays a solid outfield, but he is really impressing us as a hitter, so much so that Tim has been putting him either at the leadoff spot or in the third spot. For those of you who don't know already, if you're hitting anywhere between the 1st and 5th spots, the manager thinks you can hit.

Apparently, when we were in Mesquite, Tim and Pritch were at the same Blackjack table, and Tim, slightly intoxicated, was saying to Pritch that the only reason he was on the team was because of a favor to someone. Nice to know, huh, Pritch? Great confidence builder. I don't know if that story is true or not, but does it matter? Mike Piazza was drafted in the 62nd round by the Dodgers as a favor to Piazza's dad, who was good friends with Tommy Lasorda, LA's manager at the time. I suppose you could say that the "Pizza Man" has done okay for himself. I'm not attesting that Pritch will be wearing a big league uniform anytime soon, but as we say in the WBL, "Anything can happen as long as you have a uniform on your back." Also, Pritch has shown some manifestation of a brain, at times going back and forth with me with trivia questions, and he is quite the artist. He is continuously drawing caricature-esque sketches of certain people, and they're always funny. Maybe the best part about him, though, is that at 24-years-old, he, like the other young kids on the team, is very humble and very eager to learn.

We played Long Beach yesterday and again today, and they won both games. Last night, Mike Saipe beat us again, throwing a complete game and giving up only a solo homerun to CP in the bottom of the ninth. He blew our doors off in Long Beach, too, leaving me wondering from whence he came. Steve Yeager, the Breakers' manager and 3rd base coach, told me that he has about one week of big league time with Colorado. Mostly, he's a AA-AAA guy, and I can honestly say that he is one of the top two or three starting pitchers I've faced in my three-plus years in the WBL. When you face a guy like Saipe, when he's on his game, it's one of those "take your medicine" nights. We had only five hits, and CP had three of them. Evidently, CP wasn't too impressed. After experiencing a night of futility against a top-notch pitcher, a hitter's maturity—or lack thereof—is brought to the forefront. Maturity, in my opinion, is *such* a huge factor is becoming a good hitter. You have to say to yourself, "Look, Saipe was just better than I was tonight, but I'm not going to alter my approach to hitting just because of one bad game." I told some of the younger guys that before today's game. I told them that I feel that the key to becoming a good professional hitter is to find an approach to hitting that works for you and stick with it, come Hell or high water. I heard Bobby Bonilla say one time that he was screwed up for a week after facing a knuckleballer. While I am not questioning his maturity, I want the young guys to understand that you can't let the anomaly pitcher—the knuckleballer, the submariner, or the tough pitcher who is simply on his game—screw up your approach as a hitter for four or five days.

Unfortunately, Saipe must have screwed up a lot of guys since we came out today and lost 2-1, garnering only four hits as a team. I didn't feel that their starter had outstanding stuff, but he mixed up his pitches well. Still, though, four hits? Maybe we just need a day off, which is what tomorrow offers. The game was tied at 1-1 until we gave them an unearned run in the top of the eighth (incidentally, the other run was unearned as well). I'm not saying that I'm perfect, but I would like to play one errorless game this year. Is that too much to ask? I just want a good, clean, well-played game from the Crushers, and let the chips fall as they may. It's so damn frustrating to watch mental mistakes and routine errors every freakin' day. If we could catch the ball *at all*, we'd be 16-8, not 12-12. Oh well.

As I said, tomorrow is our first full off day. The previous three involved travel off some kind, rendering the day half-wasted. It will be nice to wake tomorrow with a full day ahead of me. My goal this year—hell, every year—is to play every inning of every game. My knee has been fine most of the time, but on days like today, a day game after a night game, it gets a little tender. I've told every manager that I've ever had at any level that I do *not* want him to give me a day off and that I will never ask for one. I don't believe in them. When I see in the paper that so-and-so got the day off for some "mental rest," I always cringe. Can someone explain to me what the term "mentally tired" means? The brain is a bundle of nerves, not muscles. Maybe I'd think differently if I were in the big leagues, but until then, I refuse to accept it.

I have a pretty decent, compact swing from both sides of the plate—as a switch-hitter, I don't have to worry about a pitcher with a tough slider—and at this point in my career, in this league, I'm basically slump-proof. Furthermore, I've made only one error in the last 15 games, and the last thing we need as a team is another defensive liability on the field. I hope that Tim will take this all into consideration when he makes out the lineup card each day, especially when we play 24 days in a row starting on June 22. Yes, my knee will undoubtedly bother me a bit, but it won't affect my hitting or my defense. As for my footspeed, well, like Bob Dylan said

in *Like a Rolling Stone*, "When you got nothing, you got nothing to lose."
Out.

Friday, June 15, 2001 (11:45 PM)
Rohnert Park

Well, it happened. It's every player's worst nightmare. It's makes you
feel about as comfortable as David Duke at the Million Man March.
Tonight, I had a conversation with Tim—in the shower! Why do certain
managers feel the need to converse with players while wet and naked?
Can't the discussion take place under different circumstances? Most players will do **anything** to avoid being the only player in the shower when the
manager is in there, myself included. Unfortunately, McAffee was on his
way out as I entered, so I was trapped. Egad!! After a few minutes of
silence, Tim asked me where I am from, and when I told him, he said that
was recruited as a quarterback by the University of Pittsburgh when he
was a senior in high school in 1973. In fact, he said he flew into Pittsburgh
on January 1, 1973, the day after Roberto Clemente died in his tragic
plane accident. Tim was evidently quite the high school quarterback,
according to a story on him in the local paper, and he even tried out for
the USFL when the league opened back in the early 1980's. I wanted to
say, "Gee, thanks, skipper, for that information, but couldn't you have
waited to tell me that when we were both clothed?"

Last night, during our off day (when I slept until 3:30 PM), I went out
on the town with one of our players, and something happened that was
way too funny to keep from my journal. I picked up one of our players
because this player is married and without wheels. This player, call him
"Joe," is one of those few-and-far-between married ballplayers who doesn't
cheat on his wife. He wears his wedding band everywhere he goes and
makes it no secret that he is very much happily married (is that an oxy-
moron?). Furthermore, he sends a chunk of each paycheck home to his
wife for their joint bank account. That may seem like small potatoes to the

non-professional athlete, but such loyalty and forthrightness is pretty uncommon in the baseball world. Anyway, "Joe" went to Old Navy earlier this week to buy a pair of shorts. Now, since Old Navy shorts aren't cheap and since we're a few days away from our next payday, he was a little short on cash. You know what he did? He went to Old Navy to return the shorts so he could get some drinking money! Is that priceless? I said, "Joe, can I please put that story in my journal?" He said, "Sure. Just don't put my name." Consider it done and done.

On the diamond, the Crushers dropped their third in a row to Yuma today, 9-6. They hit Pickford around a little, but once again, if we could play defense at all, the complexion of the game would have undoubtedly been changed. For example, in the first inning, "Pick" has runners on first and second, nobody out, and one run in already. The cleanup batter hits a hard shot to my left, which I field cleanly and flip to second base for what should be a routine double-play ball. It wasn't. The relay to first was off line, leaving runners at first and third with one out, not two, and the next batter's fly ball to centerfield should have been the third out of the inning. Instead, it was a sacrifice fly and another earned run against Pick.

I came in from the field after the third out, and I asked Scottie if that was a routine double-play ball (which I suspected that it was), and he said, "Hell, yes, it was." I said, "That's gotta be turned," and he said, "I know. You're the leader out there. Tell them that it has to be turned." As it turns out, I *am* the leader out there, if for no other reason than that I am the old man in the infield. Our normal starting infield includes four 23-year-olds and me. I am a bit leery about assuming the role of "leader" for two reasons. One, I haven't been around *that* long; in Chico, I was considered somewhat young compared to the experience of some of the guys on that team. Two, baseball is hard enough for me to master myself, let alone trying to help other guys do their jobs. As I mentioned in the last entry, most of the younger guys seem willing to learn from the older guys, and that's definitely a good trait. The problem is that I don't want to step on the toes of guys like Mitch and Tim, guys who are paid to teach.

Our new second baseman, Rene Capellan, is a 23-year-old Dominican who played in the Detroit Tigers' organization for five years and last year with Yuma. He's a damn good hitter—he was always near the top of the league leaders in hitting last year—but he made a ton of errors defensively for Plummer in 2000. Today, during BP, I asked whether the majority of his errors last year were fielding or throwing, and he said throwing, due in part to a sore arm. It appears that it is still bothering him a bit this year as well because he doesn't make the good, crisp throws that good second basemen make. "Cappy" is a good, humble kid who has some ability, but until he irons out his throwing problems, he'll still be suspect defensively.

One of the pitchers, in the wake of our failure to turn the seemingly routine double play, asked me how we can improve our shortstop and second base positions defensively. I said simply, "We need better players." That's not a knock against Patty, Cappy, and Brian Zepeda, our new middle infielder. It's no different than my being a third baseman with only one homerun; you don't see too many AA third baseman with less homerun power than I have. Our guys just aren't good enough. Patty was a Division II shortstop/second baseman in Southern California, and Zepeda just joined us from Cal State-Dominguez Hills (another Division II school from SoCal). While the caliber of baseball is decent at that level, you can't expect a young kid from that level of competition to compete day-in and day-out at the WBL.

I often wonder how pitchers like Scottie and Pick can deal with our shoddy defensive performances. These guys have been AA/AAA guys for the last few years, and at that level, you just don't see glaring defensive weaknesses. No, there aren't many superstar glovemen in AAA, but I have to believe that everyone is a solid, professional defensive player. I would bet that you could knock an entire run off our team's ERA because of our defensive woes. Little stuff, like double plays and baserunners taking the extra base on our outfielders from time to time, can add up, but since no errors are involved, the pitchers' ERA's are inflated. It's frustrating. I guess all I can do is do my job and offer as much encouragement and instruction as I can for the younger guys. Help may not be on the way. Out.

Saturday, June 16, 2001 (9:30 PM)
Rohnert Park

Crushers 6, Yuma 5. Scottie came into a tie game with runners on first and third with one out in the top of the ninth and struck out their three-hole hitter. On the strikeout pitch, the runner on first went to second, so now there are runners on second and third with two outs. Up to the plate stepped Hector Roa, a solid, veteran switch-hitter who has played in the big leagues, Japan, and Mexico, I believe. He battled Scottie for about 10 pitches, and then he hit a seemingly routine groundball to Zepeda at shortstop, who promptly threw the ball away, allowing both runners to score. Scottie got the next guy out, but the damage was done. Somehow, though, in the bottom of the ninth, we managed to scrape across one run, and then Sasa, in the tenth, hit a pinch-hit, game-winning homerun. Unbelievable. We needed that.

Now for the good stuff. After the game, Tim called Zepeda into his office to tell him that he is now released and Villalobos and Longmire in to tell them they'd been traded to Yuma. Obviously, none of them was too happy. But wait, it gets better. One of the Yuma players (the other one being right fielder Diego Rico), catcher Jose Montenegro, refused the trade, saying that he wouldn't report to us, and he "snapped," apparently breaking a few things in the visitor's clubhouse. Thus, Plummer had to come over to our clubhouse to tell Tim that Montenegro wouldn't report, in effect canceling the transaction. Tim then called out to "Villa" and Boat not to pack up just yet and to Zepeda that "you might not be released." Nice, huh?

Zepeda is now on the emotional roller coaster of 1) finally getting a chance to play pro ball 2) getting to play a few games 3) making a crucial error in a key situation 4) being told that he was released and 5) being told that he may still be on the team. Is that fair? Life is a bed of roses compared to what baseball can put you through. People wonder why I have never been in love with a woman, and the answer is quite simple: I have burned out all my emotions on this God-forsaken game. No, nothing as blatantly inhumane as Zepeda's scenario has ever happened to me, but I've lost more sleep and cried more tears over baseball than over all the women I've ever known—combined.

Being traded is an interesting part of sports, not just baseball. What it means is that basically, some team thinks you're good, and some team thinks you're expendable. In baseball, it usually means that your current organization thinks that you've "maxed out" your potential and that you won't get any better. The other organization, though, feels that you still can become a productive player. That's why scouts can be seen at minor league and major league games across the country; sometimes, all a player needs is a change of scenery, and he's on his way to the big leagues. Personally, I think of myself like this. Most managers, once I get to play a month or so for them, find me to be a pretty solid player, someone who's going to drive in some runs, score some runs, and prevent some runs with my defense. No, I don't have that jaw-dropping homerun power that a typical third baseman has, but I think deep down that most managers see the combination of being a run producer and an above average defensive player as a reason enough to keep me around. Furthermore, I've always been a hard worker, someone who is always taking extra hitting or fielding practice, and I think that has a positive effect on their opinions of me.

For example, when I first found out that I wouldn't be playing in Chico this year and that I'd be playing for the Crushers, I spoke with the GM Bob Fletcher, and he told me that he had tried to trade for me in the past. That was quite comforting. To me, it meant that not only did Sonoma County want me, but also that Chico didn't want to let me go. In a career filled with disappointments, a double-whammy of good news was refreshing.

One side note to my rambling: In light of Charley's comments about me in the Chico newspaper, Tim told our radio guy, Steve Bitker, that he "wishes that he had twenty more players like me." When your current team is a carousel like ours has been, knowing that you have a vote of confidence from your manager goes a long way towards maintaining sanity. I guess I'm like the same, average-looking girl you see every night in the bar but you don't really pay much attention to: she won't exactly knock you off your feet, but after a while, her effort and consistency kinda grow on you. Out.

Sunday, June 17, 2001 (6:30 PM)
Rohnert Park

Crushers 5, Yuma 4. Do two wins in a row count as a winning streak? We almost plucked defeat from the jaws of victory, but we held on. Roque (pronounced roh-KAY) Roman, our 34-year-old Colombian pitcher, threw a gem today. "Rocky" is 6 feet tall, and on a good day—soaking wet and on a full stomach—he weighs 150 lbs. I call him *El Flaco*, which means "the skinny one." He throws an assortment of pitches from an assortment of arm angles, and while his stuff is not overpowering, he is very difficult to hit. He had given up only one hit through 7 2/3 innings, but with two outs and no one on base, Yuma rallied for four runs, cutting our lead to 5-4. Fortunately, JT closed out the inning, and we turned it over to Scottie, who threw a perfect ninth. Rocky, for this league, has "good stuff." You hear that term a lot in baseball, but no one quite knows how to define it. Well, here is my definition: A pitcher who can make good hitters take bad swings has good stuff. There are three hitters in Yuma's lineup that I think are pretty good—Joe Kilburg, Roa, and Alex Sutherland—and not one of them took very many quality swings off Rocky today. Now, just because you have "good stuff" doesn't mean that you will automatically be a good pitcher; you still need to throw strikes and keep hitters off balance. But when you can prevent the good hitters from taking those really aggressive swings, you are on your way to becoming a good pitcher.

One side note on Rocky. He actually pitched for Chris Catanoso, former Plummer bench coach in Chico in 1998, when Catanoso was managing in the Colombian Winter League in the winter of 1999-2000. Catanoso was impressed enough with him to invite Rocky to the Tri-City Posse last year, an invitation that Rocky readily accepted, and he threw well enough that we acquired the rights to him after Tri-City folded. Thus far, he has done very well for us. His case is just another example of how a player needs breaks to make it in this game. Had there not been a league that winter and had Catanoso not been his manager, Rocky may still be toiling in obscurity in the Colombian Professional League, where he labored for six summers. No, Rocky won't be pitching in the big leagues any time soon, but you can bet the ranch that he's making a lot more money here than he was in Colombia.

I wrote yesterday about how our trade may have fallen through, but in fact, it did not. As a result, Villalobos and Longmire, two guys who were in our clubhouse and on our lineup card yesterday, were wearing the black and green of Yuma today. Montenegro and Rico joined us, but only "Monty" played. I think the happiest person of all about the trade was McAffee, who has caught all but two games for us this year. The kid is only 23, but that's still a lot of games. Today, he just basically chilled, with the exception of warming up the relievers in the bullpen. Also, Zepeda was released. I feel bad for the kid and the way he has been put through the wringer. He is average at best—even for this league—so he probably doesn't have much of a future, but seeing how Tim jerked him around made me and a few others feel for him. I wished him luck and told him to keep working hard.

Finally, I have written now for four of the last five days, and I actually enjoy and look forward to coming home and cranking out my entries. Sometimes, my carousing prevents me from diligently updating my journal, but other times, I like the peacefulness and calming influence of writing over the bar scene. Road trips are the best, though, because most towns offer little to do for entertainment, so what better way to kill idle time, right? Today's entry will put me over the 50,000-word plateau, and when you consider that we have at least two months of the season left, I could have quite a journal when all is said and done. Now, if I can only find someone to publish it.... Out.

Wednesday, June 21, 2001 (11:30 PM)
Bus from Solano to Yuma

Swept. The momentum that we built after two, close-fought, one-run victories against Yuma has vaporized. The three games were 5-2, 5-2, and 8-1. Tim thinks we're afraid of Solano. Mitch thinks that once we fall behind, we're done. They may both be right. I don't know. Offensively, we were positively impotent in the series, though; scoring only five runs over three games is inexcusable. Solano has a good pitching staff and an imposing lineup—maybe the equal of Chico's—and maybe we're just not good enough right now to compete with them. I'm not sure if Tim has any further connections up his sleeve, but if the guys we have now don't start playing better, we're in for a long season.

Just like the last time we played in Solano, we commuted by rental vans. As usual, it was a first-come, first-serve situation as to who was on which van, and it was amazing to see how diverse the three vans were. Dolf's van consisted of all the veteran pitchers except JT. The "minority" van consisted of, well, the minorities: all the Spanish speakers and Chief, who was driving. I called my van ("my" since I drove) the "Klan" van, as in Ku Klux Klan. Mitch accused me earlier this year of being part of the KKK, and I said, "Mitch, just because I'm a small town, white boy doesn't mean I'm in the Klan." He responded, "Don't let me see you at a black rally 'cuz I'll rip that sheet off you and whoop your ass." Anyway, I called it the Klan van, but it could've been the W.A.S.P. van with some of the surnames involved: Patterson, Oglesby, Thompson, Hansen, etc.

Pritch drew the shortest straw, unfortunately. Not literally, but Tim talked him into driving Tim's convertible for him. If you think being naked in the shower with the skipper is awkward, I can't imagine having to carry on a conversation with him for over an hour. Tim originally asked JT to drive, but JT realized that the ribbing he would take from the older guys would be far too intense and politely declined. Tim wasn't too happy with JT's refusal, so he put the full-court press on Pritch. Being a rookie, Pritch basically had no choice, so he became the butt of innumerable jokes over the past few days. Poor kid.

From the ever-changing roster department, we had the previously discussed trade and one addition. Montenegro played for the now-defunct Valley Vipers of the WBL in 2000. He was primarily a catcher last year, but he had played first base and shortstop as well for Plummer in Yuma. He even played second base for us tonight—he was originally drafted by Milwaukee as a third baseman—and was solid defensively. He's a tough little hitter whose versatility should be a big plus for us. Rico, in my opinion, had perhaps the prettiest swing in the league last year but had a miserable first half, hitting maybe .200. After a mid-season eye exam, though, he hit the heck out of the ball in the second half. He played in Class A for the Cubs for two years, and his left-handed bat should be a nice addition to our righty-laden lineup. Finally, Nate Hansen just joined us from the collegiate ranks—he attended The Bible Institute of Los Angeles, a.k.a. Biola—and he made his pro debut today. I don't know what kind of pitch repertoire he has, but he retired a lot of their good hitters, so he must be doing something right. Thus far, he's been quiet, so therefore I don't know a lot about him yet.

You know, I don't know if coaching is in my future, but one thing is for certain: I will **never** forget the talent disparity that exists in the baseball world. There are guys here who can't run, can't throw, can't hit, or can't play defense, and Mitch asked me about having a players-only meeting in Yuma to get us to play better. While I'm not saying that it wouldn't work, I had to question Mitch's motives. In every players-only meeting I've ever attended, it ends up being just a lot of hot air and clichés: "hey, guys, we have a good team"; "we just need to relax and play"; "we're pressing too much"; and "just everyone do his job." I told him that now as a coach, it's his nature to try to do *something* to get us going, but he has to realize that maybe we're just not good enough from a talent standpoint. All the meetings and pep talks and quality instruction in the world won't change one universal truth: you can't make chicken salad out of chicken shit.

Along these lines, there's been a lot of talk in the basketball world of coach Phil Jackson's role in the LA Lakers' back-to-back championships. Some say that Phil Jackson is a great coach because he took a talented, underachieving team to consecutive titles. Others believe, however, that he's simply riding a wave of the prodigious talents of Shaquille O'Neal and Kobe Bryant and that all the Zen teachings and meditation and books wouldn't do Jack Squat in post-Jordan Chicago or Vancouver. Who knows? It's probably a little from column A and a little from column B. As I've implied several times before, however, baseball is the one sport where a manager or coach has the least amount of influence. What I'm saying is that neither Joe Torre nor Felipe Alou nor Bobby Cox nor the venerable— and deceased—Connie Mack can make a bad team good.

On the bright side, I received an e-mail yesterday from ESPN radio. Evidently, Louise Cornetta, producer of Todd Wright's late-night talk show, got word of my writings on *Baseball America's* website, and she was impressed enough to invite me to be a guest on his show. I couldn't believe it. I will converse with him via telephone, and the show will air at about 3:45 AM EDT on Friday, June 29. I'm sure we'll talk about life in the minors, my writing, and my website, and I'm really looking forward to it. I don't know what, if anything, will come from it, but the publicity certainly can't hurt.

Finally, we are on our way to Yuma, where we play Friday night. That means we get basically all of Thursday off in the desert. Yeah!! Nothing like sitting in a hotel room for a day and a half. Actually, it's better than having gone back to Rohnert Park and then leaving at 10:00 AM

Thursday morning. The best way to handle a twelve-hour road trip is to get it over with as soon as possible. At least in Yuma, where there is nothing to do—trust me, I've tried—I can catch up on my writing and on my e-mails. Plus, being there will be monumentally better for my wallet; all that carousing can become quite expensive. Out.

Saturday, June 24, 2001 (11:45 PM)
Yuma

One for the good guys, and one for the bad guys. Last night, we were shut out 3-0. It was the fourth game in a row in which we scored two runs or fewer, and I think we had only five hits as a team. As if I couldn't illustrate to you how crazy and ephemeral this game can be, we proceeded to come out tonight against Jeff Sobkoviak, fourth in the league in ERA, and win 14-3. Go figure. We had scored a grand total of five runs in our four previous games combined, yet tonight, we scored six runs in one inning—twice. Sasa did most of the damage early, hitting a two-run homerun in the first inning and a three-run triple in the fifth, but other than that, we just chipped away at them. Regardless, it was nice to win a game for once.

Last night, we had our first bench-clearing incident of the year. Brad Moore, Yuma's starter, hit Monty in his first at-bat, and on the first pitch of his second at-bat, Moore "buzzed the tower." Monty took exception to the close shave and started out toward the mound. Alex Sutherland, Yuma's catcher, intervened, and Monty took out his frustration by shoving Sutherland. Those two then squared off but were separated by the players before any punches were thrown. No one's really sure if Moore meant to hit Monty, though according to Rico, who played with Moore last year and part of this year, he's a quiet, low-key guy. Most of Yuma's players didn't think it was intentional, for what it's worth, but Monty wasn't too pleased.

Baseball fights are funny. Even in such a non-enemy sport, the alpha-male can occasionally rear its ugly head, yet all the pushing and shoving amounts to is a bunch of hot air. Usually, the two parties who initiated the whole thing are immediately separated by other players, and they spend the rest of the time yelling at each other while being restrained. Last night was funny because Monty, a native Mexican, and Sutherland, a native Venezuelan, were cursing each other in Spanish, and I know enough Spanish to know that they were really pissed off at one another. Monty was suspended for three games, and that stinks for us because we are short-handed as it is. Oh well. Never a dull moment in the WBL.

We also picked up a new shortstop—shocking, huh? His name is John Storke, a Fresno State product, and I think he played in the Baltimore organization. He looks solid defensively, but we've had enough turnover this year that no one's job—especially a middle infielder's—is safe. Other than that, there's not a whole lot to report. I just figured that sitting in a hotel room in Yuma, freakin', AZ, is a most opportune time to do something productive. Out.

Tuesday, June 26, 2001 (2:30 PM)
Long Beach

Stop the presses. There must be some mistake: the Crushers have won three in a row. I believe that's called a winning streak, isn't it? We beat Yuma 7-5 on Sunday in a cleanly played, good professional game. Unfortunately, I can't say the same for last night. We won 5-3, but it was u-g-l-y UGLY. We committed five errors in all, with four of them coming early in the game. Yours truly, the Fat Kid, had two of them, both on bare-handed plays. The first one was a mental mistake, as I was playing very deep on right-handed pull hitter, and he dribbled one down the line. Not a third baseman in the world could have made that play, yet I tried to be Superman and squeeze blood out of a turnip. I ended up throwing the ball down the right field line. Later, their leadoff hitter bunted, and I don't know what happened. I grabbed the ball cleanly, but my throw sailed into the runner, allowing him to advance to second. Ouch. After a 22-game stretch with only one error, I've made three in the last three games. That's baseball for you.

Long Beach, though, bailed us out. In the top of the ninth, down 3-2, Patty led off with a single to center. Their pitcher, in an attempt to pick Patty off first, threw one that got away from the first baseman, so Patty advanced to second. Mac then bunted him to third, but the pitcher hand-cuffed the second baseman (who was covering first on the bunt) with his throw, causing him to drop it, so Mac was safe. After Cappy flew out weakly to right field, Rico hit a two-hopper basically right at their third baseman, and instead of a game-ending double play, Patty scored to tie the game. The *coup de grace* came three batters later when I came up with the bases loaded and the score tied. I hit a first-pitch fly ball right down the right field line, and their right fielder, who had run a long way, overran it, and it fell for a two-run double. Like I said, u-g-l-y. Scottie came on for the bottom of the ninth, and Cappy made an error on a routine play on the first batter of the inning. I was thinking, "Here we go again." Fortunately, Scottie was "bringin' the noise," and they didn't score.

Games like that make you think, "Jeez, what the hell am I doing still playing baseball." The game was just so pathetic, borderline embarrassing. The games that appear to be AA-caliber seem to be fewer and fewer, and the games that appear to be high school-caliber are becoming far too frequent. I had a former High Desert Mavericks teammate and road room-mate, Scott Glasser, come to the game with his girlfriend, and I was literally embarrassed that he had to watch the debacle. If I were a fan, I might have asked for my money back. Part of me, the realistic part, says that while I may not have AA-level ability, I know I could go to that level and not embarrass myself. No, I won't hit 20 homeruns or steal 20 bases, but I can make the routine play at third, and I can run the bases as if I've been there before, and I can hit the baseball. Some guys in this league, though.... It's just so frustrating, and I don't know how guys like JT, Scottie, and Pick—guys who have been in AA and AAA—can put up with it. I guess all they—and I—can do is just do their jobs as best they can and hope someone's watching. It's not likely, but you have to keep your focus or WBL baseball will drive you nuts. Out.

Thursday, June 28, 2001 (6:30 AM)
Rohnert Park

Yes, you read that right. It's 6:30 in the morning, and I am updating my journal. I had been writing—literally—certain journal entries while on the bus and typing them when we reached our destination, but I was unable to do so on our trip home from Long Beach. Several players were joking with me on the bus about how they can't sleep with my overhead light on while I'm indulging in my incessant writing, reading, and cross-word puzzle-doing, so I relented. Cancer, huh? You are probably thinking that I, having received little shut-eye on the bus, should be sleeping now since we have a game tonight, but I will as soon as I am finished. I was compelled to write while the information is still fresh in my mind.

The first topic is from the "Am I seeing what I think I'm seeing?" category: CP slept in a hammock. You heard me. Somehow, he managed to tie the two ends of it to the overhead luggage racks. If that's not a first in sports travel history, please tell me who did it originally. Every time some-one climbed over him to use the restroom, he just gave a shit-eating grin, implying, "Don't you wish *you* would have thought of this?" The other main topic was the speed at which the bussie was driving. We picked up a pitcher, Brian Rose, formerly with Yuma, and he and Rico drove up from LA in Rose's car. According to them, we were traveling at roughly 85 MPH when we passed them. Several of us, the Fat Kid included, were nearly thrown from our seats while the bussie negotiated mild turn after mild turn. Eventually, about an hour out of Rohnert Park, most of us were awake and discussing the celerity of the trip. I mentioned that since we were approaching the speed of light, we weren't aging very quickly, to which JT responded, "Is that why my arm doesn't hurt right now?" Also, Patty asked if we needed amusement park-style restraints to keep us

seated. I think in the back of all our minds was how much financial compensation we would receive if we survived a rollover. It was that bad.
Fortunately, though, he got us to church on time.

Finally, the guys were grilling Mac about his home state of Wyoming,
especially after he was trying to convince us how wonderful it is. I
explained to him that after driving across the state on I-80 last spring, I
wasn't too impressed. He said that I didn't see the good parts. He estimated that only 500,000 people live in the whole state, and Patty, who's
from San Diego, wondered what Mac could see in such a desolate place.
When Mac mentioned the hunting, fishing, and general outdoorsiness, I
told him that Patty is from the concrete jungle and that he has about as
much interest in that kind of stuff as I do—*nada*. Different strokes for different folks, right?

In my last entry, I lamented about the shoddy play in our opening
game in Long Beach. The second game couldn't have been a greater rever-
sal. It was perhaps the fastest, most cleanly played game I have been part of
in my three-plus years in the WBL. The contest was over in two hours and
fifteen minutes, and we won 3-1. There were few walks and only one
error—by their pitcher—and when those two totals are low, games tend to
move quickly. It was simply amazing to see the turnabout. I was joking
with BG after the game about how on certain nights in the WBL, a game
can look like a junior college game and on other nights a AAA game.
Tuesday night's game could have been a big league game, as far as I'm concerned, because it was so well played. Once again, the problem is that
games like that are far too infrequent.

Last night, we faced Mike Saipe—again—and he beat us—again. This
guy is good. He throws three quality pitches for strikes (usually if a pitcher
can throw *two*, he'll win in this league), and I have to say that he is probably the best starting pitcher I've seen in the WBL. The final score tonight
was 11-3, but it wasn't that bad. It was a 2-0 game until the bottom of the
seventh, when they scored four runs, in effect, with Saipe still going
strong, ending the game, and they tacked on five more in the eighth. We

pushed across three in the ninth, but obviously, too little, too late. According to Long Beach's first baseman, Saipe was supposed to go to Korea to pitch in the major leagues there, but the deal fell through at the last minute. Damn! Let's get him the hell out of here.

It's good to be home. We have a nice little stretch here in NorCal. We play six at home, then three in Chico, then six more at home, and despite having no days off, it's still pretty convenient. Even though we were blown out tonight, we have been playing better. Perhaps the marked increase in quality of play can be attributed to our having the same roster for about a week now. I don't know. Other than giving Mac a rest behind the plate with Monty, we've had a pretty consistent lineup; however, I overheard Tim and Mitch talking today about acquiring a new outfielder—Rocha has decided to go to Italy to play—and I think they're not too happy with Pritch's hitting right now. If he goes, we'll definitely miss him because he's a really good guy. Anyway, the Solano Steelheads are in town tonight, and they've been on a roll ever since they fired their manager, Bo Dodson. They kicked our ass 10 days ago, so hopefully it's payback time. Stay tuned. Out.

Sunday, July 1, 2001 (8:00 PM)
Rohnert Park

Tired. So very tired. We just played our tenth game in a row without a day off (and we have fourteen more to go), but I don't think that the games are the culprit. Perhaps it's the fact that I got about six hours of sleep last night and only about seven the night before. I know, I know, "Jeez, Bo, how much do you need?" Well, I need a lot, preferably ten hours. I know, I know, "Jeez, Bo, you're gonna sleep your life away," as my dad, the quintessential late-to-bed-early-to-rise guy, has told me *ad nauseum*. The problem is that I make a living with my body, and that body needs proper rest. I've often said that I have not the perfect "baseball body" but the perfect "body for baseball," a body that allows me to play everyday. Other than the lingering effects of my knee injury, which are easily alleviated with ibuprofen, I have never even come close, in my entire career, to missing a game for reasons other than stinking up the joint. I am immune to any type of sickness—at least in the summer—and I'm so slow afoot that I'll never pull a leg muscle. Furthermore, my dietary habits are such that I will *never* pull an oblique or abdominal muscle, a somewhat common injury among well-muscled athletes, bringing to mind a quote from former major leaguer and beer-guzzling redneck John Kruk: "I thought I pulled an abdominal muscle one time, but then I realized that I don't have any abdominal muscles."

Anyway, my little sister came to town for the game yesterday, along with some friends and relatives, so naturally the two of us had to head out to The Office to shoot pool and drink some Coronas. Later, we went to a late-night party and didn't get home until about 3:30 AM. We awoke at about 11:00 AM, and it wasn't too easy to get up. Hell, during the game, I was standing out in the hot sun thinking about how good it will feel to get some sleep tonight. I know, I know, "Jeez, Bo, can you really play when you're that tired?" Well, let's see: 3-5, with a double, three runs, and four RBI's. I think I did okay.

On the field, we took two of three from Solano. We lost the first one, as Pickford got hit around pretty good. Unfortunately, he hasn't rebounded from his arm problems, and after Tim pulled him from the game, he apparently decided that he had enough. According to Dolf, he was just so frustrated with his performances that he is going to quit. I don't know if that means he is retiring or just leaving for the time being or what. I do know that he is a great husband and father to his beautiful wife and adorable daughter, and the fact that he's in the WBL after spending time in AA and AAA has to be quite trying on his psyche. I really enjoyed talking with Pick, and I'm sorry to see him go, but once again, that's baseball for you.

So, Solano beat us, but we rebounded to win the second game 4-3 in ten innings, which I believe was our first extra-inning game of the year. I have to think that having your first extra-inning game occur in the 38th game is rare. Yesterday's game was a laugher. It was Jimmy Buffet Parrothead Night at Rohnert Park Stadium and a TV game, so the stands were pretty full. The only thing worse than losing by a lot at home is losing by a lot at home in front of a big crowd. Solano went up 2-0 in the second inning, but we answered with three in the bottom half and never looked back. The final score was 21-6. It wasn't as bad as the score would seem, but after we went up 12-3 in the fifth inning, Solano basically threw in the towel and pitched two position players to close out the game. All six teams in the league are going through the same long stretch, so saving pitching is imperative. You always hate to acknowledge defeat, but sometimes you have to sacrifice today in order to win tomorrow.

Today's game wasn't any better, at least for the opposition. St. George, who recently fired player/manager Billy Ashley and replaced him with second baseman Brian Grebeck, came to town for the first time this year, and we thumped them 17-7. Now that I think about it, these last two games are more like football scores than baseball scores. In fairness to them, they played a day game in St. George yesterday and arrived via bus, which arrived at about 12:00 PM for our 1:35 PM game. They didn't play with a whole lot of intensity, and even though as a team they usually don't, it still looked as if some of their guys were somnambulating around the field. For instance yesterday, the score wasn't indicative of the closeness of the game. We jumped up 10-3, but they rallied in the seventh to make it 10-6. We, however, scored three more in the bottom of the seventh to make it 13-6, and they conceded, deciding to bring in a backup catcher to pitch the eighth. Believe it or not, those blowouts are not as much fun as the reader would think. Yes, it's nice to pad your stats a little bit, but I prefer a closer, more hard-fought game, like the second Solano game. To be honest, those blowouts can be on the boring side, and I found myself half-jokingly saying to no one in particular, "Damn, I gotta go hit *again*?"

Today, we lost Cappy and Derek Fahs, a good relief pitcher who just hasn't been able to get over a nagging injury. In their place we picked up Keith Mitchell, Kevin's cousin, and Winter Adames, who is a Dominican-American. Also, we added a pitcher who remembered me from my California League days in 1997; Eric Newman—no, I didn't greet him with a Seinfeldian "Helllooooooo, Newman," though I was sorely tempted—has pitched in AA and AAA for the Padres and Diamondbacks over the past few years.

Also, from the roster department, I want to comment on our 32-year-old centerfielder, Chris Powell. To put it simply, the guy can play. I would have to say that he has been our team's first half MVP, leading the league in on-base percentage and in the top three in hitting. Plus, he plays a great centerfield. I never fully appreciated his game when he was with Tri-City in 1999 (he joined the team at about the All-Star break) and in 2000, but seeing him bust his ass every day, seeing him hustle down the line, seeing him battle pitchers, and seeing him starting rallies for us makes me glad he's on our side.

There is a dark side to him, though. We have taken to calling him things like "Dr. Jekyll" and "Bill Bixby" for his schizophrenic nature on the field when it comes to the umpires. CP is the "mild-mannered reporter" off the field, the kind of guy who loves his girlfriend and is always joking around and laughing in the clubhouse. For example, he had a pretty thick beard until recently, and I used to say, "CP, you can't get chicks with that beard." He'd say, "That's okay. I already got a great one, and that's all I need. I'm not about to screw it up." I'll tell you, though, he should greet each umpire with Bixby's warning to Jack Colvin, who played the reporter on *The Incredible Hulk*: "Mr. McGee, don't make me angry. You wouldn't like me when I'm angry."

The other night, he was leading off the bottom of the tenth inning against Solano, and he verbally disagreed with the umpire's borderline strike call on the first pitch. After mildly cursing him and taking his time getting back into the batter's box, the umpire told him to get ready to hit, which caused CP to take even more time. Then, the umpire instructed the pitcher to throw the ball with CP completely out of the batter's box, and even though the pitch was a good two feet high, the ump called it a strike. (A little known baseball rule is that if you fail to enter the batter's box when instructed, the umpire can call a strike no matter where the ball is pitched). Either CP didn't know about the rule or just didn't care, but he laced into the umpire with a tirade that would have made John McEnroe look like the Dalai Lama. Within five words, CP was ejected, but, fortunately, we were able to rally despite his absence. The next day, I asked him if he blacks out in Stevensonian instances like that, and he just smiled. It's amazing to see his transformation. Normally, you want a guy to keep his wits about him, especially in an extra-inning affair, but like McEnroe, who used his tantrums and profanity to hone his concentration, you have to take the good with the unpleasant. He can be my centerfielder any time.

Finally, somebody gave Sasa some Xenadrine before the game. Xenadrine is a legal, over-the-counter amphetamine that a lot of players use for a little "pick me up." The thirty-five-year-old Sasa, perhaps struggling a little bit today after our night game yesterday, took one or two, and even though he was our DH, he sprinted—literally, sprinted—from the bullpen to centerfield for the national anthem. I gave the guys in the bullpen a look of bewilderment when I saw him—bat in hand—tear off, and JT hollered to me that he had taken some Xenadrine. Later, JT came down to the dugout, and I said, "What's up with your boy Sasa?" and he said, "He took two Xenadrine, so now we have an amped up Chinaman on our hands." Too funny, but isn't that what the game is supposed to be? Out.

Monday, July 3, 2001 (11:45 PM)
Rohnert Park

Mutiny. As I mentioned earlier, when you hear this word, you usually think of *The Bounty* and/or Henry Hudson. Rarely do you associate it with sports, but today, mutiny almost ensued. I got to the field at about 3:40 PM for our 4:00 PM stretch today, and on my way into the clubhouse, Pritch told me that Tim Ireland (Skipper) put Tim Scott (Scottie) on the "suspended" list because Tim didn't show up for PFP's (baseball jargon for 'pitchers' fielding practice'). Why Skipper called for a mid-season PFP session is beyond me, but he did. Here are the stories that were presented to me by various sources after I entered the clubhouse: 1) Scottie didn't report for PFP's; 2) Skipper suspended him for it; 3) Scottie asked for his release. Scottie had cleaned out his locker and left the premises when Skipper walked into the clubhouse and yelled, "Anyone else want out? Anyone want to be traded or released? Come on!" and then he slammed his office door. I had no idea what was going on, and all I had received was hearsay. Most of the veterans, though, were talking about refusing to play tonight because they felt Scottie had been treated unfairly. Nevertheless, we all convened in centerfield for our stretching routine when we started discussing the situation. I spoke up and said that we owe it to the Fletchers (the owners) to come out and play hard no matter who our manager is and that I would have a hard time giving in to mob mentality. One player agreed with me but said that if we, as a cohesive unit, went to the Fletchers with our grievances, they would consider replacing Tim with someone else. All the while, Mitch was in the office speaking with the Fletchers, and when he was finished, we summoned him to the meeting. Mitch is the ultimate "players coach," and any time someone feels that he has been wronged by Skipper, Mitch sides with the player. In a matter of minutes, Skipper appeared, and then the meeting really took off.

Skipper first asked if anyone had heard first-hand the conversation between himself and Scottie, and JT—incidentally, Scottie's road roomie—mentioned that he heard Skipper tell Scottie to get into his office. According to Skipper, Scottie responded with a disrespectful comment of some kind. Skipper then explained to all of us—again—that our liking him is very low on the list of his daily concerns, and he is fine with that. He admitted that he can be an asshole at times, and in fact, most of the time, teams do **not** like him, but it is because of his abrasive nature that he has been a successful manager. Getting players to do things that they don't necessarily like to do, as a matter of course, sometimes requires an asshole-like nature.

Skipper asserted that Scottie had been late or absent several other times this season, and that because Scottie has big league time, he cut him some slack. Skipper did this because he felt that we, as a team, would be resentful to him for giving Scottie preferential treatment, and when he told this to us, we, basically said that as long as Scottie continues to throw 94 MPH fastballs by hitter after hitter and save all the close games that he is being paid to save, we don't care if he shows up at 9:00 PM. Skipper didn't know we felt that way, and that is why Scottie is still on the team. I don't know what transpired on the telephone between Scottie and Skipper after our meeting, but the bottom line is that we have our closer back, and we needed him tonight to shut down the Pioneerzz in the ninth with a 3-2 lead. He did.

In a situation like today, something I've never been a part of, professionalism is the key, I think. I don't know about the other guys, but I really respected Skipper for standing in front of us and hearing our side of the story, stuff like he has been disrespectful to players at times and that he should not have talked to a BLT (big league time) guy like he did. He apologized for any negative comments he made that weren't meant to be heard, though adding that on certain days, he can't stomach watching us play. In that sense, I agree with him because we can play some downright lousy baseball. A few other guys, Mitch included, threw in their two cents, and eventually, all was resolved. At the end Skipper told us that a team from Korea was coming soon to a game to look at Scottie, saying that he has been "shopping" Scottie all over the world. The fact that Scottie chose to leave was, in Skipper's opinion, detrimental to Scottie's future because Skipper is in the process of trying to move him.

Skipper also felt that Scottie doesn't want to be here anymore, and if that is indeed the case, it is certainly understandable. Scottie is, as I mentioned in spring training, virtually unhittable, and despite being 34, he can still get people out at the AAA level. In fact, Shane Monahan of Solano, who played with Scottie last year in AAA Indianapolis (Reds), said that Scottie was throwing "phantom balls" and that hardly anyone hit him. Unfortunately, a managerial change with Cincinnati's big league team left Scottie out in the cold, and he was therefore not invited to spring training. The Reds' loss became the Crushers' gain, that's for sure. He has a ridiculous ERA, something like 0.75, and I'll bet he has at least 24 strikeouts in maybe 13 innings pitched. I'm sure Scottie's becoming more restless by the day, wondering when *someone* is going to offer him a real baseball job. He has earned a ticket out of the WBL, and the fact that it hasn't happened yet has to be weighing on his mind.

My take on the whole situation is this, and at this point in my journal, I feel as if I've said it 1000 times: I don't care who my manager is. Just put me at third base everyday and leave me alone. Give me my batting practice—and early work when possible—and my groundballs everyday, and I'll give you a solid, if unspectacular, professional offensive and defensive third baseman every day for as long as the season goes. I don't need constant validation and coddling. Certainly, once in a while a compliment is nice to hear, but I never hang on a manager's every word. My mom, once again bless her heart, will ask me from time to time what the manager says to me, and I always give her the same answer: "Nothing." In fact, I think most players will say that you should avoid as much off-the-field contact with the manager as possible, as bad tidings—"you've been traded, sold or released"—come from him far more often than good ones, such as, "You're going to an organization."

I'm curious to see where we go from here in terms of Skipper's relationship with us. Yes, there has been a lot of turmoil due to his incessant tinkering with the roster, but it's only because he is trying to find players. He doesn't—I sincerely hope not—take a sadistic pleasure in releasing players left and right, and I presume all he cares about is winning. After all, that's what the Fletchers hired him to do. It looks as if the team is stuck with him. I'm not saying I'm right, but if more of our players thought like I did, we wouldn't have any problems. Unfortunately, one of the most inherently difficult, if not *the* most difficult, aspect of managing is trying to meld 22 different egos, backgrounds, and personalities into one cohesive unit. I hope we can put all this nonsense behind us and continue to play ball. After tonight, we have the second best record in the league, which isn't too shabby considering our lack of talent. We face the Chico Heat—in Chico—in two days, and we better all be on the same page for them. Out.

Sunday, July 8, 2001 (5:45 PM)
Rohnert Park

I apologize to you, the reader, and to myself for the delay in this entry, but I can explain. As you know, we went back to my old stomping grounds to take on the Chico Heat on July 4-6, and I had a full docket of activities. Therefore, my writing took a little bit of an All-Star break, which is strangely coincidental since the end of the Chico series marked the end of the first half of the season. For the first time in four years, though, there was no WBL All-Star game—I'd like to think I'd have represented the North—so there was no midseason break. Hang with 'em.

Going into this year, I had spent exactly half of my pro career wearing a Chico Heat uniform. I will be the first to admit that had I not joined the Heat when I did, I may be out of baseball right now. It was only through the effort and faith of former manager Bill Plummer that allowed me to become a productive hitter because God knows that no one else ever told me anything worthwhile about hitting. It was through his tutelage alone that I have been able to play baseball professionally on three other continents and been able to extend my career by posting quality numbers. In that aspect, I will be forever grateful to Plummer and the Heat. However, twenty years from now, long after I've hung up the cleats, I'm certain that

I will remember Chico in the same way that a person remembers a steamy, passionate love affair: I couldn't get enough at the time, but once it was over, it was over.

I was quite anxious about the reception awaiting me for the first game back, and I was a little upset, but not surprised, at owner Steve Nettleton's, as well as his right-hand man Jeff Kragel's, failure to greet me. Apparently, Steve isn't too happy, for whatever reason, that my picture still appears on *Baseball America's* website in a Heat uniform. Oh, well. And as for Charley, he has gone so far as to warn one of their players that a fine may be imposed if he talks to me during the game. I really think that Charley feels threatened by my presence in Chico. Third base has been the least productive position in their potent lineup, with the exception of catcher, this year, and the fact that I had a damn good first half makes Charley look like he was a fool for letting me go. Believe me, I was proud as a peacock to see my stats on the scoreboard for that first game: .364, 1 HR, 39 RBI's. I had several people—both friends and fans—tell me throughout the series that Charley was stupid for getting rid of me, and that was nice to hear. As for the introduction of my first at-bat, I would say there was a "smattering" of cheers and no boos, with the cheers coming predominately from the host family section and from the 16-year-old girl section. No surprise there.

You see, one of the greatest jobs in independent league baseball fell into Charley's lap with Plummer's leaving, and the problem is that since he doesn't know Jack Squat about baseball, he has to assert himself in other ways, like getting rid of an All-Star third baseman, to show that he's in charge. The fact that such a petty feud exists at all between Charley and me is a prime example of his small-mindedness. I think the thing he's most worried about, though, is losing his job when Steve wakes up and realizes that Charley is a monarchical figure at best on that team. I think about how Plummer ran things and how he was the first to get on a player if he screwed up in some way—bad baserunning, missing a cut-off man, etc.— but I can't remember Charley *ever* critiquing someone's on-the-field mistake. When a manager lets little things slide, before long, the players recognize that and don't take it upon themselves to master the nuances of the game. Because Plummer would get on the highest paid veteran and lowest paid rookie with equal fervor after a mental mistake, I think we were a more solid fundamental team under the Plummer regime.

After the games, I went out on the town, as is customary in Chico, and I saw why I'm glad I'm now a Crusher. The bar/nightclub scene in Chico is about as exciting to me as watching paint dry. It's so "tired." I did the whole going-out thing for three years, and let's just say I'm happy I'm no longer there; I saw some of the same people I saw when I first arrived in Chico three years ago. Time to turn the page. Both nights, rather than staying in the team hotel, I stayed with Greg and Anita Miller, my old host family. They were the one bright spot in an otherwise boring return. Their son, Scott, long the "little chubby guy," has made a conscious effort to get in shape for his freshman year of high school, and he has lost thirty-plus pounds in doing so. He works out daily and eats right as well. I don't know if I had anything to do with his attitude, but if I did, I'm glad that he is reaping the benefits. After all the Millers had done for me in Chico, I could never begin to pay them back financially, so if I had a positive influence on Scott, I'd consider it to be my version of remuneration. Unfortunately, we were there in the middle of the week, so Greg had to work; therefore, during the day, Scott and I resumed the one-on-one *Scrabble* and cribbage games we used to play all the time. The next time we are in Chico, though, it will be the weekend, so hold on to your hats.

We actually beat the Heat 5-4 in the first game in front of 4,400 fans. It was somewhat surreal. We were decided underdogs, and we took a 2-0 lead into the bottom of the seventh. They scored four to make it 4-2, and then I drove in the tying run in the top of the eighth, and the Milkman (Oglesby) drove in the go-ahead run. After holding them scoreless, we took the field in the bottom of the ninth nursing the 5-4 lead. Scottie closed the door, and ironically, I fielded the last out, a high infield popup by Jon Macalutas, the Heat player currently living with the Millers.

Naturally, we kicked the ball around in the second and third games, which the Heat won 8-5 and 4-3, respectively. We hung in there for all three games, which was good to see, but we just can't seem to get over the hump. It's the story of the 2001 Crushers: so close, yet so far away.

All in all, I would say that I am satisfied with the first half of the season. I finished with a .360 BA (4th in the league), a .470 OBP (4th in the league), and 42 RBI's (5th in the league). No, I don't expect to maintain the BA and RBI pace over the second half of the season, but I'd like to, obviously. It is just so different being on a .500-level team after spending the last four years—including 1997, when I was on the California League champion High Desert Mavericks—on the best team in the league. I get so frustrated when we play like a bunch of college kids, myself included at times, but what can I do or say? Nothing. It's pretty much impossible to improve a skill—hitting, fielding, or pitching—during the season, so the general manager must find guys who are already proven at their positions. We just aren't that good from a talent standpoint. We are last in the league in hitting and fourth (of six teams) in pitching. Do I need to mention again how our continuously lousy defense negatively affects our pitching staff's numbers?

The problem is that the Fletchers will *not* do anything illegal. They, unlike other WBL organizations, refuse to pay players under the table, and because of that, we can't get the big dogs that the other teams have. People ask me if anything financially shady goes on in Chico, and I always give the same answer: not that I know of. I was always a "Limited Service" guy, as opposed to an established veteran (usually a AA or AAA) guy, so I never got any dirty money. If the veterans were getting it, I certainly wasn't privy to it. There were rumors about it, but I couldn't substantiate them. Certainly, if you don't get the talent, you won't win many games, as we are finding out. Tim, I'm sure, feels somewhat handcuffed by the Fletchers' strict adherence to the rules, but I think the Fletchers prefer a solid, finan- cially stable, rules-following organization to an illegally run cash cow. As long as both parties understand that you can't win a lot of games with inferior players, then their working relationship should be fine. I'm not saying that the Fletchers *can't* pay players more; it's just that until they do, they will have to settle for fielding a mediocre team. Out.

Monday, July 9, 2001 (11:00 PM)
Rohnert Park

Well, my frustration has reached its boiling point. I would like to think that I am a pretty upbeat, positive guy, but enough is enough. We were swept—at home—by a team that was 15 games under .500 entering the series (15-30). Our arch-nemesis, Mike Saipe, beat us for the fourth time this year on Saturday, but I really don't have a problem with that. Sometimes you just run into a buzz saw. But it's not so much that we lost the other two games as it is *how* we lost: poor baserunning, poor infield/outfield communication, and missed signs. One of my favorite sports quotes is one from Orel Hershiser: "When you focus on execution rather than results, it's nearly impossible to fail." What that means is if you go about doing your job correctly, if you take care of the little things, if you hone your fundamentals on a daily basis, then you will be successful, both as a team and as an individual. Take pitching as an example. Say a pitcher hangs an 0-2 breaking ball that the hitter smokes right at the shortstop for a line-drive out versus throwing an 0-2 fastball six inches off the outside corner that the hitter hits a broken-bat single just over the first baseman's head. In Situation A, he executed poorly but received a favorable result. In Situation B, he executed well but received an unfavorable result. Hershiser is saying that over the long haul, a pitcher will have more success if he focuses on executing his pitches properly and not worrying about the results. I agree.

Three questions: Does a high school kid have the ability to read the signs from the third base coach? Does a junior college kid have the ability to field the practice groundballs between innings cleanly and throw the ball to first accurately? Does a Division I college team have the ability to communicate properly with each other on a short fly ball? Unfortunately, I cannot convey sarcasm through the written word, but the answer to all three questions is a resounding "YES!" We are a professional team (though only because we happen to be paid), and we routinely foul up all three areas of the game. The problem is that there is no accountability. I'm surprised at Tim's lackadaisical attitude to such basic blunders. I'm at the point where I think there should be a $20 fine for a missed sign. The other stuff, like throwing the ball over the first baseman's head between innings, makes the player look like a damn Little Leaguer, but missing signs hurts the *team*. I don't know how strict Tim has been in the past when it came to missing signs, but he needs to put his foot down. I mean, it's not that hard, is it, to read signs? I don't know if I've ever missed one. We had one guy miss the same steal sign three times in one at-bat!! I just don't get it.

Look, I am not asking every hitter to bat .300 or every infielder to make highlight-reel plays nightly or every outfielder to take homeruns away. To do those things requires a certain amount of talent, and as I lamented yesterday, we just don't have it. But it takes *no* talent, none whatsoever, to do these things I just mentioned. It's about pride. It's about professionalism. Don't think for one minute, though, that I am Mr. Perfect fundamentally. I've made a few subtle mental errors at third base, things that the untrained baseball eye would never detect. I've also failed to take the extra base at times as a baserunner. Because there is no accountability factor, however, it is human nature to slack off a bit mentally. Just as a winning team's attitude has a snowball effect in the positive direction, a losing team's attitude can make everyone play below each player's ability level at times.

We have now lost five in a row, making it the third time this season that we lost four consecutive games. In my three years in Chico we lost four in a row once (in 1998), and I can't remember any other time that we lost more than two in a row. There was immense pressure to win, and while such pressure can cause tension in the clubhouse at times, the opposite corollary is that it fosters a winning mind-set. Guys take extra batting practice. Guys know the signs. When you are expected to win, you take it upon yourself to do everything you can to achieve that end. However, on this club, I don't know if the guys care that we stink on ice.

Now, here's a lesson for you non-sports fans out there: You can't expect to improve during the game. Improvement, both individually and team-wise, has to occur in a practice setting. If your batting stroke is a little bit off, then get your ass out to early BP because you can't expect to correct the flaw, whether it's mental or physical, while your batting in a game situation. If you're in a "fielding slump" (yes, that kind of slump happens, too), then grab a coach and have him hit you groundballs until you've solved the problem.

I remember hearing about how John Wooden rarely talked about winning; rather, he focused all his efforts on getting his UCLA team to practice properly. If that thought process doesn't epitomize Hershiser's quote, I don't know what does. Wooden knew that if he had his players ready to play mentally and physically come game time, he would attain the desired results. Along these lines, Bobby Knight said, "Everybody wants to win. What's important is the willingness to *prepare* to win." In any sport you have to be ready to play instinctively when the game starts. That, in essence, is what practice is for. You can't be thinking about different things out there; everything has to happen naturally. The bottom line is that until we become better practice players, we won't become better game players.

OK. Enough bitchin' and moanin', although I do feel better now. We have the Chico Heat coming to town tomorrow, and as impressive as their hitters are—eight of their nine regulars are batting over .300—their pitching is even better. My batting average has taken a slight nosedive, which was to be expected since I don't consider myself to be .360 hitter, but I wouldn't say that I'm in a slump, either. Two of three pitchers who Long Beach started pitched pretty well, and I didn't get a whole lot to hit. Regrettably, the Heat's staff doesn't offer much in the way of relief. Our five-game skid may not be over any time soon. Out.

Wednesday, July 11, 2001 (6:00 PM)
Rohnert Park

A pain in the neck. That's what I woke up with on Tuesday morning. I don't know what I did while I was sleeping, but my neck was as stiff as a board all day. I got to the park for early BP, and I got some light treatment from Keith, our trainer. Unfortunately, it didn't feel any better during regular BP, so Dolf called his wife Cathy, a physical therapist, to have her look at it. She isolated the problem—a vertebra was slightly out of line, causing a pinching when I looked to the right—and she and Keith put me through a series of treatments. All in all, they did a great job, Cathy especially, but my neck was still quite stiff during the game. I was unable to turn my head as much as I would have liked while I was hitting left-handed, and fielding groundballs was no picnic, either. As luck would have it, not one groundball came my way, and somehow, I managed to get one hit, an RBI-double, in three at-bats from the left side. Today, it wasn't too much better, but I was able to hit an RBI-double and a solid, line drive single. Maybe I should put a permanent kink in my neck.

As for hitting right-handed, I felt more comfortable than I did lefty. The lack of mobility that prevented me from easily seeing the pitcher from the left side did not exist from the right side, so the kink didn't affect me. Also, whenever I take early BP, I hit only right-handed. I get enough swings in game situations to keep my left-handed swing sharp naturally, but with so few right-handed at-bats, I really need to keep it ready for game situations. Well, Mitch has had me crowd the plate (stand extremely close to it, probably six inches closer than I normally do) from the right side and just try to make the soft-throwing lefties rethink what they want to do with me. The results thus far have been outstanding. My right side has always been weaker than my left, in part because I have never been proficient at hitting the ball to right field. To make matters worse, lefties tend to throw pitches that are on the outer half of home plate, and trying to hit those pitches where I'd like to hit them—left field and center field—usually results in getting. out.

With my new approach, though, the outside pitch is now much easier to hit to center field. Of course, I'll be slightly more susceptible to the extreme inside pitch, but the lefties in this league rarely throw the ball hard enough to make me worry a whole lot about it. In my last four or five at-bats right-handed, I have felt as comfortable as ever. Even better, with such little margin for error, my standing "right on top of the dish" will automatically cause the pitcher some anxiety. Tomorrow we face lefty Scott Navarro, who at the moment is a league-best 8-1 and is also leading the league in ERA. If I struggle with him tomorrow, I'm not going to revert back to my old ways; remember, good pitching stops good hitting. I just have to be mature enough to understand that not every lefty in this league is as good as he is. I believe that you have to develop your own personal hitting approach for the typical pitcher and not worry about the anomalies.

Incidentally, we split the first two games with the Heat, a 2-1 loss yesterday and a 15-5 win today, which ended our six-game losing streak. Now, I have meant all year to discuss one of the most unique parts of an evening home game at Rohnert Park Stadium, and that is the "Beverage Batter."

Before the game, a batter is selected from the opposing team's lineup, and if he strikes out within the first seven innings of the game, all beverages—beer included—are half-priced for 15 minutes. The funniest part of it all is that whenever the Beverage Batter begins his stroll from the dugout to home plate, the PA guy has the sound of a beer being poured in a glass transmitted over the loud speakers. The Pavlovian response from the crowd is priceless. All of a sudden, throngs of people stand up and begin cheering wildly as the batter gets into the batters box. Each strike is greeted with a lustful howl of delight while each ball results in questions about the umpire's heritage. Once the count reaches two strikes, everyone stands and claps in anticipation of the third strike. If the poor batter does strike out, a huge roar emanates from the crowd, and immediately, human beings from ages five to ninety-five sprint to the concession stands to cash in on the discount. I think back to growing up on the farm and the response of our cows when I would bang one of the plastic feed buckets against a wall as a signal to call them in from the pasture at feeding time. After about three or four "clunks," I would hear a series of far-off "moooos," and within two minutes, the cows would be running for the feed trough. With all due respect to our loyal fans, their reaction isn't too much different. Somewhere, Pavlov is smiling. Out.

CHAPTER 6

▼

CUBAN, ANYONE?

Friday, July 13, 2001 (2:00 PM)
Long Beach

Wow, where do I begin? Let's start with the best part: we took two of three from the hated Heat. Last night, we won 8-2, but the game was tied at 2-2 going into the bottom of the seventh. For once, though, it was the other team's error that broke the game open. Navarro fielded a routine sacrifice bunt, and Craig Daedelow, their second baseman, was perhaps a step late in getting to first base, causing Navarro to hesitate on his throw for a split-second. His throw went down the right field line, and our runners advanced to second and third. Eventually, they, and one other runner, scored, and we tacked on three more in the eighth. It was a nice win for the Crushers.

I'd be remiss if I didn't mention the most important event of the last two days: the arrival of two Cuban players who had recently defected. Apparently, they had been working out in Juarez, Mexico, and Tim convinced them to come to Rohnert Park. I think they both played for Havana's *Industriales* team in the Cuban league, for which they received approximately $25 per month. As is customary for defected Cubans, they become free agents and can go to the highest bidder among the major league teams. Atypically of Cuban defectors, though, these two guys, pitcher Mayque Quintero and second baseman Evel Bastida, are not considered top-notch talents. According to reports, Quintero was offered $1,000,000 by somebody upon arrival to the States, but he refused it, the thought being that once he could prove his stuff, he could earn far more than that.

So, the Cubans arrived on Wednesday, but neither of them played. Yesterday, however, Quintero started and Bastida played second base. Wednesday night, *Fox Sports Bay Area* aired a small piece on the two Cubans, giving the Sonoma County Crushers more national TV exposure than they had ever received in their previous six years combined. For Thursday's game a horde of scouts and media representatives gathered for the game. Quintero pitched three innings, and despite not having faced a batter in over two weeks, he threw quite well. He showed a lively fastball and an above average curveball. He gave up one run in the three innings, but he also made several quality pitches—against a very formidable Heat lineup, mind you—to work out of some jams. Bastida had roughly four groundballs hit to him at second base, and he fielded them all flawlessly and smoothly, causing me to yell to him, "Oye, las manos de algodon!" (Hey, hands of cotton!). He didn't do anything exceptional offensively, but the lefty showed a pretty good eye in battling a tough left-handed pitcher in Navarro. I don't know how long we'll have them, but I hope it's as long as possible.

One observation about the Cubans is that they play with a lot more emotion than their American counterparts. I remember when I went to

Australia two years ago and how the Cuban team played. They talk a lot and throw the ball around the infield after an out for seemingly an eternity. Our players, partly due to getting our ass kicked by a noticeably better team, were complaining about their mannerisms, saying that it was "bush league." I wanted to say, "Look. These guys don't make Jack Squat financially in Cuba, they live in a Communist country with little freedom, and they have virtually no chance of leaving their native country (unlike the Dominicans, Puerto Ricans, the Colombians, et. al., who, if good enough, can sign with a major league organization) to chase the riches of America. They get maybe one chance a year to leave temporarily the Castro regime, so of course they are going to play with a ton of emotion; you would, too.

Also, the way the Cubans interact on the field with one another is decidedly un-American. Now, I realize that when you spend three days on a raft, as Evel and Mayque did in December, with someone, there is an intrinsic bond that will probably exist for an eternity, but again, I saw it in Australia, too. Quintero fell behind in the count to two consecutive batters, causing Bastida to yell, "*Arriba!*" which means, "On top!" (Get ahead of the hitter!) Quintero didn't hear what he said the first time, so Bastida yelled it again. The only time you hear an American infielder talk to an American pitcher is to tell the pitcher who's covering second base on a comebacker to the mound or to discuss the pitcher's responsibility in a bunt situation. This may be a stretch, but I think it may have to do with whole socialism/capitalism idealisms. The socialist Cubans genuinely pull for one another, believing that the whole can be no greater than the sum of its parts. A capitalistic American, especially a minor leaguer, tends to feel that the surrounding players on the field, while necessary, are of no major advantage to his advancement to the big leagues and that it's an "every man for himself" situation. I know I may be reaching, but throw me a bone, will you?

Off the field these guys speak very little English, which naturally allows me to practice my Spanish until my heart's content. They seem to be pretty impressed with my grasp of their language, so they are willing to go back and forth with me. Monty has been their interpreter for the press thus far, and that makes me a bit envious because I wish I were that good. Alas, I shall continue my pursuit of bilingualism. Also, Mac and I have been playing the card game Casino during free time in the clubhouse, and I noticed Quintero watching us. Therefore, I explained to him the rules of the game, and something tells me that before long, he'll be playing, too. Bastida then performed a lengthy and impressive card trick for us—I was the guinea pig—and upon his revealing of the hidden card, I yelled, "*Ladron*!!" (Thief!), and everyone was howling.

As I said, I don't know how long we'll have these guys, but they did make the trip with us to Long Beach, so that's a good sign. I told them last night, as we were packing for our road trip, that I welcome them to America and that they *have* to stay with us for the whole season because we need them. They just laughed. I'm sure that figures of dollar signs are dancing in their heads right now, and that has to be a pleasant thought in light of the financial situation from whence they came. Inevitably, the scouts and agents and other hangers-on will be coming around, so we best enjoy them while we have them.

Now, I'd like to extend a long overdue "thank you" to my mom and dad for raising me not to be racist. You see most American ballplayers are very standoffish to the foreigners who populate our national pastime because these "imports" are taking the jobs that "belong" to the Americans. Fortunately, mom and dad reared me to treat people as equals, regardless of skin color, nationality, or mother tongue. I don't give a damn if you're a Martian; if you can help me win a championship, c'mon! Out.

Saturday, July 14, 2001 (1:15 PM)
Long Beach

This one will be short and sweet. I would like to comment on the Japanese media in the wake of what happened recently in Seattle. For those of you who aren't as into baseball as others, Ichiro Suzuki is the 27-year-old Seattle Mariners rookie from Japan—the first Japanese-born position player to make it to the American major leagues—who was a seven-time batting champ and seven- or eight-time Gold Glove winner in the Japanese major leagues. He is easily the midseason favorite for the AL Rookie of the Year and quite possibly an MVP candidate as well. Unfortunately, Ichiro is hounded daily by a Japanese media contingent that looks like a flock of buzzards on a buffalo carcass. Well, apparently, a news crew went to Ichiro Suzuki's townhouse the other day, and he almost ran over one of the members as he backed out of his garage. That was the final straw. He and Kazuhiro Sasaki, the Mariners' closer, said that they will no longer speak with the Japanese press. For a country as enthralled with the success of one of its own as Japan is, such a moratorium could be devastating. Mariners games are often broadcast live in Japan, in spite of the fact that they appear on TV early in the morning. Ichiro is basically Marco Polo, Charles Lindberg, and Babe Ruth (the ambassador, not the slugger) all rolled into one. I don't know how long the freeze will last, but it could be for a while.

Because of this situation in the Pacific Northwest, Steve Wendt, one of our radio guys, is anticipating a spillover effect with the Japanese media in Rohnert Park. As I mentioned before, Makoto Sasaki had a damn good big league career in Japan and is still pretty much a household name there. Therefore, if last night was a harbinger of things to come, Sasa may become the Ichiro of the WBL. There were three cameras and at least seven media reps around him all game, and two guys with one camera came onto the bus after the game to film Hide Koga, our Japanese coach, just sitting in his seat (Sasa had already left with a friend). The scene of two guys using one camera to film a coach begged the question, "How many Japanese does it take to shoot some footage with one camera?" Well, Mitch, at the very moment he saw the two Japanese guys on our bus, yelled for them to basically get the hell out of there. Mitch wiggled his way past them to get into his seat, and still the cameraman kept shooting Hide (pronounced like Heidi), much to his chagrin. I was sitting in the very front seat spouting out my limited Japanese, words like "sayonara," "wasabe," "samurai," and "arigato" (thank you) to the Japanese guys. Well, we were just about ready to pull out, and they still hadn't disembarked, so Mitch started shouting out Spanish/Japanese phrases, stuff like, "El gato arigato" to expedite the process. The poor guys obviously had no idea what Mitch was saying, but the guys on the bus were laughing our asses off. Eventually, they exited, probably because Mitch basically scared them away.

We play tonight and then tomorrow afternoon in Long Beach, and then we have a day off on Monday, our first one in 24 days. Excellent! We've won three in row (5-3 last night) and been playing pretty well. Let's keep it rollin'. Out.

Tuesday, July 17, 2001 (11:45 PM)
Rohnert Park

Can you believe it? Six in a row. Six *wins* in a row, that is. Right now, we are the hottest team in the league, and unlike our first big winning streak of the year (in May, when we won six straight), we are beating teams as opposed to winning due to the opposition's mistakes. Our infield defense—or more apropos, our middle infield defense—is without question the reason. Yes, Bastida has played well, even though he has only started one game for us, but more importantly, Monte has been outstanding at second base. As a former third baseman/shortstop/catcher, he has been the pleasant surprise of our team in the second half. He has also been hitting the ball well, too. And Winter Adames, our diminutive shortstop, has been unbelievable, even more so when you consider that he joined us right out of college, and a Division III college at that. I mentioned before that we would be roughly 5-8 games better in the standings if we could improve up the middle, and with the three guys we have there now, I feel like Carnac the Magnificent.

We swept Long Beach in Long Beach over the weekend, returning the favor for when they swept us up here. I have forgotten to mention how much I enjoy their manager/third base coach Steve Yeager. For those of you who don't remember, he was co-MVP of the 1981 World Series for the victorious Los Angeles Dodgers, and after a brief coaching stint in the Dodgers' minor league system, he was hired to lead the Breakers. Furthermore, if you have seen the movie *Major League* (with Tom Berenger, Charlie Sheen, Wesley Snipes, etc.), he played "The Duke," the Yankees intimidating relief pitcher. Steve told me that he also did all of the "baseball" stunts for Berenger, as Berenger "threw like an old woman." I asked him how much he made for the entire film, and well, let's just say that he did okay for himself. He is really a cantankerous old guy, but in a good way. He is constantly yelling at the umps when they miss a call and at his own players when they do something that he doesn't particularly like. In between innings, while I'm making my practice throws to first base, I'm always chewing on his ear about something, whether it was how he did against Steve Carlton's slider or how he did with the ladies. In regards to the latter subject, I asked him if we was married while he was in the big leagues, he replied, "Hell, no!!" I think that pretty much sums up how he did with the ladies. He was a lot of fun to chat with, and, unfortunately, we have only one more series with the Breakers. I'll miss him.

Today, the St. George Pioneerzz came into town, and we beat them 13-2. Chief gave us a sterling performance, throwing eight complete innings and allowing just the two runs. Chief is a neat kid. If you remember correctly, he is of Piute/Navajo heritage, and in fact, his "Indian" name is "Dancing Bear." One day in the clubhouse, I asked him where Indian names come from, and he told me that they're usually based on how you acted as a child. He was quite an animated kid, so his grandfather bestowed "Dancing Bear" upon him whereas his brother cried a lot as a youngster, so he received a name like "Singing Hawk," or something along those lines. Interesting, huh? Chief doesn't say a whole lot, but if you want to talk to him, he'll go back and forth with you. I can't believe Tim didn't keep him right out of spring training, but basically, Chief didn't throw all that great. Since we reacquired him, though, he has been awesome.

Finally, yesterday was our first off day in almost a month, and it was nice to relax a little. Our game in Long Beach on Sunday was at 1:00 PM, so we estimated that we'd get back around midnight. We probably would have except we blew a tire on the way home. That knocked us back about two hours, but we still got back around 2:30 AM. After checking my e-mail, I went to sleep around 3:30 AM and awoke at about 2:00 PM. I felt so good, and I felt even better today. My legs were rejuvenated. In what other line of work can an employer make you work 24 days in a row without a day off while incurring 14-hour bus trips in between? You know, unfair labor practices, sometimes-shoddy labor conditions, and meager pay—are we in a Laotian sweatshop? Obviously it's not *that* bad, and by the way, you can dispense with the Don Rickles comments. Anyway, the day off must have helped because we looked good today, and I really want to be playing well going into Chico on Friday. I was telling some of the guys that I want to win three straight one-run games in Chico. That would be my version of heaven. Out.

Thursday, July 19, 2001 (11:45 PM)
Rohnert Park

Let me start with a funny story. During BP today, Sasa and I were debating on who was going to hit first in our group. Since neither of us cared, I suggested "rock-paper-scissors" to decide. He won. Afterwards I asked him how to say that in Japanese, and he told me "guh" is rock, "pah" is paper and "chookie" (like 'bookie') is scissors. I spent the entire round yelling to Sasa "guh-chookie-pah" every time he hit the ball (I rearranged the words because Sasa said that's what they call the game in Japanese). He and Hide were laughing. My Japanese vocabulary has increased considerably since Sasa came to town. In addition to the ones I mentioned earlier, I now know the following words: "ee" (good), "dah-may" (bad), "okota" (pissed off), "ah-ho" (crazy), and "ha-nuk-so" (booger). I am not sure why I know the last one, but for a while, I was calling Sasa "wasabe," and he would answer "ha-nuk-so." I don't know if he was referring to me, though I certainly hope not. I think he was referring to the suddenly omnipresent media; evidently, he ranks the Japanese press right up there with encrusted globules of mucous. Sasa is funny. He knows a lot more English than he lets on because Mitch was golfing with him the last time we were in Yuma, and Mitch told us in the clubhouse that night, "Don't let this sonofabitch fool you. He knows every damn swear word in the book."

One day recently, I was shagging balls in the outfield during BP with Sasa, and I was asking him about Japanese stuff. For example, did you know that in Japan, the teams are named after corporations? When I first heard of the Japanese team the "Nippon Ham Fighters," I wondered, "What in Sam Hill is a Ham Fighter?" Well, the team's name is Nippon Ham—as they deal in, well, ham—and their nickname is "Fighters." Another team is the Yomiuri Giants, the team made famous by the Babe Ruth of Japan, Sadaharu Oh, and Yomiuri is a train-related company (though I'm not sure if they build them or operate them or whatever). Anyway, Sasa, when spoken to slowly, can basically understand and speak broken English with anyone. He also refers to himself as "old man," who has "no power" and "no speed." Hide is constantly on his case, telling him he should quit because he's no good anymore. Whenever I hear Hide berate Sasa, I automatically think of my Taiwan experience, where they believed that yelling at a guy will sufficiently motivate him all of a sudden to start playing better. Alas, I guess the old saying is true: "East is east, west is west, and never the twain shall meet."

On the field, we took two of three from St. George, though we were aided considerably by former Crusher shortstop John Storke, now St. George's shortstop. I think he made three errors yesterday and three more today. Some of the guys on the bench were saying that Storke was still a Crusher after all. Ouch! We didn't win pretty, but we won nevertheless. We're now "ready for the Heat," a double *entendre* meaning that we are

ready to take on the best team in the league because we're playing perhaps
our best baseball of the year and that we're ready to get out of this unbelievably cold weather. I'm serious; it's been damn chilly the last few nights.
Hell, I've hardly even been sweating during night games, and that's scary
because as you already know, I usually sweat like Homer Simpson at a
smorgasbord. The days here are very mild, and the nights, while good for
sleeping, are tougher to play in than the heat and humidity of Chico. I am
looking forward to resuming my profuse perspiration tomorrow night.

Personally, I haven't been hitting too well lately, as my average has
dropped probably ten or twelve points over the last week or so. I'm still
driving in runs—going into today, I was fourth in the league in RBI's—
but my constant barrage of singles is becoming frustrating. I wish the
baseball gods would reach down and touch me and turn me into a power
hitter, at least more so than what I'm doing now. In the last six games
against Long Beach and St. George, I think I went a combined 5-23, with
no extra-base hits, and it's times like these that test your maturity as a hitter. When you struggle, there are basically four reasons why: 1) The other
team is simply pitching you tough; 2) you're getting good balls to hit, and
you're not hitting them hard; 3) you're being either too patient—letting
too many good pitches go by and waiting for a perfect pitch—or too
aggressive—swinging at balls that are nearly impossible to hit hard; or 4) a
team has started pitching you a certain way, forcing you to alter your
approach. The latter one has happened to me recently.

Both Long Beach and St. George kept throwing me inside corner fastballs, and I normally take that pitch. Unless I'm looking for it, it's a very
tough pitch—for me—to hit hard. Part of me says, "OK, Bo, they keep
pounding you in, but these pitchers are not good enough to throw it there
consistently, so just hang in there, and before long, these pitchers will start
making mistakes over the middle of the plate." The other part of me of
me, however, says, "OK, Bo, every time you go up there, because you're
waiting for the pitches you're used to getting, you're always behind in the
count (0-1, 0-2, 1-2). You have to be more aggressive and maybe even

cheat a little—look for the ball on the inside corner and hammer it." It's a tough call. Like Ted Williams said, if you start swinging at pitches that aren't in your "happy zone," before long, the edges of your "happy zone" become blurred, and now you aren't sure *what* to swing at.

All I know is that Chico's pitching staff, even though I've actually done pretty well against them this year, is very good, so I better figure it out quickly. In consolation to myself, I do not feel as though I am a .360 hitter in this league (I finished the first half at exactly .360). I knew that my average would most certainly come down from that mark, but boy, I'd love to creep back up to at least the .350 mark by the end of the season. Jeez, wouldn't everyone? Out.

Monday, July 23, 2001 (1:00 AM)
Chico

Right now, I am sitting in my hotel room licking my wounds from a tough series. The Heat took two out of three from us, and I had a disappointing weekend. I actually hit a homerun—my second of the year—on Friday night, to the delight of some Chico fans, but we lost the game 20-4, I think. As I've said many times, losing 20-4 stings a lot less than losing 5-4; games like that just sometimes happen. When one team does everything right and the other team does everything wrong, the score will end up like that from time to time. In a one-run loss, though, you beat yourself up over wondering if there was anything else you could have done to turn the tide.

On Saturday night, my roomie, TD, threw like the TD of old. Even though his stats may not show it, he has really thrown the ball well in his last few outings. He got banged around pretty badly at the beginning of the season, which severely damaged his numbers, but he threw a peach of a game on Saturday night, limiting the Heat to only two runs through six innings. Remember what I said in early June about "riding the storm out" with him? I was 0-2 with three walks, so I would consider that a fair night for me personally, but we won 7-3. I like that last part. Sunday was the rubber match, and I *really* wanted to win this series. Chief gave up four runs in the first inning, but that was it. God, he pitched a great after that first inning, but, unfortunately, we could manage only one run against them, and that's how the score ended, 4-1. I was 0-4 with a walk, but I had three chances to drive in runners in scoring position and failed all three times. The worst part is that we had runners on first and second with nobody out in the ninth, and I grounded into a double play, effectively ending the game. The momentum we had just built was suddenly gone, and it was my doing.

Games like yesterday's, even for a guy like me who stays pretty calm and collected most of the time, really gnaw at you and make you question your ability. I'm continually amazed at how bipolar my perception of myself as a ballplayer is on a day-to-day basis. When we win and I have a good game, I think I'm a pretty good player. However, on a day like yesterday, I think, "What the hell am I doing still playing baseball?" Yes, the negative vibes go away by the next day, but my transient feelings nevertheless shock me. Mike Schmidt, in his book, *The Mike Schmidt Study*, talks about the "kinship" that professional baseball players have with each other. It's a "bond," if you will, that we all share, and it centers on the extremely frustrating nature of playing baseball for a living. Can you handle the highs? Can you handle the lows? Do you have the intestinal fortitude to bounce back after repeated failures? Can you turn a lousy yesterday into a productive tomorrow? If you can, then you can call yourself a professional because as I mentioned earlier this season, "These are the times that try men's souls."

On the brighter side, I have been enjoying my almost daily games of Casino with Mayque (pronounced "my-KAY), the Cuban pitcher. Anyway, I explained the rules to him about two weeks ago, and we've been playing each other tooth and nail since then. In fact, I'm even swearing at him in Spanish now whenever he wrongs me. *Que bueno!* He's a really congenial guy, and we trade barbs back and forth, all in good fun of course.

We usually play for two dollars a game, so no one is going to the poor house, but I love hearing his expressions. I told him today how unbelievably similar his actions are to those of Florida Marlins pitcher Vladimir Nuñez, a Cuban pitcher with whom I played in the Diamondbacks organization. They make the same gyrations and use the same "words of displeasure," and even Mac, a former D'back, noticed the similarities.

On another good note, Tim Scott signed a Triple-A deal with the Yankees. He got the phone call on the way to Chico on Friday, and everyone is very happy for him. When you lose your unhittable closer to an organization, your feelings are the same as if you heard that your mother-in-law just drove your new Porsche off a cliff (no, I didn't make that up, though I wish I could take credit for it). If anyone in this league deserved to be signed, it was Scottie. He is one of those born-again Christians, and he has no qualms about telling people about his life before and after his day of enlightenment. He was admittedly quite a hellion for the vast majority of his pro career, but now he is a model teammate, husband, and father. His son Preston is a great kid, and at seven-years-old, he appears to be following in his old man's footsteps athletically. Hell, the kid looks better in a uniform than most of our players. Anyway, to a man, we were all genuinely happy for Scottie and wish him nothing but the best.

Finally, we are leaving Chico in about four hours for Sacramento, where we will fly to Las Vegas. From there, we will commute to *The Oasis* in Mesquite, NV, for our series in St. George, UT. I can't decide what's better: leaving immediately after the game and driving through the night or flying. Either way, we'll get into Mesquite at about the same time, so I guess the latter way is better because we won't be on that damn bus. True, we won't get much sleep with our 6:00 AM departure, but most players will do *anything* to avoid a 12-hour bus trip. Unfortunately, we will be returning to Rohnert Park via bus, which will give us only half a day off on Thursday. There were rumors of $120 tickets for one-way flights from Vegas to Sacramento, but who has $120 lying around? Wait a minute: maybe I can try to win it on the Blackjack table.... On second thought, after my last attempt to become rich by gambling, I nearly starved to death. Better get on that freakin' bus, huh? Out.

Wednesday, July 25, 2001 (12:15 AM)
Mesquite

I just got back from eating a $1.49 breakfast—you gotta love meal prices in gambling towns—at the *Casablanca*. Technically, since I *am* the Fat Kid, I had to order two breakfasts, but my tab was still only $2.98. Now, the will power issue comes into play: do I write or do I gamble? I will write for now, but after I finish this entry, I don't know if I can resist the myriad sounds that call to me like a Siren in the night. We shall see.

Two days ago (Monday) we had the day from Hell. We awoke at 5:30 AM in Chico, left at 6:00 AM, arrived in Sacramento at 8:20 AM, boarded the plane at 10:00 AM, landed in Las Vegas at 11:30 AM, left for Mesquite at 12:00 PM, and arrived here at about 2:15 PM. Of course, Tim canceled BP and gave us a 4:15 PM bus time. Since we actually have to cross time zones to get to St. George, we arrived at 6:15 PM for a 7:05 PM game. This is what baseball players refer to as a "strap-it-on" day, meaning after a long road trip, there is no BP, no infield, and everyone warms up for the game on his own. A lot of times, "strap-it-on" days result in big offensive games for the visiting team—which sometimes make you wonder about the importance of BP—but Monday was not one of those days.

The state of California has the famous "three strikes" policy for felons, and on Monday night, the Sonoma County Crushers faced a different kind of "three strikes and you're out" situation. Strike 1): We faced two-time WBL Pitcher of the Year Mike Smith. Smith has a sneaky fastball as it is, but on Monday he had a little extra giddy-up on it. Strike 2): The home plate umpire had perhaps the largest strike zone I had ever seen, especially on the outside part of the plate, where he was calling strikes on pitches 6-8 inches off the corner. Strike 3): Our legs—or at least mine—felt like 117 pounds of tree sap. My knee ached, and I felt as though I were running in a swimming pool—even more so than normal. Anyways, three strikes and we were out. We lost 10-2, I think. I came back from the game, ate, and went to sleep at midnight. I didn't wake up, not even once, until noon. By the end of Monday, I was picturing big, fluffy beds in my mind's eye.

Now, I need to ask a rhetorical question: Why do two-bit gambling towns attract the dregs of society? Why does the ratio of old, beat-up people to young, attractive people in casinos have to be 138:1? At least in Las Vegas, celebrities make occasional cameos, but in a town like Mesquite, forget it. There is also the "time-warp" problem. You see, the people who gravitate to casinos tend to dress as if they've just returned from a Billy Squier concert. I haven't seen so many tight blue jeans, "wife-beater" T-shirts, and big hair since *The Wedding Singer*. I suppose I shouldn't talk, though; if I were living in a town like this, I may become one of the destitute. Something tells me, however, that once I looked into my closet and saw 8 pairs of faded Levi's and 5 white, sleeveless T-shirts and into a mirror and saw a "mullet" haircut, I would wake up and smell the cigarette smoke.

We play tonight, and after the game, we will leave for Rohnert Park. My plan is to stay up late tonight, so I can be nice and tired for the bus trip. The only way to alleviate the boredom of a 12-hour drive is to sleep as much as possible, and that is my plan. It appears that the only way to achieve that end is to hit the tables. I, in light of last month's debacle, have put myself on a strict limit financially; unfortunately, seeing that will power through to fruition is an entirely different story. Out.

Thursday, July 26, 2001 (8:45 AM)
Rohnert Park

First, the good news: We were "rained out" yesterday in St. George. I use that term loosely, as we sensed some foul play. After the game on

Tuesday night, the fans were treated to a fireworks display, and as is customary of minor league baseball, the owners expected quite a smaller crowd for last night's game. It therefore occurred to several of us that since the game didn't really mean anything to them—the Pioneerzz won the first half in the South division, clinching a post-season playoff berth—the day of rest for their players may prove to be more beneficial. Also, their pitching staff is somewhat depleted. I don't know if they engineered a "rain out" in the *Bull Durham* sense (when Crash Davis, et. al., artificially induced a rain out by turning on the sprinkler system in the middle of the night) but they canceled the game nevertheless. We were just as happy, too; days off late in the season are always welcome.

Now for the bad news: It took us 16 hours to get home. Why? I have no idea. For some reason Mack, our bus driver for the vast majority of our trips this year, decided to take a "short cut." I use *this* term loosely because it was in fact a "long cut." Instead of taking the conventional route of going south through Las Vegas, over to Bakersfield, and then up on I-5 to northern California, he had the bright idea of going north from St. George on I-15 and then west on Rte. 50. I could understand if we were in cars, but trying to negotiate a 10-ton bus on winding, back roads in the middle of nowhere is absolutely insane. Can someone please tell me why in Sam Hill our bus drivers never know where they're going? It's like being a waiter or waitress and having no idea what your restaurant serves. Our guys were really pissed off and with good reason. We should have arrived at about 4:00 AM, which would have allowed to us to get a full night's sleep and enjoy our off day. Unfortunately, our late arrival will now force many of us—especially me—to sleep the day away. As we always say, it's just another reminder of where we are: the WBL.

Bus trips are a necessary evil—perhaps the ultimate evil—of life in the minors. They are just no fun. A minor league team on a long bus trip vaguely resembles the Bannockburn battlefield in the movie *Braveheart*: lots of bodies lying around, moaning in agony, wanting to be put out of their misery. Guys will do anything to get comfortable. I already mentioned CP's hammock, but Monte took the cake today. He actually climbed into one of the overhead compartments and slept there for a while. Like I said, *anything* to get comfy.

Here are a couple sights and sounds from the trip. We put in the movie *Liar, Liar* (starring Jim Carrey), and in the opening scene of the movie, Carrey's son Max is in a kindergarten class where the teacher is asking the kids what their parents do for a living. You know, "My dad does this," and "My dad does that" type of stuff. All of a sudden, JT chimes in with, "My dad's in the WBL, and he sucks." I was howling. Also, I don't know how the topic came about, but at one of our rest stops, we started discussing the "chupecabra." For those of you who don't know, the chupecabra is an animal(?) who has mutilated dozens of farm animals through South Texas and Mexico over the past five or six years. Some people say it's the devil reincarnated while others think it's a cross between a goat and a coyote. Who knows? Anyway, Diego and Monte, two Mexican-Americans, were proffering their opinions. Diego said it was a half-goat, half rabbit (not exactly an intimidating hybrid), and Monte talked about, jokingly, an alien presence. I just said, "Hell, it's probably just a couple of vatos (a street name for Mexican-Americans) drunk and high on tequila and peyote." They just laughed.

Right now, I am running on about eight hours of sleep—six from Tuesday night and two of intermittent, wholly unsatisfying bus sleep. I am dragging ass big-time. Thankfully, I am not one of those people who needs to "do something constructive" so I don't "waste the day." (Yes, Gabby, that's a poke at you.) I will soon nod off to sleep, and, well, I guess I will wake up when I wake up. On Tuesday night Dolf asked me if I hunted, and I said that other than shooting a groundhog or two, I never have. He mentioned how much he loved surfing as a youth growing up in Long Beach and how he'd be on the beach at the crack of dawn waiting to catch some waves. I told him that for me, any "hobby" that requires rising before the sun is definitely not a hobby. I suppose my motto is then, "Late to bed, late to rise, leaves you broke with bloodshot eyes." Out.

Friday, July 27, 2001 (11:30 PM)
Rohnert Park

One of the topics I want to discuss when I eventually write my "life in the minors" book has to do with the sacrifices we ballplayers make in pursuit of the Holy Grail. You know, just about every pro ballplayer gives up something to chase the dream. Some leave behind a quality girl somewhere, some are aren't able to start the family they would like, and some miss out on important family events. It is this last one that I would like to discuss now.

Two weeks ago my father's older brother Val died of a massive heart attack. He was actually playing basketball in preparation for the Senior Olympics, and things we're going quite well until then. Being on the west coast and in the middle of baseball season, I was unable to attend his funeral. My absence at this funeral is simply another family function— albeit an extremely difficult one—that I can say I missed due to baseball. I have missed so many important events—weddings, funerals, Bar/Bat Mitzvahs—that I feel so selfish at times. I mean, what's really more important? Baseball is pretty damn small in the grand scheme of things, isn't it? The problem is that you become so focused on your goal of reaching the major leagues that too often, major productions fall by the wayside. It really stinks at times, but it's part of the sacrifice we all must make. Eventually, though, the line between what's important—friends and family—and what's small potatoes—baseball—becomes blurrier and blurrier after failure to attend, and, pretty soon, you don't know what's important anymore.

One of earliest recollections of Uncle Val was when he pitched batting practice to my 11-year-old Little League All-Star team. If I remember correctly, he threw me the first curveball I ever saw, so maybe I owe part of my success as a hitter to him. Apparently, he was quite the pitcher himself as a youth, and the Pirates supposedly offered him a tryout when he was in high school. In one of those fabled stories told at family gatherings by balding men with large bellies, he declined the offer because he had to stay home and help bail hay. Is that true? Who knows? Hell, who cares? Another story my dad told is about the time Uncle Val was late getting to a summer league game, and he was supposed to be the starting pitcher. Well, he arrived five minutes before game time, and since the umpire wouldn't allow him to warm up his arm properly, he walked the first batter on four pitches. He then proceeded to get loose by making 20 or so pickoff attempts to the first baseman. Classic.

As much as he loved his sports, Uncle Val was even more renowned for his love of Budweiser. My parents, the epitome of teetotalers, knew damn well that when Uncle Val and Aunt Carol came to town, there better be a case of beer in the fridge. Originally, Uncle Val had to drink Coors Light since my dad felt obligated to keep the Coors Company in the black; he roomed with Jeff Coors, Adolph's grandson, at Cornell. But Uncle Val was a Bud man, and in the rare instance that he left a few remaining, I'd sneak a few just to see what all the hubbub was about. The rest is history. Again, maybe I owe part of my success as a—what's the opposite of a teetotaler?—to Uncle Val.

Like his brothers and sister, with the exception of Uncle Frank, Uncle Val was on the quiet side, but when he spoke, it was usually worth listening to. My dad has a saying: "People who don't talk aren't the only ones who don't say anything." Nobody personified that statement like Uncle Val. Whenever he and his family would travel from New Jersey to Sarver, PA, where Grandma and Grandpa lived, he was perfectly content eating, drinking, and being merry, and he left the talking to the others. One great memory I have from a certain Christmas gathering is when he and Grandpa got into a heated argument over whether, during the benediction, the Holy Trinity should be referred to as the "Father, Son, and the Holy Ghost" or the "Father, Son, and the Holy Spirit." I can't recall which term Uncle Val used, but Grandpa took exception to it. Unfortunately for Uncle Val, Grandpa Durkac could make Archie Bunker look like Edith Bunker, so Uncle Val relented, but I never forgot that incident as a microcosm for the stubbornness of the Durkac male. And yes, that "gene" is by no means recessive in me, either.

There is a saying that goes, "Wear out; don't rust out." Uncle Val, after retiring from the service, could have sat back and enjoyed a peaceful existence with Aunt Carol and in the revelry of his grandchildren, but that is simply not the Durkac way. As a Durkac, your body is bound to the Slovakian code the way a cowboy is bound to his horse: you ride that nag 'til it drops. Slowing down is not an option. When I called Aunt Carol to offer my deepest condolences, I made it a point to tell her that at least he died doing something he loved.

Finally, perhaps the ultimate compliment you can pay anyone is that he/she was a good parent, and that certainly is the case with Uncle Val. There were far too many good moments between Ty, Debi, and David and me to recount, and I always enjoyed and looked forward to their visits. Now that I think about it, perhaps Uncle Val could have been a little tougher on David, his youngest and four years my senior, when he would kick my ass on a daily basis, but why quibble? Uncle Val leaves behind these three outstanding human beings and four beautiful grandchildren, and perhaps the only solace we can take in his passing is that the grandchildren are too young to comprehend what has happened. They were definitely the apples of his eye. Remember not Uncle Val for the abrupt ending to his life; remember him for the quality of it. I once read an American Indian proverb that goes like this: "When you are born, you cry and the world rejoices. Live your life in such a way that when you die, the world cries and you rejoice." From what I was told, there wasn't a dry eye in the house at the funeral. This Bud's for you, Uncle Val. Out.

Sunday, July 29, 2001 (7:00 PM)
Rohnert Park

We lost today 2-1 to Long Beach, so we had to settle for a series win rather than the desired sweep. Oh well. After 65 games, we're 34-31, and

11-9 in the second half. To be honest, we have our work cut out for us over the last 25 games of the season. We play Chico and Solano six times each, and they're our division rivals. Our six-team league is divided into a North division (Chico, Solano, and us) and a South division (Yuma, St. George, and Long Beach), and the playoff format is as follows: the first half winner plays the second half winner in each division in a best-of-five series, and those two winners meet in a best-of-five finals. In the event that one team wins both halves, the team with the better overall record between the other two teams in that division receives the other playoff berth. If that is indeed the case, then the first round playoff format becomes a "one-and-four" series—the first game would be played at the runner-up's field, and the remaining games would be played at the 1st place team's field. Follow?

It sounds complicated, but it really isn't. The reason the WBL uses a "two-halves" format is the same reason that the minor leagues use it: it doesn't penalize a team for its own success. Let me explain. Let's say you're on a AA team that goes 45-25 in the first half of a 140-game minor league season. Well, to have that kind of success, you have to have good players on your team, and when a minor league player has a good first half, he usually receives a promotion to a higher level. Therefore, a minor league team that enjoys a successful first half will sometimes have a lousy second half because the players that are brought in to replace the departed ones may not be nearly as good. The baseball system, though, owes it to the fans of this minor league team—and to the players who stayed on the roster for the whole summer—to allow it to compete in the playoffs. The WBL has followed suit, but not for the same reasons. In our league players often flee to a foreign country to chase the "big bucks," so once again, in order to avoid shortchanging the fans and owners, the WBL has instituted the current format.

At this point in the season, Chico, who won the first half, is on its way to winning the second half. If we are to make the playoffs, then we have to have a better overall record than Solano. Right now, that is not the case. I believe they are three games ahead of us. The good news for us, as I mentioned, is that we play them six more times, meaning we "control our destiny," as the sports phrase goes. I don't think I've ever been involved in a playoff race in my pro career, but it appears there will be one this year. During the last four years, we had locked up playoff spots in early August, so I don't know what it will be like to have every mid- to late-August game mean something. It should be fun and interesting.

One thing I neglected to mention in my past few entries was the conversation a few of us had in St. George while stretching before the game. Somehow, the topic turned to capitalism vs. socialism, and Evel and I were doing most of the talking. He was trying to get me to believe that socialism is a better form of government than capitalism, and the device he used was health care. If I understood him correctly, in Cuba, if you need an operation, the government pays for it; he apparently liked the idea of not having to pay a penny for it. In my retort, and I can't believe I actually quoted Homer J. Simpson, I told him, "Communism works—in theory," I then proceeded to explain to him that in a capitalistic society, you have the opportunity to make as much money as you are willing to work for, and with that money you can buy health insurance to pay for operations. Plus, you don't have to deal with all that poverty, killing, and lack of freedom that can really put a crimp in your lifestyle. Furthermore, if socialism were such a good idea, millions of people would flock to Cuba and China every year, not to America. As appealing as a national health care system sounds, I think I—and Evel—will take the good ol' U.S. of A. Mind you, the entire conversation took place in Spanish—rapidly-spoken Spanish at that—so I was quite pleased with myself. At the end, after I told him, "Comunismo es estupido!" he just kind of smiled. By George, I think he's got it. Out.

CHAPTER 7

▼

AN INSURMOUNTABLE TASK

Wednesday, August 1, 2001 (12:00 PM)
Rohnert Park

"Pitching is 75% of baseball." "Pitching and defense is 90% of base-ball." While I am not a mathematician, I do know that quality pitching —and the defense that plays behind it—is the key to a team's success. On Monday, "El Flaco" (Roque) took a no-hitter into the ninth inning against the hard-hitting Solano Steelheads. He was unbelievable. His ball was dancing all over the place, totally befuddling their lineup. I call it the "dragonfly" ball, and if you've ever seen a dragonfly, start, stop, start, stop, and generally bounce all through the air, you know what I'm talking about. He must have broken six bats with a fastball that was probably no better than 85 MPH, but that fastball was moving, and his changeup and slider were equally impressive. We had afforded Roque a comfortable

6-0 lead after three innings, so by the time the ninth inning rolled around, the game was, for all intents and purposes, over. Wayne Kirby, a former major leaguer, ended his no-hit bid by hitting a homerun to lead off the ninth inning. After a triple and an error, the Steelheads had scored two runs, and the game ended. At least Kirby's hit wasn't a "bleeder." He smoked it. Most pitchers would agree that they would want a no-hitter to end on a clean, sharply hit ball as opposed to one that is a borderline error or a broken-bat infield hit. Regardless, Roque threw a helluva game, and we drew first blood against the team we are fighting for the second playoff spot.

Not to be outdone, Mayque—whom Mitch calls "Fidel" (as in Castro), which would be like calling Bill Clinton "Monica"—threw a perfect game through 4 1/3 innings, and Kirby ended *his* chance at WBL immortality (tongue in cheek, of course) with another homerun. Damn him!! Mayque pitched into the sixth inning and left with a 3-1 lead. Tim then gave the ball to BG, who gave up an unearned run (which unfortunately was charged to Mayque) and to Rosey. The two of them combined for 3 2/3 innings of shutout baseball, and we hung on for a 3-2 win. To win the first two games of an important series like this one in their park is huge for us. To hold their team to a total of six hits in those two games is remarkable. We are a pretty good baseball team right now. It's about freakin' time.

Let's talk about "no-hitter etiquette." When a pitcher reaches about the sixth inning of a no hitter, his teammates usually treat him like a leper. Baseball players are so unbelievably superstitious, and no one wants to jinx the pitcher by talking to him. You *never* mention the no-hitter: "Hey, Winter, do you know that Roque is throwing a no-hitter?" Of course, the opposition and the fans are keenly aware of what's going on, so they are making comments like, "Hey, this guy has a no-no going," or "C'mon, someone break it up." In the battle of superstitions, the vociferous usually defeats the silent; otherwise, more no-hit bids would end as no-hitters, not one- and two-hitters. Playing behind a no-hitter is fun, too, as every pitch is a life-and-death situation. No one wants the no-hitter to be lost as a result of his own physical shortcomings, *i.e.*, lack of range, speed or arm strength, so on every pitch, even more so than usual, the fielders are *really* on their toes.

Finally, I want to speak about the demons that I wrestle with on a daily basis. You see, in the beginning of the season, you don't think a whole lot about the upcoming offseason. You're too focused on having a good year, both individually and as a team. On August 1st, however, the offseason looms ahead like a huge abyss. Without question, the toughest part of the year for a minor leaguer—especially an independent leaguer—is that first month after the season ends. You start to question whether you'll do it all again next year. You have to find a "real job." And, you leave the camaraderie of your teammates, the solidarity that has grown with each other during the season. It's not a particularly fun time. I certainly wrestle with these issues, but the concern I have now, more than ever, is if I'm any good or not.

Am I good? Am I no good? In baseball statistics are hugely important— but they don't tell the whole story. Here are my stats, roughly. Over the past three years, I've hit .330. I have averaged, conservatively, 67 RBI's and 5 homeruns. Projecting these numbers over a full minor league season would put me at .330, 104, and 7. If you hit .330 in a minor league season, you had a helluva year. If you drive in 100 runs in a minor league season, you had a helluva year. If you hit 7 homeruns, as a third baseman, in a minor league season, you have no power. I have come to grips with the fact that I will never hit a ton of homeruns, but my problem is this: If I have so little power, how do I drive in so many runs? For example, Vic Sanchez, Solano's catcher and arguably the most dangerous hitter in the league, has 20 homeruns (to my 2), yet I have more RBI's than he does. Half of me wants to say, "Jeez, Bo, if you can't hit more than 5 homeruns a year off WBL pitching, how could you ever expect to hit any off legitimate AA or AAA pitching?" The other half says, "Damn, Bo, if you ever got good, quality big league bats in your hands in parks where you can actually see the ball and faced pitchers who throw the ball over the plate a lot more often, your power numbers might go up considerably." If I can drive in 57 runs with only two homeruns in 67 games, what would my total be if I hit ten homeruns? Who knows? Maybe the pitching would be so much better that I may hit only .270 and drive in only 70 runs in a full season. Who knows?

The point I'm making is that a player has to realize that he simply is *not* going anywhere. At that time, he should probably consider moving on to another line of "work." But it's not that easy. Lots of people stay in relationships with no future. They have fun. They enjoy themselves. And, yes, they kid themselves into thinking that something is there when in fact it really isn't. Baseball players are no different. Out.

Saturday, August 4, 2001 (1:00 PM)
Chico

We did it. We beat the Heat last night 3-2, and the game ended with the league's leading hitter, Ray Brown, flying out to deep left-center field with the bases loaded. The Heat left a WBL-record 19 men on base—including four times with the bases loaded—last night, so needless to say, we did our best *Molly Hatchet* impersonation: "Flirtin' with Disaster." Regardless, we beat the Heat by one in Chico, and I loved it.

Right now, the Heat are very vulnerable. The have lost two key players to injury (they should be activated by the August 6 playoff-roster deadline) and a pitcher who signed with an organization. After tearing through the first half and winning it easily, they have finally shown some weaknesses. In a way I feel bad for a lot of their players—guys whom I've played with and liked—because of the "cloud of tension" that hangs over Nettleton Stadium an a daily basis. The Heat organization has been *the* team to beat in the WBL since it arrived in 1997, and the fans have come to expect winning. Unfortunately, I don't think the fans here in Chico are knowledgeable enough yet about pro baseball to understand that even the best teams are going to lose one out of every three games. I don't think they realize that injuries, and the subsequent moving of players to foreign positions, can really wreck a team. The fans don't want excuses; they want victories. Sorry, but it just doesn't work that way.

It's funny seeing the reaction of the Heat players after a narrow defeat. When I played here, if we lost a nail-biter, a lot of us would remain in the dugout licking our wounds. In Sonoma County we rarely react that way to a loss. I hate to say it, but when you lose as often as we did through parts of our season, you almost grow to accept it. I know that sounds bad, but it's true. When we win, our highs are just as high in Sonoma County as they were in Chico, but when we lose, our lows aren't nearly as low. Whether our complacency about losing is good or bad remains to be seen, but it certainly makes for a more enjoyable clubhouse atmosphere.

Finally, my parents made their annual west coast baseball trip and were here last night for the game. They will be here until next Sunday, so Gabby will get to see his fair share of games, nine in all. I just hope I don't have any bad games while they're here. It is still very difficult for me to lose the game, go 0-4, and make an error and still act as though everything is hunky-dory. Although it's not as long as it used to be, I still need a sufficient cooling-down period after a tough game. I guess the best way to avoid getting the red ass is to get two hits every game, go error-free, and win nine in row. Yeah, that's the ticket. Out.

Monday, August 13, 2001 (11:45 PM)
Mesquite

Hiatus over: After nine days of no writing, I'm back in the saddle again. There is a lot to cover over the past week, so bear with me. First of all, we took two out of three from Chico in Chico. I was extremely happy about that, as you could imagine. Even better, in our two victories—both by one run—they left the tying and winning runs in scoring position. It couldn't have happened to a better team. It was also nice to have my entire family, as well as the Millers, there for the weekend. We carried on as if I had never left, drinking and playing cards and partying until all hours. On

Monday, an off day, we played golf in Paradise (about 30 minutes from Chico), and that was fun also. We returned to the Bay Area on Monday night, when we met up with Jon Yackmack, a good friend of mine from Kittanning. He had flown in Sunday night, and Brandi picked him up at the airport. "Turk" had never been to California before, so my parents invited him to join them. Also traveling with them was my 11-year-old, second cousin Spencer. His mom and my mom are cousins, and as the only male among six children, he relishes his time away from Estrogen Central. He has taken a bit of an affinity to me, especially my love of lumberjacking. I tell him he is going to be the "World's First Jewish Lumberjack."

Anyway, we had quite the Bo contingency in Rohnert Park for our six-game homestand. If it wasn't another group of relatives showing up at the stadium, it was a sorority sister of my mom's from her Cornell days. No matter what day it was, there seemed to be at least 10 people on the complimentary pass list under my name. I suppose I should take this opportunity to thank the Fletchers for their generosity and compliance with the Durkac Invasion. Then again, since they named their new feline "Bo Dur-cat" and my dad's a veterinarian, maybe it wasn't that big a deal.

I had a decent homestand, with only one really bad game. It was on Thursday, and we lost to St. George, 5-4. I was 0-4, and I left at least three runners in scoring position. It's games like that that are really hard to deal with, even more so when family's around. I once read how the Yankees' Paul O'Neill, when he was playing in front of his hometown crowd of Cincinnati earlier in his career, could no longer take all the commitments thrust upon him by friends and family. It's kind of a Catch-22: It's nice to have them around, but after a tough game, it's difficult to leave the feelings on the field. Well, it took me a while after Thursday's game to cool off, but I think I did reasonably well. I mean, I don't know how to react "properly." I'm sorry, but I can't turn off my emotions like a switch; bad games, even seven years into pro baseball, still burn my ass. I had another "oh-fer" on Saturday, and even though we lost, I took it a lot better. A group of about 12 of us went to Denny's after the game, and I even amazed myself at how well I did in light of my poor performance. Could I be maturing? God help us all.

Baseball players, like all athletes, are slaves to routine. Perhaps the biggest reason why professional sports teams perform better at home than on the road is because they can institute the same pattern on game days. They sleep in their own beds, they eat the same meals (if so desired), they leave the house at the same time, and they generally feel more comfortable. Michael Jordan, during the height of "Jordan-mania," said that the only peace and solace he had in his life was while his game was being played. Now, I am not suggesting that I am anywhere near the status of His Airness, but I feel the same way. If anyone is a slave to a routine, it's Gabriel Bo Durkac. I want to wake up when I want. I want to eat when I want. I want to leave the house when I'm good and ready. This is not to say that I'm some *idiot savant*, a 21st century *Rainman*, if you will. It's just that I like to come and go as I please. One week out of each summer to spend with my parents is easily doable, but to have daily commitments would be positively unbearable. In fact, Sasa and I were joking about that the other day when his family was in town from Japan. He said, "Everyday, kids… pool. Wife…shopping. Very tired." I was howling. As much as he loves his family, I think he was relieved to see them go. I could not imagine having to "wake up" and "visit" and "spend time" every single day. If that makes me self-centered (I prefer that term to "selfish," which to me implies putting oneself in front of others and causing them pain in doing so), then so be it. At least I'm honest about it, right? I simply am not ready for the around-the-clock job that is family.

Here are some sights and sounds from the past week or so, in no particular order. JT had a set of fake "summer" (as in some are here, some are there) teeth, and he had all of us rolling on the bus to Mesquite. Tim was joking with me during batting practice on how ethnically diverse we are. Even though I commented on it during spring training, with all our roster moves, it is worth rehashing. We have Sasa (Japan); Evel, Mayque, and

Andy Morales, another defector and Yankee castoff (Cuba); Diego and Gabe Garcia (Mexican-Americans); Neboyia (Native American); and Winter (Dominican-American). Tim actually said that Monte, who was born in Mexico, is Haitian. I chuckled. We discussed how unfair it is for us that Solano fields the team it currently has. They have three ex-big leaguers and two AA/AAA guys in their lineup. We have Keith Mitchell, who has about two years in the majors and that's it. McAffee has a couple of months each in AA, but as for the rest of the everyday players, we are all Class A guys at best. Hell, Winter, our regular shortstop, is just out if college, and Evel was on a boat not too long ago. It's just tough to compete when you don't have the horses.

From the personnel department, we gained Morales and lost Monte. Andy defected from Cuba in December, I believe, and the Yankees gave him a $4.5 million, four-year contract. Unfortunately, he never hit at any level within their minor league system, and they apparently released him. Tim signed him on Wednesday, and he was in the lineup on Thursday. He looked okay, but he hadn't played in over a month. Tim penciled him into the lineup again on Friday, and after another so-so performance, he hasn't played since. Monte's situation, though, really put the screws to us. He decided on Sunday that he wanted to quit and go to Mexico to play. In doing so, he left us no opportunity to add someone in his place. WBL rules state that no player can be added to a team's roster after August 6 unless the team loses a player to injury or to an organization. Since Monte's departure doesn't fall into either category, we simply have to play out the season with a 21-man roster. Everyone, especially Bob Fletcher, was really pissed. As if we weren't shorthanded enough…. Finally, we added Jeff Rhein, with whom I played in 1998 in Chico. He's a high-energy outfielder who brings speed and a little power to the lineup. He actually finished in the Top 5 in the league last year in extra-base hits, but this year he never got untracked. Bill Plummer released him, and Tim scooped him up in a hurry. "Rhino" will definitely be a nice addition to our squad.

Anyway, we are currently 1½ games behind Solano for the second play-off spot. We had a chance to put some distance between them and us over the weekend, but they took two of three. I mentioned before about our being in a "pennant race" in late August and how exciting it should be. What I just realized is that we have only 12 games left in the regular season, and now more than ever, every game counts. Making the playoffs means at least one more week of (measly) pay; if that's not incentive enough to get some damn wins, I don't know what is. Out.

Friday, August 17, 2001 (2:00 PM)
Rohnert Park

Boy, we had 'em. We lost the first game in St. George 9-1, but then we had a doubleheader scheduled for Tuesday and a single game on Wednesday. Well, Garcia threw a gem for us, going all seven innings (most minor league doubleheaders consist of two seven-inning games) and allowing only three runs. We won 6-3. The second game, however, really hurt us. BG, who is currently second in the league in ERA, got a spot start, and he made the most of it. (A spot start is when a reliever starts a game because either a scheduled starter is unable to go that day or the staff is short on pitching). He struck out the first six batters he faced, didn't give up a hit until the fourth, and didn't allow a run until the fifth. He was unbelievable. We jumped out to 4-0 lead, but the wheels came off for us in the fifth, and it all started with an error by Morales (he played third base and I played first base) on a routine groundball. From there, they added three runs, all unearned, to make it 4-3. We added one in the sixth, but they added two more in the bottom of the inning to tie it. We were held scoreless in the seventh, and Benny Craig, their leftfielder, led off the bottom of the seventh with a homerun. It was horrible. It was, without question, the toughest loss of the year for us. We had a chance to sweep the doubleheader and blew it. Fortunately, though, we won on Wednesday, but still, we could have taken three out of four and put ourselves in a nice position to compete for the last playoff spot. Oh, well.

Now, I hate to criticize other players. In fact, a lot of my past and current teammates say that I give other players too much credit for their abilities. But Andy Morales should get 5 to 10 years for armed robbery. How the Yankees gave him $4.5 million is beyond me. He has really ticked off some of us players. For example, in Monday's blowout loss, he was undressing in the clubhouse before the final out in the top of the seventh was made. That is a cardinal sin in the baseball world, saying in essence, that we have no chance of catching up. Furthermore, his pregame practice habits are lackadaisical at best. I understand that not everyone has to field 50 groundballs everyday and run around like a madman, but if you don't, then you better be able to play once the bell sounds. CP never takes extra BP, never takes BP when Tim makes it optional, and never throws a ball until game time, but he is hitting .350 and plays arguably the best center-field in the WBL. Therefore, he is given a lot of latitude. According to Tim, Andy hadn't played for a month before he joined us, so if anyone should be busting his ass during practice, it should be he. We've lost all three games he started for us, and I just wish he at least *acted* as if he wants to be here. I joked after the second game on Tuesday that I'm going to move to Cuba, play there, and then defect so I can get my hands in George Steinbrenner's pockets.

On a lighter note, it's time for a Mitch update. On Monday, I hit a homerun—my third of the year—so I engaged in a little trash-talking in the dugout, stuff like, "Jeez, you guys are bunch of banjo hitters" and "I'm tired of having to hit all the damn homeruns around here." Naturally, my tongue was firmly imbedded in my cheek while saying all of this, but Mitch was giving me the "What in the hell are you saying?" look. Later, we were discussing being hit by a pitch and how infrequently I am hit. I then added, "Well, I never get hit because I'm a switch-hitter. The ball doesn't ride up and in on me." Sure enough, in my fourth at-bat on Wednesday, I was hit in the leg. Mitch said it was because I angered the "baseball gods" with my popping off. He was even chirping at me from the bench when I was at third base. Finally, D.G. Nelson, the Pioneerzz's third base coach, asked me, "Damn, Bo, why is he all over you?" I said, "He is always riding somebody, and today it's my turn." Then, during a pitching change, I told Nelson about some of Mitch's better needles, like the one he dropped on McAffee a few weeks ago. Mac has been hovering around the Mendoza Line (.200) all year, but he's a strong kid who can hit the ball a long way when he hits it just right. Well, he hit a long homerun in Rohnert Park, and when he returned to the dugout, Mitch deadpanned, "Damn, Josh, I guess they missed that hole in your bat." We were rolling. Or in Chico last week, when Mitch found out that I have my own website where I sell a hitting manual. He said, "Bo, you got your own website? What is it, 'Swingingunderwater.com'"? Ouch. I also told Nelson about how I told Mitch that I wanted to go to Japan and make the kind of money he made and how Mitch said, "Not with a swing like that." He liked that one.

Anyway, we have six games at home—Yuma and Chico—followed by three in Yuma to end the regular season. I figure we have to win at least six of the nine to make the playoffs unless Solano has a collapse of Van de Veldeian proportions. Yuma has been struggling lately, so we better beat them. It should be interesting. Stay tuned. Out.

Sunday, August 19, 2001 (9:15 PM)
Rohnert Park

I love playing day games on Sunday. It's weird because Saturday night usually lasts until Sunday morning, and last night was no exception. I took advantage, being the intelligent consumer that I am, of the $2.00 Coronas at The Office last night, rendering me lightly intoxicated at last call. Yeah, yeah, you're thinking, "Jeez, Bo, you guys are in a dogfight to make the playoffs, and you stay out late the night before a *day* game? What are you thinking?" Well, as Greg Miller, my "host dad" in Chico says, "Stay in the car." In other words, relax. I got to the field at 12:30 PM, stretched at 1:00 PM, and was ready to play at 1:35 PM. I had two hits, an RBI, a run scored, and two nice defensive plays in the field.

The real reason I like Sunday day games, however, is because it frees up Sunday night for me. I can get home around 5:30 PM and do whatever I want. Usually I like to write, but if I wanted to, I could go out on a date or go into the city or simply catch up on stuff. Tonight's writing, though, was delayed by the Crushers Booster Club award dinner. We all went to a local recreation center for a dinner thrown by the tireless Booster Club members, and it was a good time. All of us players received scrapbooks filled with newspaper articles from this summer, and they gave each of us a humorous little prize. When Bob Proctor, the head honcho, announced my name, he said that I was competing for the "cute" award, whatever that meant. I made my way up to the stage, where Bob told me that the competition wasn't between another player and me but rather me and my namesake. You see, as I already mentioned, back in spring training, the Fletchers got a week-old kitten and promptly named it "Bo Dur-cat," so they presented me with a picture of myself and a picture of the feline and the question, "Who wins the cute contest?" The frame was plaster baseball, complete with seams on it, and a rectangle cut out to display the photo. It's cute. Also, among some of the prizes were two Chico Heat garbage bags, and one of the recipients of one actually threw it down on the floor. When I went up to receive my prize, I said, "You know, Bob, I just thought of a good use for those Chico Heat garbage bags. After we stomp the guts out of the Heat this week, we'll put their remains in the bags." Everyone loved that.

From a personal standpoint, I was happy to hear that I was selected to the WBL Postseason All-Star team. Although we didn't have an All-Star game this year, the league's managers—and general managers, I believe—vote for the best player in the league at each position, and this year, like in 1999, they selected me as the third baseman. Actually, let me clarify that: I'm pretty sure one certain manager didn't vote for me. Whatever the case, after being released by two different teams on two different continents in less than two weeks, I was extremely satisfied to receive the award. (If you think about it, though, being selected the best third baseman in a six-team independent league is probably a bit like being told you have the best smile in Sheffield, England: Don't let it go to your head.) I remember back in 1998 when former Crushers third baseman Eric White received the same award, and the Crushers presented him with the plaque before a game with us. Do you see where I am going with this? I hope like hell that they do the same with me because we all know who's coming to town. In an occupation where rejections and failures run rampant, I'm allowed to strut like a peacock once in a while, right?

From the corrections and retractions department comes the following: Reports of Andy Morales's death have been greatly exaggerated. If Bo must criticizeth, then Bo must praiseth as well. Morales has been hitting the heck out of the ball over the past three days. I shouldn't have been so shortsighted in my assessment of him. No, he isn't the most intense guy you'll ever see on a baseball field, nor does he have the greatest practice habits, but one thing I've learned through my years in baseball is that every player is different. A player may not play with the same fire as a Pete Rose, but that doesn't mean that the player can't be as good as Rose. Maybe Andy just needed a little more time to find his stroke. What I am trying to say is that while he may have received a few million dollars more than his market value from the Yankees, he is not the bumbling buffoon that I made him out to be. Next time, I'll exhibit a little more patience before I cast the first stone of criticism.

Now, I mentioned that I felt we had to win six out of our last nine to have just an outside chance of reaching the playoffs. Well, we can now make that three out of six. We swept Yuma this weekend in three pretty exciting, playoff-style games. On Friday, I drove in our first run in the first inning, drove in our second one in the eighth to put us up 2-1, and then scored our third and final run. It was a nice win. Today's game was a weird one. We made six errors—to their one—yet we won 12-6. Go figure. We jumped out to a 6-1 lead after four innings or so, but the errors let them back into the game. The score was tied at 6-6 when I put us ahead with an RBI single in the fifth inning, and it was 7-6 going into the bottom of the seventh. Yuma brought in Pete Schourek, a former 19-game winner in the big leagues, in the seventh. After striking out CP and Morales, I came up with no one on and two outs.

Now, what happened next is one of those little things that I do on a day-in, day-out basis that baseball people understand and appreciate. Schourek also pitched one inning yesterday, and I think he struck out two of the three batters he faced, so despite being in the WBL, he obviously has a few tricks left in his bag. He was throwing a dirty curveball as his "out" pitch, and that's what he was trying to throw to me. One thing I have always been able to do, and I'm not sure why, is to lay off the breaking ball that is thrown for a ball. Let me explain with the following excerpt from my hitting manual why this ability is so important in becoming a good hitter:

First of all, I never saw the point in swinging at balls. Making solid contact is tough enough when you're swinging at pitches in the strike zone, let alone ones that aren't. One thing I've always been good at is not swinging at breaking balls out of the strike zone. I have a theory about breaking balls and it goes like this: if you could monitor the total number of breaking pitches thrown over the course of a major league season, it is my guess that only 33% or so of them would be called a strike if the hitters didn't swing at them. My point is that most of the time, a breaking ball is designed to *look* like a strike, but by the time the catcher catches it, it is a ball. Hence, if you can train yourself to take those pitches, you'll eventually find yourself in more hitters' counts, which will ultimately make you a better hitter. When you find yourself in a lot of 2-0 and 3-1 counts, you know that your approach is working well for you because those counts usually mean a fastball is coming, and just about every good hitter who ever played lived for those counts.

Anyway, Schourek threw me a first pitch curve for a strike. Then, he threw me a changeup away for a ball. Then, he threw me two more curveballs for balls—the same pitch that he had struck out Morales with two days in a row and the same pitch that a lot of WBL hitters would swing at. With the count 3-1, he threw me a fastball on the outside corner to make the count full at 3-2. What does he throw now? The same curveball, again for a ball, and I walk. Oglesby followed with a single, and Keith Mitchell hit a clutch two-run double, effectively ending the game. What's the big deal, you ask? Well, had I swung and missed at any of those breaking balls, as a lot of hitters would have, Oglesby and Mitch never would have hit in the inning, and perhaps the whole outcome of the game would have been different. I'm not fishing for compliments here; I'm just pointing out that in spite of my constant self-deprecation, I feel I am a pretty decent ballplayer. If I must eternally disparage about my shortcomings, then I must also be permitted to point out the things that in fact I *can* do.

Finally, Tim knows about my journal, and if you remember, he asked that I leave him out of it. Well, that was when my journal was appearing online. Obviously, I have included him many times since, and he told me that I had to put the following story in the journal, so here it is. On Saturday, I came up in the first inning with CP on second and two outs. Tom Bergan, Yuma's starter, jammed me pretty badly with a fastball, but I hit just enough of it that it bounced right behind second base on the dirt. Yuma's shortstop, Richy Leon, grabbed the ball on the edge of the outfield grass and made an off-balance throw to first base. I was burning (and I use that term loosely) down the line, and I was safe by barely a step. CP, on the other hand, never stopped running and by the time Yuma's first baseman had received the throw and turned and fired to home, CP was safe. Therefore, I got an RBI single with a runner on second. It gets better.

Then, Oglesby came up next and hit a 1-1 fastball right over the first baseman's head. With two outs I'm running on contact, and I knew that I could make it to third easily. I, as any good baserunner knows, never slowed down when approaching third base, *i.e.*, I anticipated being sent home. I was nearing third, and I kept wondering when Tim was going to give me the stop sign. I knew Oglesby didn't hit it well enough for me to score, so I was getting a little anxious. Well, apparently, Yuma's right fielder didn't exactly bust his ass to retrieve the ball—my "blinding" speed doesn't evoke much trepidation in outfielders—and when he gently tossed the ball into the second baseman, Tim waved me home. I thought, "Oh, boy, I better kick it into overdrive; it's gonna be close," and I peeked over my shoulder to see where the ball was. When I saw their second baseman wind up to throw it, I knew I better pull off the slide of my life to make it, and I did just that. Fortunately, the throw was just off to the right of the plate, enough that their catcher couldn't block the plate, so I dove head first—usually a no-no at home plate—and caught the back corner of the plate with my fingertips, just barely under the catcher's tag. Safe!! The crowd was going wild. Naturally, I had to go into the dugout and spew out some more trash-talk like, "Boys, you just can't teach speed" and "You see, guys, I only run fast when I have to."

I, Bo Durkac: Speed-demon, got an RBI on an infield single with a runner on second, and then I scored from first on a single. A *single*! Now, here's where Tim's assessment comes in. He said in almost twenty years of managing, he has seen each play happen maybe—*maybe*—five times, and I'm involved in it *in the same inning*. Furthermore, I am slower than a seven-year itch, and I still pulled it off. He was totally amazed, as was the rest of Western civilization, but like former major league pitcher and über-freak Joaquin Andujar said, "Baseball can be summed up in one word: You never know." Out.

Monday, August 20, 2001 (11:30 PM)
Rohnert Park

What a freakin' game!! I can't remember the last time I was so pumped up after a win. We beat the Heat tonight 7-4 in dramatic fashion, and coupled with Solano's loss, we are now one game behind in the playoff race.

The Heat took a 4-1 lead into the bottom of the fifth, but CP hit a clutch two-out, two-run homer to make it 4-3. It stayed that way until the top of the eighth, when Tim elected to bring in Scott Reeves to face arguably the best hitter in the league, Ray Brown, with two outs and runners on first and second. Tim apparently felt that the young, side-arming lefty had a better chance of getting the lefty Brown than did righty JT, a ten-year veteran. Reeves was still in middle school when Brown won MVP of the Pioneer League—a rookie league predominately for kids right out of college—in 1994, and Brown hasn't slowed down since. He is a two-time, all-WBL first baseman, and, to put it bluntly, he can flat-out hit. Well, Reeves threw his first pitch for a ball, and then he proceeded to strike Brown out on three consecutive pitches. The place went nuts as Scottie practically sprinted to the dugout. It was awesome.

Then, in the bottom of the eighth, CP hit a hard grounder to right field, where it was misplayed by Chico's right fielder. CP, having never slowed down, went all the way to third and landed on third with his trademark, Pete Rose-esque headfirst slide. All 1000 fans (maybe) at Rohnert Park Stadium were on their feet. Morales followed with what looked to be a simple game-tying, RBI groundout to second base, but their guy kicked it, and so Andy was safe. I came up and hit a single to right, putting runners at first and second with one out in a tie game. Up stepped the Milkman. He worked the count to 3-1, and former AAA pitcher Jeff Harris, who started the game, threw a fastball on the outside corner to make it 3-2. Then, in a scene right out of Hollywood, he hung a slider to the Milkman, and the Milkman hit it over the wall in centerfield. It was awesome!! I didn't think 1000 fans could make that much noise. We took the 7-4 lead into the top of the ninth, and Brian Rose, who has evolved into our *de facto* closer, pitched a 1-2-3 inning. Crushers win, Crushers win!!

Talk about a game! It definitely had a playoff-style atmosphere. To be honest, I don't know what the playoff situation is. Bob Fletcher put the playoff scenarios on the wall in the clubhouse—you know, stuff like if

Sonoma County wins X number of games and if Chico and Solano finish such and such. I really didn't know what the hell was going on, and Pritchard remarked that he got a migraine trying to figure out the situation. All I know is that we have won five in a row, and Solano lost tonight. You should have heard the crowd, all 1000 of them (maybe), erupt when the PA announcer said, "This just in from St. George, UT: Pioneerzz 9, Steelheads 5." I can't remember being so charged up after a big win. Hell, I drove home as if I had just stolen something.

Another bit of humor from the Chico games is the constant battle that ensues between Charley and Mitch. They were opponents in the epic National League Championship Series of 1986, and as everyone knows, Mitch's Mets beat Charley's Astros and later went on to win the World Series. They seem to be good friends, as they are always joking around with each other. Well, every time I get a hit, Mitch, our first base coach, always pats me on the back, looks into Chico's dugout, and says, "I told you Charley: This kid can flat-out hit. He's my dog!" I never look into the dugout for Charley's reaction, but Mitch ends up laughing his ass off. And, yes, I gloat internally a little bit, too; I'm only human.

One thing I'm glad about this year is that I have hit pretty well against Chico. They have the best pitching staff in the league, so I would not assert that I have "raked" them, but certainly, I have had my share of hits. Right now, I am sixth in the league in hitting, third in on-base percentage, probably eighth in RBI's, and according to my postseason award, the best third baseman in the league. Charley, meanwhile, has had a revolving door at third base. That's not to knock the two or three guys that he has played there; third base is simply not an easy position to become good at in a few months. I often wonder if Charley will ever admit that he messed up. In the newspaper article that aired our grievances, he said that I would never play in Chico as long as he is the manager. Those are some pretty strong words. My mother often complains about the "male ego" and how if egos weren't such a predominating factor all the time, people would make better decisions. As I grow older, I see her point. If I were that much of a cancer that Charley would turn his back on a two-time, All-Star third baseman, then I must be a real horse's ass. I just think Charley thought he could get by without me, and to be truthful, he has. The Heat is still the team to beat in the league without Bo Durkac, but I have to believe that the Heat would be better **with** me. Perhaps he wanted to show his authority and make an example of me, saying that no one player is above the team (not that I ever acted like I was). I just think he needs to adhere to one of my all-time favorite quotes, by John Wooden: "Who's right isn't nearly as important as what's right." Out.

Tuesday, August 22, 2001 (11:45 PM)
Rohnert Park

We beat the Heat again tonight in an action-packed game, 6-5. I scored the winning run in the seventh inning on an RBI groundout by Morales, and Rosey pitched a scoreless eighth and ninth for the save. Rosey has been lights out this year for us since being released by Yuma. On paper he doesn't seem to be that imposing, and during a pitching discussion at The Office on Saturday night, I told him that. As most pitchers do when you question their fastballs, he was quick to point out that he hits 90 MPH every once in a while (for all you Freudians out there, intimating that a pitcher has a weak fastball is the baseball version of penis envy). Whether that's true or not is irrelevant—at least to me. He has been unbelievable in his role as our closer, and that's all that matters. In the ninth he had to face Ray Brown, Brad Gennaro, and Jon Macalutas—currently, three of the Top Ten hitters in the WBL—and struck out Gennaro and Brown and got Macalutas to hit a soft line drive to center. Well done, Rosey.

Now, let's talk about wrestling. No, not Greco-Roman wrestling. Not WWF. I'm talking about wrestling with reality. During the game tonight, I hardly even noticed our lack of fan support. In yesterday's entry I mentioned that we had maybe 1000 fans in attendance, and we had about the same tonight. When the final out was made and we all slapped high-fives,

I walked over to the bench, and I have to admit that I was let down a little bit by our lack of fan support. Certainly, we have our die-hards, namely the members of our Booster Club, who would never **dream** of missing a game at this point in the season with a playoff spot on the line. But then it hit me: What's the big deal?

If we, by some minor miracle, win the WBL Championship, what have we accomplished? It's not as if we are a team of research scientists who discovered a cure for cancer or a way to repair a severed spinal cord. It's not as if we have 40,000 fans who live or die with each pitch. We have our regular fans, but beyond that, there's really nobody outside the organization who would give a rat's ass. I doubt they'll throw us a ticker-tape parade in Santa Rosa; all we can hope for is a free round of booze at The Office.

I guess with every peak, as a matter of course, there has to be a valley. Perhaps my coming down from last night's high was inevitable. In my seventh pro season, I still love competing as much as ever. I still love winning. I still love doing well. Unfortunately, the demons can still creep into my mind occasionally and derail the train. We have won six in a row, have a chance to sweep the hated Heat tomorrow, and are on the verge of coming out of nowhere to make the playoffs, so I should be a little happier. Sometimes, though, the big picture can rain on the parade. Even if we win it all, we're all still broke and unemployed.

OK, OK, enough already. See, this is why I could never be married while still playing baseball. I couldn't imagine having to explain to my wife why, in spite of our big win, I'm not all "chipper." I need and relish my time alone, and I simply could not bear trying to make sense of how I'm feeling. I guess I just had to vent a little, and it actually felt good. I suppose it's like being on an exotic vacation with a girl whom you know is going to break up with you upon your return. In other words, you better have fun while you can. You may never have it so good again. Out.

CHAPTER 8

▼

COMING UP SHORT

Thursday, August 23, 2001 (10:45 PM)
Yuma

We lost yesterday to the Heat, 6-3, on Fan Appreciation Night. We had probably 3000 fans in attendance—and it was a TV game as well—but we had to face WBL Pitcher of the Year Greg Bicknell. He was on his game last night, holding us to no runs on six hits through eight innings. We managed to scratch across three runs in the bottom of the ninth and actually had the tying run on first base before we succumbed. The fans gave us a rousing ovation as we left the field, partly because of our effort in the ninth and partly for an exciting season. A lot of them wished us luck in Yuma in the hopes that we'll do well enough to earn the playoff spot.

We left after the game last night for Yuma, and we noticed that Tim wasn't on the bus. I think he flew down. JT and I started talking about him and how, if we make the playoffs, he should unquestionably be the Manager of the Year in the WBL. Solano and Chico dwarf us from a talent standpoint, but going into the last weekend of the season, we are on the verge of making the playoffs. Whether it was changing pitchers or giving a steal sign late in the game, the vast majority of his stratagems have worked out well, as evidenced by our 17-7 record in one-run games. It's funny because JT and Tim have had their run-ins, but JT was saying that he genuinely likes him as a manager. Even on the *www.crushersbaseball.com* website discussion list, a few fans have questioned his people skills, but not his managerial ones. Look, this isn't a youth soccer league, where your "coach" better possess some congeniality. In pro sports, the bottom line is winning, and with our roster, Tim has won a lot more than most managers would have.

Here's another good one from the bus. Sasa and Hide flew to Yuma, so they obviously weren't on the bus. Well, Steve Wendt, our radio guy, found a tape of Sasa from his Japanese days. Apparently, the Dodgers had considered signing him, and the videotape was footage that one of their scouts had shot of Sasa. Watching the tape, we were dying. Sasa has a pretty pronounced leg kick now, but 10 years ago, it looked like something out of Bruce Lee film. A left-handed hitter, Sasa would turn his hips back towards the catcher, and no joke, his right foot would sometimes travel in a direct line for the catcher's face, stopping a foot and a half short. The tape showed him hitting line drives all over the yard, oftentimes on pitches most Americans wouldn't even swing at. You sometimes hear announcers on TV, when discussing a good hitter with an unorthodox style, "You wouldn't teach anyone to hit like that, but it works for him." Trust me: You would *never* teach anyone Sasa's style. It was funny as hell. CP shouted out, "Jesus, why did Sasa ever leave Japan; he was hitting 1.000." Unfortunately, Sasa wasn't on the bus to enjoy it with us, but something tells me that the tape may find it's way into the VCR from the hotel to the stadium.

Anyway, we have our final three games of the season in Yuma, and the playoff picture is still murky. It's my understanding that if Solano, Chico, and we all have identical second half records, then we go to the playoffs. Actually, there are too many possibilities to count right now, but rest assured that if we sweep the Bullfrogs this weekend—a very real possibility—we go to the playoffs. Hopefully, I'll have something juicy for tomorrow night's entry, so wish us luck. And stay tuned. Out.

Friday, August 24, 2001 (11:15 PM)
Yuma

Crushers 3, Bullfrogs 2. What a game! We scored an unearned run in the fourth to go up 3-1, and Yuma responded with one of their own to make it 3-2. That was it for the scoring. Their starter, Brad Moore, threw a pretty good game, allowing only four hits, but he walked a few guys. Evel delivered a big two-out, two-run single in the second inning, and he hit the hard ground ball that Yuma's third baseman misplayed for what turned out to be the difference in the game. El Flaco threw the first four innings, giving up their two runs. BG followed with four scoreless innings, and Rosey pitched a 1-2-3 ninth. We have one helluva bullpen, and Tim hasn't been afraid to use any of them lately. Whether it's bringing in young Scott Reeves to face Brown and Gennaro of Chico or having BG throw four innings, every move Tim has made has worked out over the past 11 games, in which we've gone 8-3.

It also helped that we played error-free baseball while mixing in a few highlight-reel plays. Diego threw out a runner at the plate in the fourth, Winter made a nice play up the middle, and even the Fat Third Baseman made a nice play. With one out in the eighth, the hard-hitting Carlos Villalobos hit a hot smash down the third base line that I dove for, backhanded, and threw to first to retire him. If that ball sails by me, it's an easy double, and Yuma had the tying run at second with their fifth and sixth hitters coming up. The Bullfrogs must be tired of seeing me make these plays; over our last four games against them, I've made at least three out-standing plays against them. As I tell my opponents when they tell me that I'm killing them defensively, since I don't hit the ball over the fence, I have to make plays like that to earn my keep.

You know, I'm amazed at how hermit-like I've become this year. In the past sitting in my hotel room on a Friday night—even in a place like Yuma—would be unthinkable. A bunch of guys went over to an *Outback Steakhouse* for dinner, but I ate by myself at an *IHOP*. I actually prefer eating alone, much to the delight of McAffee, who says, "Bo, you're missing out on life with all the reading you do." He's always on my case in the clubhouse about my incessant book-worming, especially while I'm devouring our postgame spread. I like to eat alone so I can catch up on my *Sports Illustrateds* and *ESPN The Magazines* which I often don't have the time to read when we're at home. I don't mean any disrespect to my team-mates, but I like my "alone" time. I see these guys all day long at the yard, and I just don't feel the need to be in their faces all night long, too. I guess I've always been that way. In fact, one former Chico teammate said it best when he said, "You may go to a bar with Bo, but once you get in, you don't see him again." CP is the same way. He hasn't gone to The Office once this year. We all razz him a little, trying to get him out, but really, no one cares. He prefers to go home and get his rest, and if it works for him (it does), then so be it. Most of the time, I would rather do some writing than go out. God, what's next, domestication?

Let me tell you how hot it is in Yuma. Yuma is right where Mexico, California, and Arizona all meet. On the way home after the game tonight, a marquee thermometer read 95°F. During BP today, I think it was 105°F, and needless to say, I was sweating like Gary Condit during a Connie Chung interview. Tim told us starters to get our groundballs, get our hacks, and then get our asses into the air-conditioned clubhouse. That works for me. It was so hot that I was soaked with sweat by the end of our stretching routine. As a player, I don't know if I could play here because, as you know, I need a lot of extra BP, especially early in the year. I haven't taken early BP in probably a month, in part because of I've been feeling pretty good at the plate but also because rest is more important to me at the end of a long season. But if I were playing here, I don't know if I could handle early BP as often as I like to take it. As much as I would like playing for Plummer again, this infernal heat might prove to be too much.

Chico lost today in St. George, which means that as long as either Solano or we win at least one more game, they can't win the second half. Solano beat Long Beach tonight, so as of right now, we are tied. If we win our final two games, then we go to the playoffs, and they go home. Tim addressed that today in a brief pregame chat, stating that we can't worry what the other teams are doing. As the sports phrase goes, "We control our own destiny," meaning that if we win the rest of our games—no matter what the other teams do—we go to the playoffs. One down, two to go. Let's crush 'em. Out.

Saturday, August 25, 2001 (11:45 PM)
Yuma

Do you want the bad news or the worst news first? OK. The bad news: The Crushers lost tonight, 6-2. The worst news: Solano won, 8-7. Ryan Henderson, a former AAA pitcher, went the distance, allowing only four hits. He features a hard, cutting fastball and a nice curveball, and that was all he needed tonight. Yuma scored four in the bottom of the third after an uncharacteristic error by Evel on the leadoff batter of the inning. As it turned out, the Bullfrogs didn't need the other two runs they tacked on.

As if the last two weeks haven't been nerve-wracking enough, when I reached first base in the ninth inning, Mitch told me that Solano was losing 6-1 to Long Beach in the seventh inning. When we returned to the clubhouse after the game, Tim told us that Solano was losing 7-1, adding that assuming Long Beach holds on, all we have to do is win tomorrow and we're in. So, a bunch of us headed over to a local *Applebee's* for dinner, anxiously awaiting the official final score of the game (TD remains good friends with former Crusher A.J. Samadani, Long Beach's closer). Unfortunately, TD became the bearer of bad tidings, as Samadani's phone call provided us with the final score. We entered *Applebee's* in the driver's seat; we left holding onto the bumper as the car sped away.

This is what a whole season's worth of baseball comes down to: We need to win and Solano needs to lose. If you remember, I predicted that we would have to win six out of the last nine to have a legitimate chance but that we'd most likely need to win seven. To this point, we have won six, and even if we win our seventh tomorrow, we still need help. Three weeks ago Gabe Garcia predicted that it would go down to the last game. As it turns out, he was right. I guess all we can do is win tomorrow and pray for a Solano loss.

Win or lose tomorrow, I am so proud of this team. I don't mean to sound condescending or anything like that, but we played over our heads in the second half. When Winter and Evel became our "keystone combination," we became a good team. Our pitching staff, at least our bullpen, has been pretty stable all year, but other than that, we've had so many roster changes that I didn't know if we were a baseball team or a collection of Liz Taylor's husbands. I can't believe that we still have a mathematical chance to make the playoffs. Certainly, a tip of the cap must go to Tim, but a lot of credit is due to the players—all seven of us, maybe—who have been here since the first day of spring training. It would have been easy back in late June to say, "Ah, the hell with this; give me my release, so I can go play somewhere better." Believe me, several of my teammates were tempted and tempted often. We hung in there, though, and now we're on the cusp. Let's Crush 'em—and Break 'em, too. Out.

Monday, August 27, 2001 (1:15 PM)
Rohnert Park

Bullfrogs 5, Crushers 1. Season over. As it turned out, we could have won 147-1 and it wouldn't have mattered since Long Beach did its best "el foldo" and were swept by Solano. We needed to sweep the Bullfrogs, no easy task in its own right, and we had to do it on the road. Solano, meanwhile, had to sweep the Breakers, and they did just that. We won seven out of our last ten games, but Solano won nine of their last ten. Trying to overtake a quality, veteran-laden team like Solano in the last week of the season is like trying to climb Mt. Everest without oxygen. Or Sherpas. Or food. We just couldn't pull it off.

Believe it or not, in spite of the constant roster changes, I really enjoyed this year. The old saying, "Misery loves company" became sort of an unofficial theme for the 2001 Crushers. We started out with a bang, but after losing our shortstop and leadoff hitter James Lofton—who, reportedly, may receive a September call-up with the Red Sox—we hit the skids for what seemed like a month and a half. We had several three- and four-game losing streaks and very few winning streaks of that length. All the while, though, we regularly convened at The Office to commiserate and to drown our sorrows in suds.

Another reason I enjoyed this team is that because, across the board, we were so under-talented, we didn't have the egos and chips on the shoulder that a team like Chico has. Chico, which led the league in both pitching *and* hitting, has a lot of guys who don't belong in this league, but because they are, they don't play with the rookie enthusiasm of a Winter Adames or a Scott Reeves. I hate to use the term, but too many of Chico's guys are bitter about being in the WBL. To be sure, guys like Ray Brown and Brad Gennaro and pitchers Gabe Sollecito and Greg Bicknell *should* be in AAA, and since they're not—and since the end of the tunnel is approaching— they don't have as much fun. Hell, Winter and Scott are just tickled pink to be receiving a biweekly paycheck to play baseball, or as Pete Rose put it, "…have a license to steal." Because we had so many young kids, I became more of a "leader" (in my opinion a horribly overused term in sports,) but it was a role that I gingerly accepted and grew to like.

A lot of people have asked me if I'm going to return to Chico to live for the offseason. Well, to me, that would be like moving next door to where your ex-wife and her new husband live. That's not to say that I will never return; my brother and my old host family are still there, as well as a few other close friends. Certainly, I will visit them this winter, but I am planning on living in the Rohnert Park area. I will try like hell to get this journal published, and yes, I will try like hell to get back to Taiwan, where, according to Tim, the two leagues are considering a merger and a huge increase in salary. Tim still remains in contact with the head of the TML and has reported to him several times how well I was doing this year for him. Hopefully, Tim can pull some strings for me, and I think I left enough of a favorable impression on him that he will do what he can. As for my immediate future, as in the next month or so, well, I've decided to keep it a secret. My next entry will divulge all the necessary information, but let me repeat what I said back in April when I found out that I was joining the Crushers: "A rolling stone gathers no moss." Out.

CHAPTER 9

▼

HEADING EAST AGAIN?

Monday, August 27, 2001 (10:15 PM)
Oakland, CA

What am I doing in Oakland, you ask? Well, let me tell you. About two weeks ago, I received an e-mail from a guy named Donny Woods, my trainer when I was with Adirondack of the now-defunct Northeast League in the summer 1995. He wanted to know if I would be interested in playing for his new team, the Nashua (NH) Pride, of the independent Atlantic League, if the Crushers failed to make the postseason. James Lofton did it last year, and he helped Nashua win the league championship. I contacted Nashua's manager, Butch Hobson, about "turning the same trick," and he seemed mildly interested. Then, I got the bright idea of "offering my services" to the other teams of the Atlantic League, and I did so via e-mail. ("Turning tricks" and "offering my services"—what am

-213-

I, a prostitute?) On Thursday, Bud Harrelson of the Long Island Ducks called me in response to my e-mail, stating that he needed an everyday third baseman. Carlos Baerga, a former four-time All-Star in the major leagues, had been playing third base for them, but he opted to go to Korea to make more money. I told Harrelson that I'd have to see what our post-season chances looked like. Before I knew it, Harrelson called me again late Sunday night to find out what our playoff situation was, but due to the time zone effect, I couldn't call him back until this afternoon.

For me, it came down to one question: Do I take the role as part-time starter and designated hitter for the playoff-bound Pride—who just recently signed former major league third baseman Kim Batiste—or accept a full-time third base job for the playoff-unlikely Ducks? While the former offered a longer season (and hence more money), I opted for the latter. As much as I would like to win a championship and earn a few extra bucks in doing so, the thought of DHing and playing part-time is extremely unappealing to me. With the exception of April of 1996 with the Visalia Oaks, I have been *the* third baseman on every pro team I've played for, so I don't know if I could handle—mentally or physically—being a role player. Long Island plays in front of an average of 6,000 fans per night (as opposed to Nashua's 3,000), and Harrelson told me that basically I was going to man the hot corner for the rest of the season. Those two factors also played large parts in my decision. After being told earlier this year—*twice*—that I was no longer wanted, I certainly like feeling desired again.

I have to admit that I am a bit nervous about going to the Atlantic League. We WBL players often wonder about the caliber of play in the other independent leagues, and as the WBL's All-Star third baseman, I think there is some pressure on me to show the Atlantic Leaguers that we Left Coasters can play, too. Now, I'm not going to get delusions of grandeur and try to hit homeruns or steal bases or anything dumb like that. If I can put up the same numbers, prorated of course, over my three weeks in the Atlantic League, I'll be happy. I would also like to use this opportunity to showcase my skills—what few I have—to a new part of the country. It's no secret that the Atlantic League is better scouted than the WBL, as well it should be with such big leaguers as Jim Leyritz, Jose Canseco, Lance Johnson, and Pete Incaviglia making the rounds there. The owner of the Ducks, Frank Boulton, also told me about the AL's track record of placing players with organizations, and although my catching on is a long shot, you never know.

Whatever transpires, at least I took a shot. Naturally, my omnipresent fear of failure will be a tough obstacle to overcome—especially if I start slowly—but like Michael Jordan said when he tried to make the major leagues, "I can accept failure. What I cannot accept is not trying." I couldn't agree more. Furthermore, this will be the first time playing professionally on the east coast since that summer of 1995. I have a lot of family in New Jersey, where four of the eight teams in the league are based, and many of those relatives haven't seen me play since my college days. As if this summer hasn't already put me through the wringer enough, the same emotions are resurfacing: fear, anticipation, pride, independence, and greed (did I mention a nice little increase in salary?). Hang on folks; the odyssey isn't over just yet. Out.

Wednesday, August 29, 2001 (12:45 PM)
Somerset, NJ

Boy, where do I begin? Let's start with the travel. We left Yuma, AZ, on Sunday night at about 11:00 PM. I was able to doze for a few hours on the bus, but you know how travel sleep is—not exactly deep sleep, if you know what I mean. After confirming my deal with the Ducks on Monday afternoon, I flew out of Oakland at 11:30 PM PDT on Monday night and arrived at JFK International Airport at about 8:00 AM EDT on Tuesday morning. An El Salvador native named Juan picked me up and drove me to a town called Islip on Long Island. I was asking him about Long Island and how much farther beyond Islip the island went, and he told me about three hours more, all the way to the Hamptons. Whenever I hear the Hamptons, I think of *Seinfeld* and the house that George told his ex-fiancé's parents that he had there and how they called his bluff, forcing George to drive them all the way out there. Despite having grown up on the east coast, I have never been to the New York City area (unless you include my unrecountable trip as a seven-year-old), so it was interesting to see some of the places that I had heard about.

I arrived at Euro-American Bank (EAB) Park at about 9:00 AM, and I immediately took care of all the necessary bookwork: reimbursements, contracts, worker's compensation, and tax forms. Matt O'Brien, the club's GM, showed me around the stadium, and then I told him that I'd like to take a little nap. He took me to one of the upper-level suites (yes, a minor league version of luxury boxes, but I'll get to that) where there was a leather couch. One of the clubhouse attendants brought me a blanket, and I asked Matt to come wake me at about 12:30 PM so I could go get something to eat and collect myself before our 3:30 PM BP. Well, the wakeup call never came, and I awoke on my own at 3:15 PM. Naturally, I had to scramble down to the clubhouse, get my new gear, put in my contact lenses, and get out to the field on time—it wouldn't look too good to be late on my first day. Unfortunately, one pressing issue was on my mind: food. I ate before I got on the plane in Oakland, which would translate to about 1:30 AM EDT. Because I was running late, I couldn't eat until after BP, roughly 5:30 PM. Therefore, I went about 16 hours without food, and my pregame meal consisted of two peanut butter and jelly sandwiches and three hard pretzels. Not too bad, huh?

Don McCormack, our manager, put me at third base for the game and batted me seventh in the order. I felt surprisingly good in spite of the arduous journey I had just undergone, and I had a so-so game at best. I went 1-3 with a walk and an error. I hit two balls hard—one for a hit— but I batted twice with the bases loaded and didn't knock anyone in. In the second inning I hit a one-hop rocket right at the shortstop that he fielded and flipped to second to end the inning. Later, with one out in the seventh in a 4-2 game, I hit a weak fly ball to center that was not deep enough to send in the runner on third. I was frustrated. As I've said many times, I need to produce in those situations since I'm not going to hit a ton of doubles and homeruns for my RBI's. I had a chance to give the fans—and the team—something to cheer about and I didn't. Damnit!! We lost 5-2.

EAB Park is outstanding. According to Matt, it seats just over 6,000 fans, and there was a full house last night. The park actually features two levels, with the upper level, of course, housing the suites. I really enjoyed playing in front of a packed house, and I mentioned to one of my team-mates that there were more fans there than in one evening in the WBL—all three home teams' stadiums combined! There is a Diamond Vision scoreboard, complete with headshots of each batter and his stats. Quite big league, no? I suppose the whole ambience reminded me of the Epicenter, home of the Rancho Cucamonga Quakes of the California League; two or three times I played there in front of 6,000 or more fans. In my first at-bat, I was introduced as Bo Durkac, "the new guy"—yes, the PA guy actually said that over the loud speakers. The weather was very humid, and I was sweating a lot. I even had to go behind the pitcher's mound and grab the resin bag in order to dry the sweat off my hands. In my short stint here we have nine more home games, and I am looking forward to playing at EAB Park again.

After the game I packed up most of my stuff for our nine-game, all New Jersey road trip, which began today. Leaving Long Island, we drove through NYC, and I got my first peek at the Brooklyn Bridge. I think we took Route 278 down here to Somerset. We play here for three games, followed by three more games in Atlantic City, and conclude in Camden. One of the guys mentioned a nightclub in Camden called "Top Dog" that is supposed to be off the hook on Tuesday nights. I guess that's an invitation, isn't it?

During the game I was thinking that maybe they should rename the league the "Minority League." I have never seen so many blacks and

Latinos on one field. I don't know why we don't see more of them in the WBL. Obviously, I don't know everyone's history yet, but our shortstop, Juan Bautista, is a former Oriole farmhand with two weeks of big league time. Speaking with him between innings last night, he told me that he was supposed to take Cal Ripken, Jr.'s place at shortstop about three years ago, but Ripken decided that he wasn't ready to move over to the hot corner just yet. Then, they signed Roberto Alomar for second base, leaving Bautista to flounder in AAA. Ray Ricken, at 6'5, 260 lbs., pitched for the Tri-City Posse of the WBL last year, and another pitcher, lefty Brad Woodall, has some big league time with Atlanta. I remember Woodall because he was a senior at UNC when I was a high school senior visiting Chapel Hill in 1991. Other than that, everyone else is completely foreign to me. I will fill you in on the others as I learn more about them. It appears, however, that most of the players on both teams are AA/AAA guys, and even though it's early, it appears that the quality of this league is better than that of the WBL.

Finally, as "the new guy," I'm just trying to fit in and earn my keep. As a general rule, the "new guy" isn't supposed to act like one of the guys until he has done something significant—more than once. And it doesn't have to be *on* the field. A lot of new guys have become "part of the team" by hooking up with an extremely attractive young lady in a nightclub in front of his teammates. The guys think, "Damn, if this cat can hook it up with a hot chick like that, he must be all right." Credibility can be acquired in that way as well as with on-field performance. Personally, I'd like to drive in a few runs, play some good defense, and help this team win a few games to become "one of them." If, however, a situation presents itself at Top Dog, well, I'm not adverse to that, either. Out.

Wednesday, August 29, 2001 (11:15 PM)
Somerset

Ducks 11, Somerset Patriots 3. We had twelve hits and nine runs by the end of the fourth inning. I had a nice game, going 2-4 with a double, a walk, an RBI and two runs scored. All the guys on our team were saying what a good team Somerset has, but we beat them up pretty good tonight. Our starter, Robert Theodile, threw a helluva game, going seven innings and giving up only two runs. He had a hard fastball and a sharp breaking curve to go with it, and he must have struck out 12. Mike Glavine, Tom's "little" brother, hit a titanic homerun to right field—it may actually still be in flight—but other than that, they didn't hit many balls too hard. It was a nice win.

Somerset's stadium is beautiful, and like ours, it holds over 6,000 fans. There are two levels as well. Incidentally, the attendance tonight was about 6,450, though the fans didn't have much to cheer about.

I'm learning more about my teammates all the time. For example, our first baseman, 37-year-old Doug Jennings, has played in the big leagues for the Cubs and A's and also in the Japanese big leagues, where, according to one player, he "made his millions." He also played against Sasa, telling me yes, he could indeed hit. Our second baseman, Adonis Harrison, has a little big league time with Tampa Bay, and everyone on our team raves about his glove work. I've seen him make mostly the routine plays, but he made a Roberto Alomar-style play tonight. Our club is definitely more of a veteran team than the Crushers and for that matter, just about all the teams in the WBL. Part of the reason for that is that there is no team salary cap in this league. Apparently, the maximum amount that one team can pay one player is $3,000 per month, but a team can pay each player that much if it so chooses. In the WBL the salary cap is $25,000 per month **per team**, which significantly hinders a player's chances of making any decent money. Justin Davies, our leadoff hitter and center fielder, and I were talking about the attitudes of our players, and we decided that most of the guys are bitter about being here and earning a fraction of what they could be earning in AAA or in a foreign league. Davies and I both take the opposite point of view; we are both just happy to be playing baseball for some decent money. I suppose it's a glass-half-empty vs. a glass-half-full argument.

In closing, during the fourth inning tonight, I was on first base when Bautista hit a soft line drive down the right field line. I took off immediately, paused for a second to make sure the right fielder couldn't get to it, and then took off again. As I rounded third, Harrelson gave me the stop sign very late, and I stopped. Bautista, of course, had a double. Later, after we had both scored and were sitting in the dugout, he asked me why I didn't score. I had to break to him the news that I'm not the swiftest afoot. (In fact, during the last week of the season, the Milkman, after watching me gimp around the bases on a sore knee, told me, "Bo, if you were a horse, you'd be dog food by now.") Anyway, Bautista is two triples away from setting the league record, and evidently, he wasn't too pleased with my slow ass keeping him from tallying another three-bagger. I told him, "Mala mia. No puedo correr." (My bad. I can't run.) He just laughed. Out.

Saturday, September 1, 2001 (2:00 PM)
Atlantic City

Well, I satisfied my gambling "addiction" last night. Six of us piled into my roommate Ryan Gorecki's 1988 Mustang and headed into Atlantic City. No, it wasn't as comfortable as I would have liked, but beggars can't be choosers, right? Pulling into AC at about 1:00 AM, Ryan and I—the other four decided to do the dance club thing—hit the tables at Trump Marina and then Harrah's. I was amazed to see that the minimum bets were $15, as opposed to the $5 tables I'm used to in Mesquite. I overcame my reluctance and walked out $36 richer on the night. I can live with that.

As for on the field, I don't want to say I'm struggling because that would imply that I'm getting good pitches to hit and not hitting them. I also don't want to say that I'm overmatched because that would imply that I've been looking, well, overmatched at the plate. In actuality, it's somewhere in between. I'm telling you, folks, the pitching in the league is *far* superior to that of the WBL. In the WBL, you can count on one pitcher per team having really good stuff. Here, the middle relievers have better stuff than most of the starters I've faced in the WBL. If I had to guess, most of the right-handed pitchers throw in the upper 80's, and two of the three lefties I've seen both have better fastballs than WBL lefties. Right now, I'm hitting .250 after 16 at-bats, and the bottom line is that I'm going to have to recalibrate my timing if I want to hit in this league. Whether I can do that in three weeks remains to be seen.

Now, in spite of the increased caliber of play in this league, it's good to see that ballplayers are ballplayers no matter where you are. For example, we watched the movie *Wild Things* on the way from Somerset to Atlantic City last night, and during the famous "testosterone-inducing" scene of the film, I could see the drool forming on the mouths of every guy on the team. Also, Tony Amin, one of our trainers, is one of those guys with a thick "New Yawk" accent, and his mouth goes a mile a minute. If he's not ragging on the age of a player from the other team, he's ragging one of our guys. After the game in Long Island on Tuesday, we traded one of our pitchers, but that pitcher's meal money appeared on the bus on Wednesday morning. Naturally, the guys were trying to decide on how to spend it. Before they eventually settled on buying some movies for our bus trip, Tony told Ricken, "I'd give the money to you, but you might go out and buy a buffet table." The behemoth Ricken then slowly rose out of his seat and proceeded to turn Tony into a human pretzel.

One final story. The other day in the dugout during our 5-1 loss to Somerset, I saw something I'd never seen before: two Dominicans getting into a shouting match. You see, when you've played in the low minors and in lesser independent leagues as I have, birds of a feather *really* flock together. Because the Latinos are usually quite young, their English isn't very good, and, therefore, they stick together like glue. Most of the black guys tend to hang out with the other black guys, too. Yesterday, though, I was shocked to see two veteran Dominicans vehemently arguing over a pitch that was hit for a homerun by a .220-hitting catcher. Even more amazing was that part of the arguing was done in English and part in Spanish. I mentioned earlier about the chips on the shoulder that a team like Chico has with all its talent. Well, when several of your players were either on the cusp of the big leagues or actually in The Show, the chips become slabs. Out.

Sunday, September 2, 2001 (2:45 PM)
Atlantic City

Am I in Taiwan again? I feel as though I am since I'm hitting like I did when I was there. I am 5-21 right now, a robust .238, but even worse is that two of those five hits were bleeders. In other words I'm hitting like Ally McBeal again. This time around, however, I know what the problem is.

As John Wooden once said, "Physical superiority negates all theory." In basketball terms, this means that you may have the ideal game plan to break a full-court, man-to-man press—a scheme that worked to perfection in practice—but if the pressing team's athletes are too big and too quick for your team, then all the planning in the world isn't going to help. Now let me explain how it pertains to me.

All hitters base their approaches to hitting on the speed of the pitcher's fastball. If that day's pitcher isn't throwing particularly hard—anything less than 86 MPH—then the hitter doesn't have to worry about the pitcher's fastball blowing his doors off. When discussing this type of pitcher, we say, "He won't throw his fastball by you." We hitters can follow the ball slightly longer before we decide to swing, rendering us less likely to be fooled by a pitch. If, on the other hand, the pitcher is throwing 90 MPH or more, then the hitter has to respect his fastball because unless the pitcher throws it right down the middle, he *can* "throw it by you." Consequently, the hitter has to start his swing a split-second earlier than he is comfortable doing in order to catch up to the fastball. The hitter's natural, ingrained timing mechanism then becomes fouled up, and he loses that comfort zone. All of a sudden, the hitter, because he has to start his swing a tad earlier, is now unable to follow the ball for that extra few feet to determine what pitch is coming. Therefore, he becomes susceptible to anything that isn't a fastball. I would guess that 80% of the lousy swings—at sliders or split-fingers in the dirt or at fastballs at the chin level—you see in a major league game are a result of the hitters' starting their swings early to catch up to a good fastball.

You see, that's why organizations like to draft pitchers who throw over 90 MPH. The brass figures that if the young hurler can learn a curveball, a slider, a changeup, or a split-finger fastball (or any combination of these pitches), then he can become an effective major league pitcher. The problem for a hitter isn't the 90+ MPH fastball; although it sounds difficult, believe me when I tell you that it's not that hard to hit a straight, 92 MPH-fastball when you know it's coming. The problems start when the hitter isn't sure what's coming, and if he's trying to catch up to the good fastball and the pitcher throws something else, the hitter is usually beaten.

Having played in the WBL for the past four seasons, it appears that the average fastball is roughly four or five MPH slower than that of the Atlantic League. No, not everyone in this league throws 90 MPH, but the speed itself is not what's important. What's important is the *change* of the speed. Over the last four years, my hitting instincts have been honed to hit WBL pitching, and I've been successful in doing that. My instincts have told me that I can follow the ball for "x" number of feet—I don't know exactly how long I track it—before I make my decision to swing or not swing. In this league, however, I must make my decision before I would like to, and this change in velocity has necessitated a change in my instincts. The problem is that such a change cannot occur in a few weeks.

When I joined the Visalia Oaks of the Class A California League in 1996, I started out hitting 6-36. I had played the previous spring in college and the previous summer in the Northeast (independent) League, and neither level of competition offered me the type of pitching I would see in April of 1996. To put it simply, I had to get used to seeing 90 MPH fastballs everyday. Once I did, then I started hitting. I finished the year at .298, but after my lousy start, I hit .309 over the rest of the year. Unfortunately, with the Ducks, I don't have four full months to turn things around.

We have roughly fourteen games left, and I don't know if there's anything I can do to expedite the learning curve. All the batting practice in the world won't help. I need to "change my instincts," and that is not an overnight proposition. I need to face these pitchers everyday, for four or five at-bats a day, in order to find my timing again. I suppose there is a chance that I could come around in the next week or so, but we'll have to wait and see. I hope you enjoyed—and were able to follow—today's hitting tutorial. Out.

Tuesday, September 5, 2001 (1:00 AM)
Camden, NJ

My batting average has fallen to its professional nadir of .226. After seven games, that's the best I can do. I'm telling you, the pitching in this league may not be great, but it's better than anything I've seen since my California League days. Actually, let me clarify that statement: It's *harder* than anything I've seen in the WBL. Remember, everything starts with the fastball, and if you can't hit that, you're in trouble. Right now, I can't, and it's frustrating. Just to show how odd this experience has been, I actually prefer hitting right-handed now. In my entire baseball career I've been a better hitter from the left side—I would guess my career averages would be in the neighborhood of .330 vs. .280—but with the increase in velocity of the right-handed pitchers I've been facing, I feel much more comfortable from the right side. The average lefty, even in this league, throws approximately four to five MPH slower than the righties, so my right-handed instincts haven't been as affected as those from the left side. I think I'm 3 for 10 from the right side, and all three hits have been line drives, unlike the other side, where two of my four hits were bleeders. It's not as though I've always dreaded hitting right-handed; it's just that I am a better hitter from the left side, and I would prefer batting from that side.

The attitudes of the guys on this team are decidedly different from that of my teammates in the WBL. You may not believe this, but a lot of these guys *don't* want to play everyday. We have two utility guys, Ryan and Tom Caputo, and it seems as though every time we get to the park, one of them is bitching about being in the lineup. I don't quite understand why they don't want to play. I suppose the fact that we have only 12 games remaining and we're basically out of the playoff race might have something to do with it, but for some reason, they'd rather be on the bench from time to time. Regardless, the Ducks still pay them. Personally, I couldn't stand—no pun intended—riding the pine. I've now played in 671 of 692 possible professional games. Of the ones I missed, only one was due to injury, and not once have I ever asked for a day off. I missed the others because I may have been struggling or because the manager wanted to play someone else. Now, I could say that I want to play everyday because I believe in the (unfortunately) horribly antiquated notion "I'm being paid to do a job, and I owe it to my boss to show up at work ready to go," but that's not why. I want to play everyday basically for two reasons: 1) The pride that comes with being "dependable" and "consistent" and 2) not playing—*i.e.*, watching a baseball game—would make me so bored that I'd probably go clinically insane. The situation here is a classic case of "to each, his own," and even though I don't quite understand the attitude, it nevertheless exists.

Also, hustle, another outdated part of the major league game, is sorely lacking here, too. What happened to running out groundballs and fly balls? What happened to running on and off the field? I've never seen so many guys "jake it" down the line after hitting a weak pop-up or grounder. Certainly, it's okay to jog down the line if you're nursing a leg injury, but as far as I know, the players in this league are healthy. I know this because when they want to run—when they "smell a base hit" or when they try to stretch a double into a triple—they can turn on the burners. What happened to running hard *all* the time? At the ripe old age of 28, maybe the game is passing me by.

Atlantic City's stadium, The Sandcastle, is quite a step down from the other two stadiums I've seen thus far. Apparently, the owner of the Ducks, Frank Boulton, also owns the Surf, and since he's selling the Surf at the end of the season, he has decided to put as little money into the field and stadium as possible. We played in front of about 2,800 fans on Sunday (naturally, the postgame fireworks display was the culprit), but the other two games featured Sonoma County-like crowds. The smell of seawater and the sight and sounds of the sea gulls flying overhead, as well as the casinos making up the skyline beyond the outfield wall, let you know exactly where you are. Typical of a minor league team in a gambling town, Atlantic City doesn't draw a lot of fans—there is just too much else to do—but players still want to play there, and visiting teams still like and look forward to the road trip.

Finally, we have three more games on this road trip, followed by three at home, and then we have a day off. So far, in spite of my struggles on the field, I've enjoyed my little excursion into the Atlantic League. Not to sound as if I've "conquered" the WBL, but I have liked the challenge that this league has afforded me. It has shown me that the WBL is pretty small potatoes in the big baseball picture; every once in awhile, the white kid from the suburbs needs to go into the inner city so the black guys can show him how good basketball *really* is. Out.

Wednesday, September 5, 2001 (11:30 PM)
Cherry Hill, NJ

I am now below the "Mendoza line." For those of you who aren't familiar with that term, the Mendoza line—named after former light-hitting shortstop Mario Mendoza—is .200, and right now, I'm under it. I can't believe it. I never thought I could hit this poorly. The pangs of frustration I felt in Taiwan are similar to the ones that I feel now, but the ones I'm experiencing now are far more debilitating. Failing to hit in Taiwan was due to a different pitching style (and my own rustiness), not as much to an increase in the quality of pitching. My ineptitude here in the Atlantic League, however, means one thing: I simply am not very good. Certainly, given a full season in this league—with ample time to adjust my timing—I think I can hit .260 or so, but what good is that? I have minimal power and no speed, and the numbers that I put up in the WBL would be severely curtailed in this league. The guys in this league are mostly AA/AAA guys, and they can play. And they can pitch. Our little world known as the WBL has ill-prepared me for this league—and blinded me as to how good baseball players can really be. I mean, if the guys in this league are, well, in this league, how can I expect to further my career? I am going to have to do some serious thinking this offseason.

Last night we went to *Top Dog*, and it was pretty much what I expected: A bar downstairs, an outdoor section, and a dance club upstairs. The big drink special was $1 Bud Lights, and, believe me, the barley and hops flowed throughout. Having been in California for basically the last six summers, I took for granted the "no-smoking" policy that exists in the Golden State. In *Top Dog*, especially in the dance club part, the thick fog of cigarette smoke filled the air. I walked out last night, and my clothes smelled like smoke, a sensation I haven't smelled in quite some time. All in all, I would say that the club scene here is no different than what can be found on the west coast. To me, no matter where I'm "clubbing," the whole scene is so passé; I'll take the scene at The Office any day.

One other thing that drove me nuts tonight is New Jersey's "no left turn" rule while driving. My mom, who is leaving for a cruise with my dad on Monday, drove all the way to Camden with a relative so I could have a car (way to go, Lani!). Tonight, after the game, I went out to get a bite to eat and to fill up with gas. Apparently, New Jersey, on major roads, forbids left-hand turns across traffic. Instead, they have these "jug handle" turns. If you picture a jug handle, that's the kind of route you have to take when you want to either turn left or make a u-turn. I knew where I wanted to go tonight while I was driving, but every time I was ready to turn left, I had to take one of those infernal "jug handles." Before I knew what was going on, I was traveling in an entirely different direction from where I wanted to be going. After stopping to ask for directions—and to curse a blue streak to no one in particular—I eventually made it back to the hotel. Fortunately, this entire experience took place at night; otherwise I may have ended up in a fender-bender. The whole time I was thinking of the scene in *National Lampoon's European Vacation* when Clark Griswold can't switch lanes while driving around in a circle in London. After each lap, he says, "Look, kids, Big Ben. Parliament." By the time the scene is over, it's dark out, and Clark is horribly frustrated. As Yogi Berra once said, "It was déjà vu all over again." Out.

Friday, September 7, 2001 (11:00 PM)
Long Island

What's it called when the game ends and your team has more runs than the other team? Oh yeah, a win. The only thing more pitiful than my hitting is the Duck's record in the "Durkac era." Actually, my batting average is worse than our team's winning percentage—.190 vs. .272—but who's counting? We beat the Lehigh Valley Diamonds, 5-3, tonight in front of 6,000+ fans at EAB Stadium. Lehigh Valley is one of those unfortunate teams that is playing its entire season on the road. From what I've heard, plans for building a stadium in Lehigh, PA, were interrupted due to lack of funding; therefore, the stadium isn't complete. Rather than dump the team altogether, the league opted to make Lehigh Valley a traveling band of ballplayers. Naturally, they're not a very good team, not so much because of the travel schedule but more so because not too many quality ball players would want to play in a situation like that. Regardless, right now a win against Danny Almonte's Baby Bronx Bombers would have sufficed nicely.

Lehigh Valley threw a knuckleball pitcher against us tonight, and he tossed a pretty good game. We got to him for four runs in the second inning, but other than that, we really didn't do a whole lot against him. Knuckleballers, as you can imagine, are weird to hit against. The ball comes in around 60 MPH, and it dances all over the place like a feather in a tornado. Former major league catcher and funnyman Bob Uecker, a.k.a. Mr. Baseball, once said, "The best way to catch a knuckleball is to let it roll all the way to the backstop, and once it stops, pick it up." When a knuckleball is thrown properly—as guys like Hoyt Wilhelm and Phil Niekro used to throw and Tim Wakefield currently throws—it's next to impossible to hit. Hell, if the catcher can't catch it, how can a hitter hit it?

I had a sharp single to right field and a hard grounder to first tonight against the knuckleballer, and it brought back memories of my High Desert days. Back in 1997, a guy named Kevin Pincavitch, under the tutelage of former major league knuckleballer Charlie Hough, was learning how to throw it. He pitched for San Bernardino, a Dodgers farm team, so we faced him probably three or four times that year. Well, in an otherwise undistinguished season, I made my mark by hitting the snot out of Pincavitch's knuckler. It got to be a damn joke. Our big hitters—guys who hit 30+ homeruns to my 8 and batted .310 to my .280—couldn't do squat against him, but I raked him. I'll bet I was something around 7-11 against him that year, with a homerun, a couple of doubles, and probably eight RBI's. When I went to Australia in 1999 with that independent league All-Star team, Pincavitch was on it, and the first thing he said to me was, "Jesus, Durkac, I could *never* get you out!" I just laughed. I think my legacy with the Diamondbacks came down to three things: destroying knuckleballs, chasing skirts at *The Blue Parrot* and drinking gin-and-tonics by the gallon. The latter one was brought to my attention by McAffee, who told me that the Diamondbacks players who played with me that year would see the green sweat stains on the underside of my hat, and they figured it was from all the gin-and-tonics being purged from my body. Oh well, I guess it's better to leave a triumvirate like that as a legacy than nothing at all.

For the record, I am staying at a posh Hilton hotel in Huntington on Long Island. These rooms go for around $249 per night, but since this is the official hotel of the Long Island Ducks, I have to pay only $60 per night. I will be on Long Island for a grand total of nine nights, and as part of my contract, I will be obligated to pay for each night out of my salary. If can find other living accommodations, of course, then I would get to keep the $60. Honestly, though, I don't know if I would do it. I like the fact that 1) I'm by myself, 2) someone cleans my room daily and 3) I'm living large. Certainly, it would be nice to pocket that extra money, but I'd only leave if the other situation were rather nice. After kicking around in the minors for seven years, I'm allowed to "live it up" for two weeks, right? Out.

Monday, September 10, 2001 (5:30 PM)
Long Island

Today is the first off day we've had since I came here. We played thirteen straight days, so a day of rest is nice. Some fans of the Ducks offered to buy lunch for any interested players at a local *Outback Steakhouse* today, and as expected, the turnout was huge. Minor league baseball players rarely pass up a free meal. Charlie and Pat (I didn't get their last name) have become big fans of the Ducks, and they wanted to show their appreciation by throwing us a little shindig. I was thinking that we should be thanking *them* for their generosity. We all stayed for about two hours.

During lunch, Ricken asked me why I was being so quiet. I told him that he was doing all the talking. I wanted to tell him about the two week statute of limitations on a new player: A new player must wait at least two full weeks before he is allowed to express himself freely. Tomorrow will mark the end of my grace period, but since I have been positively lousy on the field, I may extend it for one more week. Hell, if I don't start pulling my weight around here in the next week or so, none of my teammates will be privileged enough to hear any of my hair-brained theories.

As I said, on the field, I haven't, well, been on the field too much lately. I started the second game in Camden on Wednesday last week, and since then, I've started only one game. I guess my ineptitude has caused our manager, Don McCormack (Mack) to play Tom Caputo, the guy I was supposedly brought in to replace. When two players like Tom and I are competing for a starting position, there normally exists an inherent tension between the two players. Tom hadn't been hitting too well when I arrived, and he knew that I was supposed to become the everyday third baseman. Now, he can deal with the news in one of two ways: He can either "big league" me and ignore me, or he can accept the situation for what it is. Fortunately, Tom chose the latter option, and there has been no friction between us whatsoever. In fact, he is one of the first to congratulate me after making a nice play or after getting a base hit. Now that he has been playing more frequently, and in the spirit of reciprocity, I am quick to compliment him. Most of the time, a situation like this can be quite tense, but both Tom and I have handled it quite professionally.

Looking at my joining this league from a distance, it would initially appear that I made a mistake in coming here. I hit better than .330 in each of the last three years in the WBL, and I'd like to think I've made my mark as one of the best all-around third basemen in the history of the league. But I was insulated from the "real world" of professional baseball. After two weeks, I am still amazed at the talent disparity between the two leagues. Since the WBL hasn't properly prepared me for the Atlantic League, my career stats will take a minor hit. Furthermore, as much as I hate to think it, I've given the WBL a bad name. As I mentioned in my first entry about going to the east coast, I was afraid that people of the Atlantic League would say, "Jeez, if Durkac is the best that the WBL has to offer, then that league must be lousy." Certainly, baseball people have every right to say that. I will not apologize, however, for my failure to hit in this league.

I would have to equate my leap from the WBL to the AL to a jump from college to independent league baseball. I feel I can comment on the latter comparison because I took that step, too. I am simply not enough of a natural hitter to make a seamless transition. Maybe WBL guys like Gennaro, Brown, league MVP Vic Sanchez, and CP could do it, but I haven't been able to. Secretly, I thought I would be able to come into the AL and hit .300. Unfortunately, I both overestimated the WBL and underestimated the AL.

I don't know how much playing time I will receive over the last nine games, but whatever the case, I can handle it. I'm not one of those guys—believe me, there are *tons* of them—who can't accept their own failures and come up with a plethora of excuses to explain them. For example, I've seen .220 hitters complain about having to sacrifice bunt in a close game, asking, "Doesn't he (the manager) have any confidence in me?" Well, my man, how much confidence can he have in a .220 hitter? Just do your damn job. If Mack wants to use me as a pinch-hitter, so be it. If he wants to play me everyday (my preference, in spite of my struggles), then let's go. I believe in the adage, "My worst day at the ballpark is better than my best day at a real job." Out.

CHAPTER 10

▼

THE ULTIMATE METAPHOR

Tuesday, September 11, 2001 (7:30 PM)
Long Island

Today started out as a normal day. I awoke at 8:30 AM, showered, packed, checked out of the hotel at 9:00 AM, went to *McDonald's* for some take-out breakfast, and after pulling out of the parking lot, I flipped on the radio. I could not believe what I heard.

The baby-boomers of America all point to the John F. Kennedy assassination in 1963 as *the* event of their lifetimes. Just about every living 40- and 50-something can recall exactly where he/she was and what he/she was doing upon hearing the news. I have often wondered what event the children of the baby-boomers will one day view with the same pinpoint detail. To me, the O.J. Simpson car chase in 1994, the Oklahoma City bombing in 1995, and Princess Diana's death in 1997 were all candidates. That is, they were until today.

When I arrived at the clubhouse today to catch our team bus to Somerset, the TV was on. I thought I was watching a cross between a Tom Clancy book and a Charles Bronson film, but, alas, it was reality. First, I saw both World Trade Center buildings burning. Then, I saw the South building collapse. Later, the North building collapsed. CNN showed footage of a jet flying into—and through—one of the buildings. The worst part came last: the dead and missing persons count.

Reporters tramped through the wreckage, which looked like the Pacific Northwest in May of 1980 after the Mt. St. Helens eruption. The only problem was that the two inches of "soot" covering Manhattan was powdered cement, as in the stuff left over after a building falls down. As of 8:00 PM, there has been no report of the death toll; however, one CNN reporter, after pointing out that the Battle of Antietam in the Civil War represented the single greatest one-day loss of American lives in our history at 22,000, mentioned that this horrific tragedy could conceivably surpass that total. No one seems to know whom to hold responsible, though the consensus thus far points to a radical Middle East group. Regardless, the damage has been done, and President Bush has promised a full-scale retaliation.

America hasn't been forced into a war since December 7, 1941. In the Korean War, the Vietnam War and the Persian Gulf War, we played "policeman of the world," right or wrong, to justify our involvement. We weren't retaliating for any acts committed against us. We had no need to strike back. Fortunately, that hasn't happened since the day that "will live in infamy." But today, for the first time in almost 60 years, our bluff was called.

Think of this situation as junior high school. There is the eighth grader who is the biggest, strongest, smartest, best-looking, richest, and most respected and well-liked guy in the school. He's also a Golden Glove boxer and a black belt in karate. Basically, nobody messes with him. Sure, every once in a while, one of the "little people" may talk a little smack to him, but being the laid-back, good guy that he is, he just laughs it off. I mean, the little guys are nothing to worry about, right? What does secretly worry him, though, is the short, skinny, poor, dirty-clothed sixth-grader from the wrong side of the tracks who, unlike the other wannabe tough kids, isn't afraid to make eye contact with him. This kid never says two words to the big guy or any of the big guy's friends. Once, between classes, the big guy had to step in to break up a fight between one of the poor kid's friends and one of the big guy's friends. The poor kid wasn't too happy with the big guy's intervention, and he just seethed in the corner of the hallway, his warped mind plotting revenge. Six months later, while the big guy was just minding his business during lunch, the poor kid snuck up behind him and stabbed him in the back. Everyone was horrified and pissed off. What could this little punk possibly be thinking? But don't worry. The little dirtbag—the kid nobody likes—called down the thunder and now he's going to get it; it's time for the big payback, and the whole school can't wait to see it.

I suppose it speaks volumes about the desensitization of today's society when we can watch the bloodshed and destruction of Kosovo and the Holy Land, which appears almost daily on the news, without even flinching. In fact, it happens *so* often that most of us don't normally give it a second look. We think, "Yeah, it's unfortunate and wrong, but hey, it's happening somewhere else. No big deal." Well, while watching the news all day today, I had to remind myself constantly that it was happening *here*. Whoever did this had the audacity to attack not only the two cities that represent America—New York and Washington, D.C.—but also the World Trade Center and the Pentagon, the two symbols of our "top dog" position in the world's hierarchy.

I just watched President Bush's brief address to the nation, and among other things, he mentioned America's stand in the wake of the devastation. He said that we will make no distinction between the terrorists and the countries that harbor them. I absolutely loved that. Having studied the

Vietnam War in college, I can see why the nation was split so badly regarding our involvement there. In this instance, though, whether you are a hawk or a dove, retribution is imperative. I understand and even agree with the "no negotiating with terrorists" policy that the USA practices because the old "give an inch, take a mile" adage would arise if we were to negotiate. But there was no chance for negotiation today. We were attacked—unannounced and unprovoked—and if we don't retaliate, what kind of message are we sending to the rest of the world? In the past, we have tried to keep our foreign military involvements to a minimum in order to avoid receiving the "bully" stamp and also to not rock the world's boat. Now, I don't believe a single nation on Earth would frown upon our day of reckoning. Whoever is responsible better run for the hills. Out.

Wednesday, September 19, 2001 (11:45 PM)
Long Island

We just took two out of three from the Bridgeport Bluefish. For the second straight game, I sat the bench, and I was bored out of my mind. I still don't see how people can watch baseball games live. Someone once said that baseball is the most intellectual game because most of the action takes place in your head. I suppose that's true. Baseball is a game of match-ups and percentages, with one manager always trying to stay one pitch ahead of the other. Having been around the game for so long, however, there is not a whole lot I haven't seen. Certainly, something will happen from time to time that will cause me to say, "Boy, now that's something you don't see everyday," but those instances are rare. It's not as if I am a father taking my eight-year-old son to a game and explaining to him the nuances of the double play pivot or why the third baseman bare-handed a slow grounder as opposed to using his glove. Sitting on the bench and eating sunflower seeds is not my idea of a good time. The only positive thing was practicing my *español* with the Latin players who were also on the bench. What am I going to do? Demand that Mack play me or release me? Hell, if I were managing, I wouldn't play me either.

One event, though, did make things interesting last night, and that was a brawl of WWF proportions. In the top of the ninth, with two outs and nobody on base, our Hut Smith was pitching to Dee Jenkins. We were clinging to a 6-4 lead, and Smith ran the count to 2-2 on Jenkins. The next pitch probably should have been called strike three, but the home plate umpire thought otherwise. Our bench had ridden the umpire all night long for his small strike zone, particularly when our starting pitcher was on the mound, so after the bad call, we really laid into him. The next pitch was low for ball four, and Jenkins, upset with our complaining, started yelling at our dugout on his way to first base. I won't say what he said to us, but it would have made a truck driver blush. Smith took exception to Jenkins profanity-laced tirade and went over to first base to give Jenkins a piece of his mind. Jenkins popped off to Smith, Smith decked Jenkins, and then all hell broke loose.

Naturally, the benches emptied. Smith and Jenkins were rolling around on the ground as the two teams converged. Jenkins and Smith were separated, but somehow Jenkins broke free and punched our manager (I don't know why), opening a gash on Mack's face that left him bleeding profusely. According to one of our players, Jenkins is borderline psychotic, and that label was justified when Jenkins returned to their dugout and brought a bat with him to the fracas. Thank God for Oreste Marrero.

On Monday, just before the start of the game, Tony, our trainer, told me about Marrero. Marrero is one of those rare guys on a baseball field whom *everyone* knows about and fears, as he possesses a Jekyll and Hyde personality and the strength of a lumberjack. Apparently, he is a laid back, easy-going guy until someone flips his switch. Last year, for example, after striking out on a bad call, Tony said that Marrero, with veins and muscles bulging from his neck, looked at his bat as if he wanted to break it over his leg but decided just to break it in his hands, the way you or I would break a yardstick. In all likelihood it probably didn't happen exactly like that, but you get the point. Then, Tony told me that Long Island and Bridgeport brawled last year, and Marrero was flinging guys away from the pile like a man hastily going through a laundry basket looking for his lucky underwear. Whatever the case, everyone on the field knew whom to avoid.

When Jenkins stormed out of the dugout with his weapon of choice, Marrero put him in a chokehold that Hulk Hogan would be proud of. Marrero dragged Jenkins off the field and into the dugout, where he remained. No one really knows what Jenkins would have done had he gotten by Marrero. On the "undercard," if you will, a couple of other fights broke out, but fortunately, they didn't have the intensity of the first one. I have been in three major brawls in my career, and this one was far and away the worst. On a side note Jenkins lost his gold chain, and Marrero came back onto the field to look for it. I saw him looking on the ground and asked him, "What are you looking for?" He quickly responded, "A gold chain." Then he looked at me and asked me, "What am I looking for?" as if to ask me if I was looking for trouble. I said, "No, no, no." Believe me, I wanted no part of that guy and began to help him look for the chain. It reminded of the scene in the movie *Friday* when the neighborhood bully Dee-Bo knocks out a guy and the guy's father yells at Dee-Bo. Dee-Bo then shouts back, "You want some of this, old man?!" The father thinks for a split-second and responds, simply, "No" and quickly jumps into his car.

With all the tension in America recently, everyone is a little on edge, but this fight was horrible. Early in the brawl, the stadium broke into a "USA, USA, USA" chant, but it didn't work. The fight became so bad that the police were called in to bring some peace to the situation. Some fans were throwing stuff at the Bridgeport players and inviting a few of them to come into the stands. Eventually, though, with the threat of a Ducks' forfeiture, order was restored. We lost four players to ejection, and Bridgeport lost three. Carlos Paredes came into the game to retire the next batter, ending the game. What an ugly ending to an ugly game in the wake of an ugly event.

We have six games remaining, and it looks as though, by default, I should be playing in most of the games. We lost one position player to suspension, and Harrison and Jennings are leaving tomorrow due to previous commitments. In the upcoming Somerset series I should have several family members—aunts, uncles and cousins—attending some of the games, and I'd hate to be picking splinters out of my ass with them in the stands. Out.

Saturday, September 22, 2001 (5:00 PM)
Somerset

As I write this, I am sitting in the visitor's clubhouse at Commerce Bank Park. We checked out of the hotel at 3:00 PM today, but since we didn't take BP today, we have roughly three hours of dead time. We didn't take BP yesterday, either. Apparently, BP, normally a *sine qua non* of every game day, has been fazed out of our daily routine; having been eliminated from playoff contention, what's the point, right? To kill time, I played some Casino with two Dominicans, Otoniel Lanfranco, and my roommate on Long Island, Paredes. At about 4:00 PM, I sat down to play some Solitaire when they walked by, so I asked them if they knew Casino. They both responded in the affirmative, at which point Paredes and I played. I won. Then I took on Lanfranco. He won, so now he is playing Paredes. It sounds like somewhat of an impromptu, round-robin Casino tournament. Right now, Paredes is winning, but I would rather write than play again. I told the two of them how I taught Mayque Quintero, the Cuban, how to play—in Spanish—and they were quite impressed.

As I ponder my baseball future now more than ever, I find myself focusing on the negatives—no financial security, no formal job training, etc.—and rarely on the positives. Although the positives are indeed few and far between, the one thing that I did gain from my years in baseball is my proficiency in Spanish, something I never would have attained outside of baseball. I have forced, more or less, the Latin ballplayers to speak with me throughout my entire career, creating a study-abroad environment right here in the USA. In doing so, I have picked up a good deal of the language while bridging cultural gaps at the same time. I have always gotten along with the Latinos on every team I've played on because 1) I make a genuine effort to understand their language and also the difficulties they face in coming to America and 2) unlike many American ballplayers, I have never let my own (tenuous) job security interfere with basic human interaction.

On the latter point, I firmly believe the reason that a lot of American ballplayers don't get along with their Latino counterparts is the jealousy factor. Fifty years ago, when baseball was predominately white, scouts rarely ventured outside the USA in search of talent. The arrival and subsequent success of a few Latin players, in particular Roberto Clemente, caused the baseball cognoscenti to tap the talent base of the Spanish-speaking world. In doing so, the jobs that formerly went to white Americans were beginning to go to Dominicans, Puerto Ricans, and Venezuelans, and on a smaller scale Mexicans, Nicaraguans, Panamanians, Colombians, and Cubans. In baseball, there are no quotas; you simply find the best players you can, develop them, and hope they help your big league team win a World Series.

If I may go off on a tangent, in the wake of "Affirmative Action" and other similar policies, I wish the business world would take note. You would never hear Bill Parcells or Joe Torre or Phil Jackson say to a player, "Sorry, so-and-so, but I have to let you go. You see, we have this quota to meet, and since you're a W.A.S.P., you are prohibiting a reasonably qualified minority from advancing his career. There is no doubt that you are a better player, but my hands are tied by the system." In the sports world such a conversation would be inconceivable, but such discrimination has been known to occur in the business world.

Those American ballplayers who feel shortchanged by the talent pool of Latin America shouldn't complain. As an American, you are afforded certain privileges that most of the rest of the world—and especially Third World countries like the Dominican Republic—only dream of. We all have education on which to fall back. We all speak English. We all have families we can visit or who can visit us during the season. The same can't be said for the Latinos. Once the Latinos enter the organized baseball system, they receive the same chance to succeed or fail as the Americans, but they are faced with innumerable challenges off the field that impede their progress. In a way the Americans have it easier, and if an American doesn't make it to the big leagues, he has no one to blame but himself or his own lack of talent. I am curious to find out what percentage of the Latinos who don't make it to the big leagues didn't make it because of cultural differences. I will ask some of my Latin teammates, but I bet the percentage is rather high.

I am not sure what my point is to this entry. Maybe I just needed to "vent." One of the beauties of baseball is the internationalization of the game over the past three decades. Look at the way the Japanese-Americans in Seattle have rallied around Ichiro Suzuki. Look at the pride exhibited by Dominicans and Dominican-Americans during Sammy Sosa's epic homerun battle with Mark McGwire in 1998. Look at Puerto Rico, perhaps the only country in the world whose most famous person is not a military hero or a statesman but an athlete, Roberto Clemente. The Latinos who come to America chase the same dream that we *gringos* chase. They have their own national pride, their own music, their own language and their own culture. Immigrants built America into a world superpower. Discriminating against the baseball-playing immigrants is therefore ignorant, racist and downright preposterous. Out.

Wednesday, September 25, 2001 (1:00 AM)
Long Island

Let me reflect a little bit. In 1998, after being released over the winter by the Diamondbacks, I went to spring training with the Houston Astros' organization. Going into it, I planned on making their Class A team in Kissimmee, FL, and playing there for the season. About midway through the camp, however, I began to feel very dejected. I was 25 at the time—hardly an old man in the non-baseball world—and seeing all these younger, better players frustrated me immensely. I had tried everything to make myself a better player: lifting weights, tinkering with my swing, discussing hitting with anyone who would listen. Unfortunately, nothing worked. I did a lot of soul searching, and at my request, the Astros released me. At the time I thought my baseball career was over, but then the Chico Heat came calling.

It took all of two weeks for me to rekindle my love of the game. Playing in an independent league was infinitely more fun than playing organizational ball. There is less pressure, less "looking over your shoulder," and less structure. Even though I enjoyed the game again, I still wasn't producing with the bat like I knew I could. Fast forward to the spring of 1999, when Bill Plummer and I resumed my daily hitting lessons, and before long, I was having the best summer of my life. All of a sudden I *really* loved baseball.

Looking back over the last three years, however, I realize now that all the "success" I had was merely a mirage. In one of my entries from this summer, I pondered my own ability and wondered if I am, in fact, any good. Playing in an obscure (some of the players in this league have never even heard of the Western League) independent league offers a blanket of security and confidence, *i.e.*, Linus with his blanket. Having played in the Atlantic League for the past month, Linus's blanket has been ripped out of his hands and shredded right in front of his face.

To illustrate how deluded I had become, the other day I was perusing my hitting manual that I wrote last fall, and one of the chapters deals with my career statistics. I wrote how, in spite of my paltry homerun totals, I have nevertheless been a productive hitter in the WBL. Well, that may indeed be true, but so what? Let's say, hypothetically, I return to the Atlantic League next year and with a fresh start and a better, more positive attitude, I hit .270. I still won't hit for any homerun power—I have come to grips with *that* fact—so my chances of going overseas to make any money are out. I will be 29, so catching on with an organization is out. There are tons of players in this league who are both younger *and* better than I am, so the more lucrative jobs that are out there would go to them. Therefore, what's the point of continuing to play?

The father of one of my former teammates once surmised that the reason we WBL ballplayers in our mid- to late-twenties continue to play is to delay our entrances into the real world. I think he's right. I mean if a "real job" that pays $40,000 a year magically fell into any of our laps, 99% of us would probably call it a career and take the job. As a rule, jobs that pay that amount of money don't go to underqualified baseball players. Hence, we continue to play. Certainly, those of us who perform well feel that someone is watching and will then offer us another chance in an organization or overseas. But the reality is that Osama bin Laden has a better chance of becoming president of the USA than I have of making any money playing baseball.

During my last few days of that 1998 spring training, I couldn't get the song "Puff the Magic Dragon" out of my head. While some people think the song is about smoking marijuana (or taking some kind of mind-altering drug), I prefer to think that *Peter, Paul and Mary* were alluding to the inevitability of growing up. I sensed that my impending "retirement" signified a loss of innocence, meaning "Puff no longer went to play along the cherry lane." The same feelings, though not quite as intense, envelop me today. I sit in the dugout counting down the days. I can't wait for this nightmare to end. It pains me greatly to say this, but as of 9-25-01, it appears that tonight's game may very well be my last. I have fought the good fight. I have lived the dream. After all, my deepest, darkest fears have been confirmed: I simply am not very good. After giving baseball my heart and soul for seven years, it's time to cut my losses and move on. Out.

Monday, October 1, 2001 (1:00 PM)
Chicago

I am currently in Midway Airport awaiting the second leg of my return flight to San Francisco. I have about an hour to kill, so I figure my final journal entry is the best way to kill it. I just spent three full days in Kittanning working on the farm with Gabby and devouring Lani's magnificent cooking. I labored like a mule and then ate like one. Because of all of their recent traveling, the farm was in horrible shape when I arrived on Wednesday night, and I hate to see it like that. I told Gabby that I had three days to get five days of work done, so we took advantage of his long weekend off. We put some roofing on one side of the sheep barn, mowed and trimmed the lawn, and cut some firewood. The latter chore, my personal favorite, received most of my attention. There is something about being out in the woods with a chain saw and a definite task at hand that I've always enjoyed. Even though they won't fire up the fireplace for at least another month, it's good to get a head start on the winter. I cut, split (when necessary), and stacked approximately two truckloads worth of wood, and coupled with some existing stacks, they should be set until I get home for the holidays.

Naturally, friends and family wanted to know about my baseball future. Not wanting to sound too discouraged about my stint in the Atlantic League, I generally skirted the issue, saying how much of an eye-opener it was. The admission of failure is usually something human beings tend to avoid at all costs, and even as honest and upfront as I am about my own abilities, I found it difficult to relay the actual truth: I am probably done playing baseball. Certainly, I won't make any concrete decisions until next spring, but I'm leaning that way. Also, I didn't want to incur the sympathy and pity that would undoubtedly accompany the revealing of my intentions. You know the look I mean, the one people give you when they tell you they've just divorced or lost a family member. Is there any worse feeling in the world than thinking that someone is pitying you? I think not. Therefore, until I know for sure what I will do about next summer, I shall say nothing.

Looking back, this seven-month baseball season was first a long one. I arrived in Taiwan on March 1, and I played my last game on September 25. That amounts to just about seven full months. When I think of where I've been and what I've gone through, I need to take a deep breath. I went to Taiwan hoping to play there all year, but apparently I wasn't good enough. I returned hoping to play for Chico, but apparently I wasn't good enough. I joined Sonoma County, and I must admit how nice it felt to be wanted and to play well. Finally, I went to Long Island and discovered that apparently, I wasn't good enough. If *Meat Loaf* thought, "Two out of three ain't bad," then one out of four must be downright lousy. Maybe the Agan, the Heat and the Ducks all were right. Maybe, like I say I did with the Diamondbacks, I fooled the Crushers into thinking that I am actually good. Who knows? I mentioned once before about the bittersweetness of being a two-time WBL All-Star. Well, the sweetness part has just about worn off completely and now I feel mostly bitter, not to anyone or anything in particular, about where baseball has left me. Believe me, I had a helluva ride, but right now, what do I have to show for it? Perhaps immaterially I have a few things—experiences, friends, memories—but materially, not a whole lot. "Twenty years now, where'd they go? Twenty years now, I don't know/I sit and I wonder sometimes where they've gone...."

No, it hasn't been anywhere near twenty years, but you get the point.

Fortunately, I am college-educated and reasonably intelligent, and most people, myself included, think that once I find something in the "real world" that captures my fancy as baseball used to, I will be fine. In the meantime, though, I don't really have a plan, and that's somewhat frustrating. In baseball, you play the summer, live the offseason where you choose, work, work out, and look forward to the next season. The pattern becomes quite routine. But what now? There is no "plan." I guess at some point, however, after losing the love of your life, you have to put him or her behind you and get busy living or get busy dying. Easier said than done. Out.

EPILOGUE: REFLECTIONS AND MEMORIES

When you choose a career in sports, it's all or nothing—and it's *now*. Unlike the similar "feast or famine" occupations of actors, musicians, or entertainers, there is a statute of limitations on an athlete's career. About five years ago, I heard that the length of the average baseball career is six years, and that includes the minor leagues. In contrast, look at bands like *Aerosmith* and *The Rolling Stones*, who have been cranking out hits for over thirty years. No one has ever played baseball for thirty years. Furthermore, successful bands can collect royalties that offer them the luxury of never having to work again. As you just found out, the minor league salary is meager at best, so unless you spend one of those six years in The Show, you probably won't have anything financially to show for your labor.

In the opening entry of the journal, I mentioned about how you have to "sell your soul" to baseball if you want to make it. To reach the major leagues requires the ultimate sacrifice, and what most ballplayers sacrifice is the future. Very rarely does a ballplayer enter the minor leagues with a college degree, and those who do—like me—have little chance of using it. You can't go to an employer in October and say, "Hi. Here is my résumé. You'll see that I am qualified to fill your position. Oh, by the way, I'll be leaving in four months to go to spring training." How many employers are going to hire someone like that?

But what about the vast majority of the ballplayers who either haven't completed their degrees or haven't even begun working on one? Most college fall semesters start at the end of August or in early September, and the typical minor league season can run into mid-September. Do you beg out of the last two weeks of the summer, which is probably the playoffs, to attend college? Doing so tells the organization that maybe you're not as serious as you should be about your baseball career. Or do you forsake your education to show loyalty to your team and your organization? (That organization will probably just end up releasing you anyway.) As for the spring, players report to spring training in early March, and most college spring semesters end in early May. No luck there, either.

So what do you do? I'll tell you. You work your ass off to become as good as you can be. I always say, "A baseball career is short. You have the rest of your life to be miserable working a desk job." You work dead-end jobs in the winter to make car and rent and insurance payments. You do strength and conditioning training four or five days a week. You work on your baseball skills three or four days a week. And you do this every single winter. Now for the worst part: there is no guarantee that all this sacrifice will pay off.

Medical school is no picnic. I know. I have several high school friends who are finishing right now. Becoming a successful jazz musician probably isn't very easy either. However, no one sits next to a med school student and tries to knock the pencil out of his hand while he's taking a test, and no one slashes the tires of the musician's car just before his big audition. Do you see my point? You may work tirelessly to improve your skills, but as a professional athlete, you know that someone else is being paid to prevent you from doing your job. If that person is better at his job than you are at yours, then on that day, you will lose. Too many losing days and you will probably get fired. That's what really stinks about a life in sports. All the hard work in the world sometimes just doesn't matter.

So, again, what do you do when you know your chances of making it to the majors are infinitesimal? Well, if you have no formal education or skill, you don't have a whole lot to look forward to in the real world. Therefore, you keep the uniform on as long as possible in hopes of gaining some kind of financial retribution after chasing windmills for years. You go to Taiwan. You go to Mexico. You go to the Atlantic League. Wherever. If you know that you will have to start from square one eventually, you might as well play as long as you can and make as much money as you can.

Eventually, though, most career minor leaguers have to call it quits. All the sacrifices are just not worth it anymore. You get sick and tired of moving every six months. You start to long for the things your friends have: a real job, a house, kids, general stability. Unfortunately, they have these things because they entered the working world at the same time you entered the baseball world. They have paid their dues, and they have started to climb the corporate ladder. We've paid our dues, but we have nothing to show for it. It's a bitter pill to swallow, to be sure.

I shouldn't complain too much, though. While I won't pull a Sammy Sosa and say, "Baseball has been 'bery, bery' good to me," I will say that I've had a helluva ride. I've been all over the country and all over the world. I've met tons of good guys—and even better girls. I have signed hundreds of autographs. I've had thousands of people cheer for me. And perhaps the best part is that every two weeks, I received a paycheck for doing so. The only things you can take with you when it's time to meet your maker are your memories, and baseball has provided a bounty of those for me. Fifty years from now, when I'm old and gray, I'll be able to say that I was a professional baseball player. No one can take that away.

0-595-21169-0